Changing Attitudes Towards the Death Penalty

Zoltan J. Toth

Changing Attitudes Towards the Death Penalty

Hungary's Renewed Support for Capital Punishment

palgrave
macmillan

Zoltan J. Toth
Department of Legal History and Jurisprudence
Károli Gáspár University
Budapest, Hungary

ISBN 978-3-030-47556-7 ISBN 978-3-030-47557-4 (eBook)
https://doi.org/10.1007/978-3-030-47557-4

Cover illustration: davidhills/Getty

This Palgrave Macmillan imprint is published by the registered company Springer Nature Switzerland AG.
The registered company address is: Gewerbestrasse 11, 6330 Cham, Switzerland

Contents

Part I Death Penalty Debates in the Twentieth and Twenty-First Century: Pros and Cons 1

1 Introduction 3

2 The Deterrent Effect: From An a priori Logic 9

3 Capital Punishment as an Inhumane Punishment 13

4 Necessity or Lack of Need for Capital Punishment 25

5 Miscarriage of Justice 35

6 The Goal of Punishment 49

7 Economic Considerations 55

8 Other Reasons for and Against Capital Punishment 61

Part II A Case Study of Capital Punishment in Hungary in the Twentieth Century 75

9 Statutory Regulation of Capital Punishment in Hungary during the Horthy Era and World War II 81

10 The Death Penalty in the Years after Liberation from Nazi Occupation and During the Establishment of the Soviet Dictatorship 95

11 Capital Punishment in the First Decade of State Socialism 119

12 Capital Punishment in the 1960s and 1970s 131

13 The Act No. IV of 1978 on the Criminal Code of Hungary 145

14 The End Time of the Death Penalty in Hungary: Two Steps of the Abolition in 1989/90 159

Part III The Politicization of Capital Punishment in Hungary: Renewed Controversy 169

15 Public Opinion in Hungary in the Light of the Current Legal Situation and the Facts about Trends in Murder Rates 171

16 Revived Debate on the Death Penalty in the Political Scene 185

Index 209

Part I

Death Penalty Debates in the Twentieth and Twenty-First Century: Pros and Cons

Regarding the death penalty, numerous books, articles, and essays were issued as part of the criminological and criminal law literature over the recent decades. However, almost all of these have a common feature i.e., studying only one side of the issue and attempting to disseminate propaganda for or against the death penalty, in line with specific purposes. But only a few papers exist that explain the arguments of both sides with objectivity, allowing the reader to take a stand. This part of the present book was written with the intent to fill that void and to demonstrate, as exhaustively as possible, the respective arguments (both pros and cons) that often appear in debates. Sometimes the opposing arguments are displayed in dialogues, other times the various approaches are merely outlined, while the reader can decide on the righteousness thereof.

1

Introduction

Although the death penalty was abolished in the majority of European countries by 2018, the debates concerning capital punishment continue to arise. Currently, the death penalty is only applied in Belarus although Russia still has this sanction in theory (no execution has taken place in the last fifteen years) so it can be considered a so-called de facto abolitionist state. In many European countries, leading politicians argue or have recently argued in favor of reinstatement of the death penalty. Among them, there are not only leaders of extremist parties (such as Ján Slota, former president of the Slovakian SNS[1] in 2010 or Jean-Marie Le Pen, former president of the French FN[2] and his daughter Marine Le Pen, former vice president, currently president of the party, in 2007), but moderate (mainly conservative) politicians, as well. Similarly, Lech Kaczyński, Poland's deceased president, urged a European debate regarding the reintroduction of capital punishment in 2006. His twin brother Jarosław Kaczyński, former prime minister and currently president of the leading opposition party, the PiS,[3] also announced at the end of 2011 that one of the objectives of his party was also to reinstate the death penalty. Daniel Lipšic, former Slovakian Minister of Justice, raised the issue at the beginning of 2008. John

Z. J. Toth, *Changing Attitudes Towards the Death Penalty*,
https://doi.org/10.1007/978-3-030-47557-4_1

Arthur Stevens, former head of the Metropolitan Police Service (better known as Scotland Yard) in England, after the murder of a policewoman in 2005, declared that although he was previously against capital punishment, death is the only acceptable response to brutal murder. All these persons were in favor of the death penalty partly for moral reasons and partly for practical considerations, believing that capital punishment has a deterrent effect and would serve to actually decrease the number of murder cases.

As to the controversy over capital punishment, two fundamental types of disputes—along with two kinds of reasonings supporting them—that center on the appropriateness or applicability of the death penalty can be differentiated. There exist on the one hand, philosophical or moral, and on the other hand, pragmatic (empirical and logical) reasons. Pragmatic arguments are characterized by impartiality and objectivity resting on solid, empirical, and at least partly supervisable grounds. As opposed to this, moral arguments are not formed on the basis of such requirements, therefore, they cannot be regarded as par excellence rational arguments by nature. Ethical viewpoints rest on profound beliefs that one accepts as axioms, in other words, one has a particular opinion of something without backing it up logically either by means of listing supporting evidence or refuting its counterarguments. The essence of morality lies in its status as the innermost, unquestionable, and indisputable, hence, undeniable (that is, immune to refutal) part of the human psyche, which is best described by the word "belief"[4] and nothing can dissuade those who "believe" from their own presuppositions and convictions.[5] Hence, if someone "believes" that the ultimate moral principle is to rid society of the "evil," that is, of those people who are dangerous and purposefully trespass, posing a threat to their fellow, law-abiding citizens and that the only proper way to do that is for such a trespasser to receive punishment in the same form as they have offended because there is no treatment more just than that, then this person will claim with a solid moral conviction that the death penalty is an appropriate form of punishment. At the same time, those on the opposite viewpoint who think that no human has the right to make judgments over other humans and that life is so sacred and invaluable that it is forbidden to take it away in an "ethical" society even from those people who deliberately took away others' life out of their own immorality, will emphasize the legitimacy of their own beliefs with the same vehemence. The debate between everyday people—and also between professionals with their points elaborated in a more sophisticated argumentation—on capital punishment rests on such moral grounds. As a consequence of this, it results in the mutual, conscious ignorance of the other party's reasoning and a shift from the point under discussion to personal disagreements, rendering the studies dealing with the death penalty as *weapons of a philosophical jihad* rather than inferences based on rational research. Since moral arguments as enunciations of beliefs cannot be studied rationally, that is—to put it more simply—they do not meet the criterion of scientificity,[6] I will not discuss the pure forms of the arguments raised in connection with the death penalty[7] in this paper. (The criterion of scientificity—in contradiction with its older conception—is not verifiability but, instead, falsifiability. It follows from this that an assertion cannot be regarded as a scientific statement if it does not—not even in theory—leave any room for proving its falseness, therefore, moral arguments do not constitute any part of science—just like any other declaration or conviction formed on beliefs.)

The empirical points of discussion concerning the death penalty, however, are also able to polarize people's various standpoints to an extreme. This is equally true for the issue of the deterrent effect, the possibility of wrongful convictions, the matter of humanity or inhumanity of the individual methods of execution applied nowadays, the existing or non-existing discrimination in the judicial process, or even for the financial aspects as well.

The practical arguments concerned with the applicability or non-applicability of capital punishment need to be divided into two distinct categories: relevant and non-relevant arguments. While the former either in themselves or through their relationship with one another may be used to prove the standpoint of retention or that of abolition, the latter—regardless of what the truth is about them—cannot even in theory serve as a rationale for taking a position in the discussion of the death penalty's acceptability. This latter category includes (among many other reasons of secondary importance) arguments pertaining to par excellence economic (i.e., pecuniary) aspects or arguments in connection with the public's support and since these attributes are by nature defined or influenced by a particular legal system, one can only make inferences about the state of the actual legal system in question, but not about capital punishment as such. It follows from this that the arguments dealing with these issues are only valid as long as the circumstances from which they sprang up persist and as soon as a change occurs in the legal situation, they lapse. Results obtained from the debates associated with the above-specified viewpoints cannot be perceived as conclusive arguments with regards to the theoretical discussion of the death penalty also because they only take into consideration marginal aspects thereof instead of the crucial questions that should be raised. Accordingly, this part deals primarily with these crucial questions concentrating, principally but not exclusively, on the Hungarian scene.

Notes

1. *Slovenská národná strana* (Slovak National Party).
2. *Front national* (National Front).
3. *Prawo i Sprawiedliwość* (Law and Justice).
4. The word "belief" is not used to mean or refer to faith here, it stands as a synonym for any aprioristic point of view.
5. As a result, moral conviction as belief is irrational, which simply means that, as far as its genesis is concerned, it is not a consequence of something but it depends on an aprioristic choice of values (that is, there is no rational reason or logical verification behind it).
6. The criterion of scientificity—in contradiction with its older conception—is not verifiability but, instead, falsifiability. It follows from this that an assertion cannot be regarded as a scientific statement if it does not—not even in theory—leave any room for proving (unavoidably only temporarily, owing to the current perception of scientificity) its falseness

(in the presence of appropriate conditions), therefore, moral arguments do not constitute any part of science (just like any other declaration or conviction formed on beliefs).

7. Clearly, many rational arguments build on a more or less moral base. Nevertheless, this does not necessarily entail that these are "moral" arguments, so it should come as no surprise if moral elements do occur in some or even in most of the upcoming examples that are to be analyzed without one having the obligation to call their rational/empirical nature into question because of this.

2

The Deterrent Effect: From An a priori Logic

As for the a priori logic, there are two points of view competing with each other. The so-called retentionists or revivalists, namely, the advocates of capital punishment, deem that the more severe a penalty is (imposed on a perpetrator), the greater the fear of the consequences of a crime will be. They argue like this: "I don't want to be fined 100 dollars. I even less want to be fined 1000 dollars, even less punished with one year prison, even less with prison for life and least of all to be sentenced to death." For instance, according to Alexander Deak, capital punishment has a greater deterrent effect than life imprisonment, since it is final and irrevocable and there is no possibility of escape. Then again, life imprisonment holds some hope (although very small) for freedom, either by means of escaping from prison or hoping for pardon from the President. Deak does believe that the threat of irrevocable death is in fact more dreadful than "normal" life imprisonment that does not last forever (only twenty or thirty years) or actual life imprisonment, which *might* not last a lifetime (due to the possibility of escape from prison or pardon). As he puts it: "I believe the view that a real criminal would not be deterred by capital punishment is not correct. On this basis, the entire Criminal Code should be repealed, as a notorious thief or fraud would not be deterred by

Z. J. Toth, *Changing Attitudes Towards the Death Penalty*,
https://doi.org/10.1007/978-3-030-47557-4_2

punishment."[1] Furthermore: "In my opinion a person who virtually excludes himself from society by committing a murder deserves the death penalty. … Regardless of any contrary statement, I firmly believe that capital punishment has a deterrent—i.e. preventive—effect…"[2] György Pálinkás, late Justice of the Supreme Court of Hungary had a similar opinion; according to him, if even the death penalty had no deterrent effect, then no other punishment would have it. If even the most severe punishment cannot deter a person from committing a crime, then no other, more moderate penalties can. Should this be the case, we could abolish all punishments and renounce to the special and general preventive purpose of the criminal justice sanctions, as well.[3] The late doyen of the bar, Hungary's best known defense counsel, György Bárándy also regularly made statements regarding the need to reinstate the death penalty. In addition, Professor József Földvári, the criminal lawyer who gave his expert opinion to the Constitutional Court of Hungary in 1990 in the case of the abolition of capital punishment[4] also formulated—on several occasions during the years before his death (2009), first in 2002—that if he was asked today to give an expert opinion in a similar case, he would not be in favor of abolishing the death penalty, because its application, according to him, is necessary in case of serious crimes.

In contrast to this, the abolitionists, that is, the opponents of capital punishment take the different types of murders and try to prove that in the cases of most of these the nature of the punishment does not affect the motivation of potential perpetrators.[5] For example, it does not impact on crimes of passion. These criminals, according to the abolitionists, do not deliberate in advance the possible consequences of their acts, hence, they cannot be frightened by the penalty of death. (And, of course, they cannot be frightened by any other penalty, either.) This is also true for those who commit their crimes while drunk or who are motivated by an overpowering, usually sexual, instinct (a so-called "*drive*").[6] Nevertheless, even when it comes to crimes committed under the influence of alcohol or crimes of passion, there is at least a moderate amount of deliberation behind one's actions. This deliberation may manifest itself in the development of a typical attitude (in other words, in a general state of mind) towards violence. The lack of these incentives, however, may contribute to the development of a personality that does not reject destructive behavior and is more prone to turn to violent methods in order to solve a matter, but it can also present itself in that short time span when the sudden resolve triggered by emotions is realized in the outside world, since all affective acts are preceded by a momentary consideration during which every possible scenario is evaluated that might assist the enactment of the action or prevent it. If it was not so, that is, if a perpetrator had absolutely no control over their impulses and their sexual or any other instincts, in that case the perpetrator could not be a subject for punishment at all due, to a lack of imputation and culpability.

Furthermore, capital punishment cannot deter those who themselves want to die, for example, political perpetrators (anarchists, terrorists). "Indirect suiciders" cannot be deterred, either, for the previous reason; they are those people want to die but are too cowardly to do this by their own hands, and want to get into such a situation where the police officers have no other choice but to shoot them dead, or where the authorities have the possibility to sentence them to death and execute them.[7] This undeterrability is also true for suicidal murderers who, actuated by jealousy, murder, for example, their wives and/or their wives' lovers, and, not wanting to live further, commit suicide after the murder.

In the end, the threat of death does not deter those who deem the police will not catch them. As Beccaria wrote some two and a half centuries ago: "Crimes are more effectually prevented by the certainty than the severity of punishment."[8] (In addition: "It is not the intenseness of the pain that has the greatest effect on the mind, but its continuance. The more immediately after the commission of a crime a punishment is inflicted, the more just and useful it will be.")[9] Thus, the death penalty cannot frighten the most cruel and brutal offenders, for example, the assassins, the murderers for hire and so on; or those who think they are cleverer than the police officers and will not be apprehended. Hence, as per the abolitionists, the solution is not making the possible penalties more severe, but making the investigations more effective.

The truth is that, in fact, neither the existence nor the non-existence of the deterrent effect of capital punishment can be proved. We simply are not able to know whether there were any people who planned to commit a murder, but did not do it because they got frightened of the possible penalty of death; albeit, in lack of the death penalty they would have committed this offence. Since they did not do that effectively, we can never be sure that the murder would have happened or not, simply because none of us is a fortune teller, oracle, or prophet.

Notes

1. Cf.: Alexander Deak: On Capital Punishment [A halálbüntetésről], p. 57. In: *Belügyi Szemle*, 1995/1, pp. 55–57.
2. Ibid., pp. 55–56.
3. Cf.: György Pálinkás: Requiem for a Legal Institution [Requiem egy jogintézményért], p. 70. In: *Belügyi Szemle*, 2001/6, pp. 63–73.
4. CC Decision No. 23/1990 (X. 31.).
5. Considering that the majority of the Hungarian criminal lawyers and criminologists are abolitionist, I will not provide a list of them and references to their works in the subject, herein. The interested readers may nonetheless find the list of these works—published in Hungarian—in the bibliography of the following monograph: Zoltan J. Toth: *Capital Punishment: Pros and Cons* [Halálbüntetés pró és kontra]. HVG-ORAC, Budapest, 2012, 291 p. (ISBN 978-963-258-177-4).
6. Cf.: Isaac Ehrlich: The Deterrent Effect of Criminal Law Enforcement, p. 274. In: *Journal of Legal Studies*, Vol. 1, 1972, pp. 259–276; Isaac Ehrlich: On Positive Methodology, Ethics, and Polemics in Deterrence Research, p. 128. In: *British Journal of Criminology*, Vol. 22, 1982, pp. 124–139; Joanna M. Shepherd: Murders of Passion, Execution Delays, and the Deterrence of Capital Punishment. In: *Journal of Legal Studies*, Vol. 33, No. 2, 2004, pp. 283–322.
7. Pamela Watkins, a very rare example, was such an offender. (For the case of Watkins see: Anthony G. Amsterdam: Capital Punishment, p. 357. In: Hugo Adam Bedau (ed.): *The Death Penalty in America*. Oxford University Press, 1982, pp. 346–358.) In Hungary, the famous offender of the bank robbery of Szena square committed the crime with this kind of motivation as well and, as contrasted to Watkins, actually succeeded in his plan.
8. Cesarec Beccaria: *An Essay On Crimes and Punishments* [1764]. E-book. Liberty Fund, Indianapolis, Indiana, 2011, p. 49.
9. Beccaria, op. cit., p. 51.

3

Capital Punishment as an Inhumane Punishment

According to the abolitionists, capital punishment is an inhumane form of punishment because it violates the right to life and human dignity by not only restricting but also rendering impossible the exercise and enjoyment of these rights permanently and irrevocably. In Hungary, these arguments are brought forward by referencing to the Decision of the Constitutional Court No. 23/1990 (X. 31.) AB (CC) on Capital punishment in violation of the Constitution. Namely, this decision of the Constitutional Court (CC) stated the following: "In Hungary, the right to life and human dignity … is an inherent, inviolable and inalienable fundamental right of every person. … It is the primary duty of the Hungarian state to respect and protect them. … The Constitutional Court held that the provisions of the Criminal Code applicable to capital punishment are in contravention of the prohibition on restricting the basic content of the right to life and human dignity. The provisions relating to the deprivation of life and human dignity by capital punishment not only impose a limitation upon the essential content of the fundamental right to life and human dignity, but also allow for the entire and irreparable elimination of life and human dignity or of the right ensuring

Z. J. Toth, *Changing Attitudes Towards the Death Penalty*,
https://doi.org/10.1007/978-3-030-47557-4_3

these, therefore, the Constitutional Court established the unconstitutionality of these provisions and declared them null and void."

On the other hand, the advocates of capital punishment refer to the dissent opinion of Péter Schmidt stating that the Constitution only "prohibits arbitrary deprivation of life," but deprivation of life cannot be deemed as conceptually arbitrary.[1] As Part IV of the decision of the Constitutional Court also provides: "This prohibition … does not exclude the opportunity for deprivation of life and human dignity in a manner that is not arbitrary," therefore, according to Péter Schmidt "although it falls within the jurisdiction of the Constitutional Court to interpret the Constitution, but it is the right and obligation of the Parliament having constitutional power to resolve the conflicting provisions of the Constitution. This authority may not be vested in the Constitutional Court." It must be added, of course, that Péter Schmidt was in favor of capital punishment abolition, so his dissent is a mere indication of his opinion, that this decision should be made by the Parliament rather than the Constitutional Court. Kálmán Györgyi, then Chief Prosecutor also worded similar ideas in part. The differences between their opinions are as follows. Györgyi did not deny the right or even obligation of such organ to take a position and decide on the constitutionality or unconstitutionality of capital punishment in accordance with Act XXXII of 1989 of the Constitutional Court; he only would have deemed it more "fortunate" and a solution providing more support for the legitimacy of the solution of this matter if this sanction was abolished by the Parliament. As opposed to this, according to the opinion of Péter Schmidt, the Constitutional Court did not have competence to make this decision under the given circumstances, as it had to choose from two controversial constitutional rules. In any event, based on this decision of the Constitutional Court abolitionists deem that capital punishment is arbitrary and inhuman and when used the humanity of human beings is being called into question.

In contrast, the advocates of capital punishment widely refer to the phrase of the parallel opinion of the same CC decision expressed by László Sólyom, first chair of the Hungarian Constitutional Court, who stated the following: "[T]he decision of the Constitutional Court is deliberately subjective and bound to history: even if and when the

Constitutional Court declares absolute values; it covers the meaning addressed to their own time; and its judgment ... cannot claim perpetuity either in principle." To sum up, according to Sólyom, capital punishment is not inhuman from eternity and the right to life is not always and everywhere is an inherent human right, but becomes as such if the state has recognized it and protects it. In Hungary, at the end of the twentieth century, lawmakers did so and the Constitutional Court based on such "subjective and bound to history" decisions of the lawmakers may have declared capital punishment to be unconstitutional in order to enforce it. The famous criminologist József Vígh also shares this view. He believes that "*until not long ago everyone had right to life under conditions set by society and by the state. I believe the situation is the same today.* Everyone has rights and obligation in a scope provided by society. Thus it is really not reasonable to mystically consider human rights inherent and unalienable."[2]

An additional area of concern is the issue of the right to self-defense. According to the advocates of capital punishment, if the right of an individual to self-defense is acknowledged, namely that he is allowed to stave off an attack presenting an imminent danger to his life also by killing the aggressor, then the right of the society to collective self-defense must also be acknowledged. If a person as an individual has the right to self-defense, then he must also have the right as a member of a community, namely, the society. Therefore, it is not only the right, but also the obligation of the society vis-à-vis its members to protect them against the unlawful attacks of others, and if it is only able to prevent anti-life attacks only by taking the life of the aggressor, then it is obliged to do so. In this respect, on the other hand, abolitionists expressed their disagreement stating that there is a difference between a legitimate defense situation and the execution used as punishment. In the former case defense taking the life of the aggressor precedes the unlawful taking of life, thus it is an action which is able to prevent the purpose (murder) of another unlawful action from being realized. In the latter case, however, capital punishment does not come before it and it does not even atone for homicide as it has already happened. If a person killed innocently could be resurrected through execution then—as abolitionists consider—the situation was different, but as it is physically impossible and taking someone's life subsequently (execution) is not able to change the past, thus capital punishment as a subsequent response of the state cannot be the means of self-defense (namely by taking the life of the aggressor to prevent the murder).

This idea was originally formulated by Bertalan Szemere (the interior minister of the first independent government in Hungary during the revolution and war of independence of 1848–1849) in a very descriptive way (which is much more detailed than the before-described one). His opinion is the first of its kind, but it is not the same as of the abolitionists, or of the theoretical predecessors of Szemere, Beccaria, or Bentham, because they did not even include this argument into their reasoning.[3] Moreover, the opinion of our second prime minister was also shared by Elemér Balás, among others, around the end of the nineteenth century, who differentiated between "normal rule of law" and "the situation of emergency." However, Balás did not compare them, because the methods available in emergency situations could not be used within normal circumstances (due to the main differences between the two situations).[4] (We have to add that this reason implies the acknowledgement of capital punishment within *extra ordinem* legislation and the application of law. The contrary idea, namely that capital punishment should be avoided even in special circumstances, was not formulated by anyone in Hungary till the 1980s.)

On the other hand, those believing in capital sanction scrutinize execution not only as a means of self-defense against homicides, but also draw a parallel with other state activities which—similarly to capital punishment—result in the destruction of human lives. In this regard they argue that if we acknowledge the lawfulness of such other state acts (which on top of all that substantially outdid executions in their effect), then by analogy there is no reason for not acknowledging the lawfulness of capital punishment, likewise. For example, numerous specific cases could be listed when a state tried to protect the lives of the people by means of war, while during that war thousands of people were killed. This happened during the Gulf War of 1991 and also in Bosnia, Kosovo, and is also happening now at several places in the world in full agreement with, and even with the support of, civil rights organizations. So, whilst world powers in good conscience liquidate soldiers serving dictatorships (who in turn are just obeying orders; alternatively, they were the ones who would be executed for insubordination) in order to free an oppressed nation, an occupied country, or to put an end to another dreadful war, they are unwilling to do so in respect of certain expressly identified persons (not innocent persons, but murderers at that). To sum up, in the case of murderers, they refer to human rights for which they are unprepared to kill, while in the case of war they also refer to human rights for which they liquidate thousands of people.[5]

Those opposing to capital punishment think that each mode of execution is cruel and inhuman and, therefore, no humane execution exists conceptually.[6] However quick an execution can be, there is inevitably a certain pain and suffering involved. It is not only true for the modes of execution used in some of the developing countries even today, considered by the "developed" world as barbarous (for example such as stoning) but also for hanging, the firing squad, electrocution, the gas chamber, and even by lethal injection used (also) in the USA. If, for example, hanging is improperly done, and the hangman erroneously calculates the length of the rope based on the weight and height of the convict, then as a result of falling from too high, the head of the convict may come off upon execution, or otherwise due to the short fall the spinal cord does not break and this way the convict will die from choking for several minutes. The risk from the firing squad is that if done from afar the bullets may fail to hit vital organs and so the person to be executed will die from slow exsanguinations. The same happened for example with Eliseo J. Mares in Utah of the United States in 1951, when the firing squad targeted so wrongly that none of the four sharp bullets hit the heart of Mares and so he simply died because of massive loss of blood. The problems of the method of the firing squad stems from the fact that this kind of execution is carried out by volunteers. Gunfire execution is performed in a way that five people are chosen as volunteers, all receive brand new guns with bullets, but only four have real ammo, the fifth one is filled with blanks. The person who made the preparations is not present at the execution, therefore the members of the firing squad will not know who fired with blanks. The reason for this solution is to facilitate the psychological coping-mechanism of executioners, because each may think that it was not them who actually killed a man, because he had the blanks. That is why it was often the case in volatile executions that due to an unexpected event the execution could not be carried out properly.

There are even more problems with gas chambers. According to the original plans (which were established in Nevada in 1921) the convict would have been killed by poisonous gas spread to his cell at night, while he was sleeping, without any prior notice. By this way he would have been spared from the enormous stress of days and hours preceding the execution and his death would have been painless and calm. Due to the practical difficulties (the cell has the same airspace as of the other cells, therefore, it would have been impossible to spread the gas only to the convict) the first execution was performed on February 8, 1924 on Gee Jon, a convict with Chinese origins in a specially designed chamber which could be closed hermetically. (Presently, the USA is the only country in the world to use a gas chamber.) Although originally, they intended to introduce it to enable the death of convicts to be painless, it did not succeed many times when used in practice. The person to be executed usually chokes for several minutes before they die whilst trying to escape from his bonds and there are precedents that someone managed to do so. In 1953, in the San Quentin State Prison for example, Leandress Riley freed himself from the chair and tried to break out from the chamber. After this the execution was of course stopped and he was strapped again, but he did the same for the second and the third time as well. Finally, the execution was done in front of official witnesses and wardens who were already panicking, and public officers present could no longer be persuaded to attend any execution in gas chambers. Besides, this mode of execution is the most dangerous to the persons doing and attending the execution. Namely, it may happen that the gas chamber is not properly insulated (e.g., it was badly constructed or got damaged due to the condition of not being used for several years) and so there is a danger that cyanide gas gets out from the chamber and also poisons people standing there.

Of the modern methods of execution, electric chair is the most troublesome. It often occurs that by the time the convict dies, his body has charred, his face has strained beyond recognition, his eyes have goggled or burst, and his blood vessels have burst. It also happened several times that the convict was still living after the first electric shock of two minutes and so they needed to switch on the electricity again (even repeatedly) to let him die. Theoretically, although a sudden electric shock should paralyze the brain during a fraction of 1/240 of a second before the convict could even feel any pain whatsoever, the first execution of such kind done on August 6, 1890 on a certain William Kemmler had to be repeated, because after the first electric shock of 2000 volts Kemmler was still alive. A similar case happened in 1946 in Louisiana with a minor aged seventeen, and with Willie Francis and John Louis Evans in 1983 in Alabama. After the first execution (which was repeated only one year after) Francis said "I felt a fire in my head and my left leg ..."[7] and in the case of Evans one of the electrodes blew upon the first electric shock; during the second electric shock, flames shot out from his temple and leg; given that his heart was still beating after this the electricity was switched on for the third time which then killed him definitively. In 1990 in Florida, Jesse Joseph Tafero was executed in a similar way: every time the electrocuter switched on the electricity, blue and orange flames shot out immediately from the head of Tafero. By the time Tafero died, his head has been practically burnt up.

The latest method, lethal injection, was first allowed by law in Oklahoma in 1977, officially for allowing the convict to donate his organs (as a last good act, by this compensating for his actions a bit) for medical purposes, which would have been impossible by using other methods of execution. In reality the reason was that this was much cheaper than the other two "fancy" ones, gas chamber or electric chair, because the poison cocktail cost only few dollars. (It is interesting that the "humanity" of execution was not a priority.) The method was finally applied by the first time in Texas, not in Oklahoma, where for the first time in history the convict Charles Brooks was executed by lethal injection. Lethal injection was considered for a long time as the least drastic mode of execution, however, serving an execution this way does not always take place smoothly. Namely, the cocktail of drugs is generally (in most States) made of three kinds of agents: a sedative and two substances; one paralyzing the lung and the other one the heart. If the timing of dosage is wrong or the needle is not inserted into the proper place, it may happen that the sedative does not produce its effect on time or such a small amount of sedative gets into the body of convict that upon elapse of a short time he wakes up and must suffer his own agony awake, that is, he is more or less conscious when he slowly suffocates. Recently, an opinion has become more and more common (and scientific research seems to confirm it as well), that during executions using lethal injections, there is another risk involved, namely, that the majority of convicts not only have terrible pains during such executions, but are not even able to communicate it to the outside world. Sedatives, namely sodium-thiopental (natrium pentothal) is often administered in a smaller dose than in surgical anaesthesia as a result of which the person to be executed often remains awake or wakes up. At the same time the second substance, the muscle relaxant (pancuronium bromide) aimed at stopping lung functions slackens muscles, therefore, the convict appears to be sleeping, unconscious for the outside world even if the poison designed to stop heart function, kalium chlorid produces its effect causing terrible pains. For that reason, since 2006 lethal injection executions have been suspended in several states of the US. As of September 25, 2007, that is, after the US Supreme Court accepted the arguments of the case of *Baze v. Rees* (where two death row inmates contested lethal-injection execution on the grounds that it causes "unnecessary pain and suffering" and is, therefore, unconstitutional) the Supreme Court suspended executions of death sentences imposed in Kentucky. This resulted in pending cases as the issue on whether executions carried out using such methods can be considered as "cruel and unusual" punishment (i.e., unconstitutional) has not yet been resolved. Furthermore, as a result of that the remaining States using lethal injection also did the same—voluntarily—and so executions were allowed to continue only after the decision of April 18, 2008 made in this case permitting further use of lethal injection[8] (nonetheless—notwithstanding the decision of the Supreme Court—fierce and endless disputes are still taking place regarding the cruelty of this method).

Capital punishment is inhumane not only for the methods of execution, but also because a great deal of time passes between the promulgation and the execution of death sentence. It is, of course, necessary in democratic countries to reduce the risk of *justizmord* (miscarriage of justice) to a minimum and an opportunity must be given for the convict to request a change in the verdict at all levels and to apply for amnesty. A long waiting time, however, corrodes convicts both physically and mentally. These people in the United States, for example, nowadays spend on average fifteen years on the so-called "death row," separated from the rest of the convicts and being forced to do nothing for most of their time.[9] This leads to their physical and mental disintegration. In addition, there is the feeling of waiting, one day after another, in horror to hear when the decision rejecting their application for amnesty would be promulgated and if it has already happened, when they would be notified of the date of execution. In some Central-American countries, for instance, executions to be carried out on Tuesday in the coming week are promulgated each Thursday afternoon; death row inmates sit through this day in horror awaiting every moment to hear the key scraping in the lock and someone entering the room to tell them that they would be killed in five days. Otherwise, in the months and years after being condemned to death, most of their time they are thinking of the execution; imagining every tiny detail of it, their own behavior, and the circumstances, until the outside world ceases to exist and only thoughts on their own death are left. Separation, and the fact that they are no longer considered as human beings even by prison wardens, contributes to this loss of personality; they are called "package" by the wardens; or convicts are also depersonalized by the wardens using other expressions and are in fact treated as such.

This is corroborated by the Hungarian empirical investigations, as well. According to a recent survey, "inmates become more introverted and distrustful. The extent of their self-esteem reduces. Their social activites drop and they do their everyday activities routinely. Their social connections gradually degrade, then cease."[10]

In the end, the very awareness of the fact that the convict will inevitably die in an indeterminate amount of time is psychologically unbearable. Robert Murray uses the "airplane analogy" for explaining this sense in a vividly descriptive manner: the public would surely not accept the punishment of being tossed out of a plane, albeit this is the same feeling for the condemned as the lethal injection. Yet, it is not tolerable, because of the psychological pain. As Murray puts it:

> Killing inmates by tossing them out of airplanes would of course be unacceptable to the public. But why? It's as fast and effective as lethal injection. The terror of falling two minutes isn't all that different from the terror of lying strapped to the table and neither is physically painful. There's a similar waiting process before each execution. If an airplane is used, you wait

> for the time it takes the aircraft to take off and reach the target area at the proper altitude. For lethal injection, you wait in the death house until everything's ready and all possibility of a stay of execution has been exhausted. In an airplane, a cargo door is opened; in the death house, a curtain across the viewing window is drawn back. In an airplane, you are thrown to an absolute death and witnesses watch your body fall. In the death house, you are strapped to a gurney and witnesses watch state officials inject you with sodium thiopentothal. In both cases, death is sudden and final.[11]

Due to the aforementioned, abolitionists propose the abolition, or the replacement, of capital punishment, with alternative forms of punishment. Many people prefer actual life sentence, but it is highly questionable whether being aware of the fact that they would never be released is more humane and if it is so, then how much more humane than capital punishment? Cesare Beccaria, the initiator of abolitionism, on the other hand, would have replaced capital punishment with perpetual forced labor, although the human nature of this sanction is especially questionable. Many convicts think they would not like to live in prison all their lives without any hope of being released. Of course, here and now in the twenty-first century in Hungary where capital punishment is not allowed, we can only guess how they would actually decide if they were given the opportunity to choose between lifetime imprisonment or death; any dispute can only be academic for the main part. This assumption, however, might be supported by the fact that presently more than fifty convicts serve their life imprisonment without parole and three convicts have committed suicide in the high security zone of prison "Csillag" ("Star") in Szeged, which holds the most dangerous perpetrators of those sentenced to such punishment. (Three times killer József Budai committed suicide in 2007; Péter Csepregi, convicted for two counts of murder, committed suicide in 2008; Zoltán Ember, a serial killer who murdered five victims committed suicide in 2015.)

Notes

1. See the same in the parallel opinion of Tamás Lábady and Ödön Tersztyánszky ("it cannot be stated that entire deprivation of life is conceptually unlawful, that is, arbitrary").
2. See: József Vigh: A halálbüntetés eltörlésének időszerűségéről [The timeliness of the abolition of the death penalty], p. 118. In: *Belügyi Szemle*, 1995, pp. 15–20. (Highlighted by the original author.)
3. See: Bertalan Szemere: *A büntetésről s különösebben a halálbüntetésről.* [On punishment, and more particularly capital punishment.] Halálbüntetést Ellenzők Ligája (Anti-Death Penalty League), 1990, pp. 123–126.
4. Elemér Balás: *A halálbüntetésről* [On Capital Punishment]. Révai és Salamon Könyvnyomdája, Budapest, 1900, p. 18.
5. See: Vigh: op. cit., p. 19; György Pálinkás: *Requiem egy jogintézményért* [Requiem for a legal institution], p. 67. In: *Belügyi Szemle*, 2001/6, pp. 63–73.
6. For concrete examples of flawed executions, without further details, see e.g.: Marian J. Borg and Michael L. Radelet: On botched executions. In: Peter Hodgkinson and William A. Schabas, (eds.): *Capital Punishment. Strategies for Abolition.* Cambridge University Press, 2004, pp. 143–168.
7. Cited: When the state kills ... p. 170. Amnesty International Publications, 1989 In: Ágnes Sebes (ed.): A halálbüntetésről. (On Capital Punishment.) Medvetánc Füzetek, Magvető Könyvkiadó, Budapest, 1990, pp. 95–218.
8. *Baze v. Rees* 553 U.S. 35 (2008).
9. In 2010 the average time spent on the death row was 178 months; in 1994 "only" 122 month (about ten years) and in 1984 74 months (about six years). (Find the summary chart of time spent at the death row for the period between 1984 and 2000 here: US Department of Justice, Office of Justice Programs, Bureau of Justice Statistics: Capital Punishment, 2010—Statistical Tables. December 2011, NCJ 236510, p. 12. In: http://bjs.ojp.usdoj.gov/content/pub/pdf/cp10st.pdf)
10. Szilvia Antal, László Tibor Nagy, and Ágnes Solt,: Az életfogytig tartó szabadságvesztés empirikus vizsgálata. (Empirical investigation on real life imprisonment.), pp. 63–64. In: György Virág (ed.): Kriminológiai tanulmányok 46 (Criminological Papers 46). OKRI, Budapest, 2009, pp. 54–94.
11. Robert Murray: Execution is Inhumane. In: Mary E. Williams (ed.): *Capital Punishment: Current Controversies.* Greenhaven Press, 2005, pp. 57–61.

4

Necessity or Lack of Need for Capital Punishment

One of the main arguments of abolitionists against capital punishment is that it has no greater deterrent effect than other serious forms of punishment have; consequently there is no need to maintain it.[1] Nor is capital punishment suitable to inhibit the spread of anti-life crimes and so it must be abolished and wherever it was abolished it must not be restored. Abolitionists often refer to Beccaria anyway, but in this matter, he is particularly quoted. According to Beccaria: "Crimes are more effectually prevented by the certainty than the severity of punishment[2] … A more moderate, but certain punishment will always be a more effective deterrent than the fear of another punishment that is more severe, but there is a hope of not being punished."[3]

It is beyond doubt: with this phrase, Beccaria laid down a timeless basic truth in criminal law. It is apparent that the better the ratio of detection is and the more criminals are caught, the less probable it will be that anyone would undertake to commit a crime in the knowledge of an almost certain punishment. In other words, effective law enforcement work is everywhere a greater obstacle to the spread of crime; however, we also have to see that there is no country in the world where all offenders are caught and there is no law enforcement apparatus that could have

Z. J. Toth, *Changing Attitudes Towards the Death Penalty*,
https://doi.org/10.1007/978-3-030-47557-4_4

ever been able to do so anywhere, at any time or would be in the future. Criminals are always one (or more) step(s) in front of law enforcement officers; furthermore, the capacity of the police is finite (there are many more offenders than available police officers necessary to investigate the identity of all offenders) and so the threat of being seriously punished will always play a role in the detention of potential offenders.

In addition to that, Beccaria would have replaced capital punishment with punishments that are more brutal than death; in some cases—as it appeared in the title of Article XXVIII dealing with Beccaria—he himself admitted the necessity of this sanction. "The death of a citizen cannot be necessary, but in one case. When, though deprived of his liberty, he has such power and connections as may endanger the security of the nation; when his existence may produce a dangerous revolution in the established form of government."[4] As an example of today, in order to free a terrorist leader, his gang hijack jets as well as take and execute hostages in order to enforce authorities to free their leader; or if a mafia boss continues to manage his criminal organization from inside the prison, for example giving instructions to bribe the witnesses who let police officers put him "behind bars." Within it, according to Beccaria, "[a] punishment, to be just, should have only that degree of severity which is sufficient to deter others."[5]

Of course, abolitionists of today disagree with these two phrases and emphasize that capital punishment is unnecessary in any case, as well as making the case for the entire and irrevocable abolition of capital punishment. They certainly agree that some kind of alternative punishment is indispensable no matter how little deterrent force it may have, but opinions are divided on what this alternative punishment should be. Beccaria—as we have seen—at that time proposed forced labor for life, which now would of course be unthinkable. As he put it:

> Perpetual slavery, then, has in it all that is necessary to deter the most hardened and determined, as much as the punishment of death. There are many who can look upon death with intrepidity and firmness; some through fanaticism and others through vanity, which attends us even to the grave; others from a desperate resolution, either to get rid of their misery, or cease to live, but fanaticism and vanity forsake the criminal in slavery, in chains

> and fetters, in an iron cage and despair seems rather the beginning than the end of their misery. The mind, by collecting itself and uniting all its force, can, for a moment, repel assailing grief; but its most vigorous efforts are insufficient to resist perpetual wretchedness.[6]

Koestler, at the same time, recommended imprisonment for several decades. Today fixed-term imprisonment and life imprisonment are the two alternative modes of punishment that are most widely adopted.

It is a common opinion among abolitionists that even capital punishment does not deter more people than alternative punishments do, however, this statement is certainly challenged by the advocates of capital punishment. They think it can deter maybe only a few people, but certainly some, from committing their planned wrongdoing and if there is only one single person who does not commit a murder just for this reason and if there is only one single innocent victim whose life was saved at the price of the death of other killers, it was already worth it. The question may also be raised whether the life of one single innocent victim is worth as much as the ones of several criminals. Many would answer by saying that the life of each human being is equal and must be protected in the same way; so the lives of several persons (even if they are killers) is worth more than that of one single person but others say that people are not equal and so neither are their lives. A potential victim (an innocent, guiltless person) has more right to life than those who have already proved themselves able to destroy other people, acting out of self-interest. We think that taking any position in this matter—irrespective of other pragmatic arguments in connection with capital punishment—will fundamentally determine who would take which side in the dispute on capital punishment.

Coming back to the theoretical argumentations regarding capital punishment, we must investigate whether imprisonment has in fact a dissuasive force of the same degree as capital punishment, and therefore is indeed unnecessary, or not, thus making capital punishment necessary after all. The advocates of capital punishment start from the point that persons having committed the most serious crimes must be withdrawn from society; they must not be given more chances to endanger the life of the honorable members of the society. That is why fixed-term imprisonment and not real custodial life sentences are considered to be inadequate, since there is a chance that criminals being released from prison would commit another crime. For example, with a person who poisoned someone or some people with malice aforethought, s/he will be able to commit this crime even at the age of eighty. For no physical force is needed for it and evil-doing is not a function of age. It is also possible for someone to wait to be released and to behave well in prison in order to be able to afterwards avenge all the grievances he suffered in prison; whether on society (to the detriment of victims randomly selected) or the person who let police officers put him behind bars. It is also conceivable that if the convict is no longer able to take revenge on the witness, because, for example, he died during the convict's detention, that he avenge the witness's family members and descendants. And it is widely found that the persons having committed the most serious crimes behave the best in prison. In the view of abolitionists, this is because they are compelled to spend a long time in a detention facility and, therefore, it is in their vital interest not to aggravate their own circumstances and to obey internal regulations. In fact, according to many abolitionists, these anti-life criminals actually wake up to the seriousness of their act and its consequences in prison and their good behavior is evidence that they have regretted their act. The advocates of capital punishment, on the other hand, deem this behavior as pure imitation with the single real aim to be released as soon as possible, after which the convict will present the same danger for society as before. Anthony G. Amsterdam, however, gives an answer in the name of abolitionists to the question suggesting that those conditionally released would present a further danger to society. He denies it and relies upon the expertise of those people who decide on their release. Whoever assumes—he thinks—that these functionaries (judges, wardens, psychologists, and parole officers) wrongly assess or can assess as to how big a danger the accused could present to the society in the future, that they themselves furnish an argument against capital punishment. If we acknowledge the opportunity for human error and mistake in exoneration cases, then we must also acknowledge the existence of similar dangers when someone is being sentenced to death. This latter is, consequently, at least as much if not much more dangerous in the event that capital punishment is imposed wrongly and consequently an innocent person is executed.[7]

The advocates of capital punishment, however, intend to protect society in all circumstances from anti-life criminals and so they completely rule out alternative modes of punishment that provide opportunities for released convicts to commit another crime. After all, for the same reason (in terms of the protection of the society) they do not consider real life imprisonment[8] to be proper; namely, if the most severe punishment is real life imprisonment, then—for the lack of any threat by capital punishment—criminals can do anything in prison, they stand to lose nothing, as more severe punishment may not be used against them even if, let us say, they kill their fellow prisoners or a warden.

An example of this is György Matula, who was serving his imprisonment for a definite period of time for homicide, when with a cellmate Lajos Raffael he killed their third cellmate in 2010 on New Year's Eve, without any particular reason, just for fun. At the same time, it is not obvious whether the violence between murderers serving their prison terms is indeed more frequent than violence among the general prison population or among criminals at large. For example, as per Wendy Phillips Wolfson, "in 1973, the inmate's risk of being killed in prison did not exceed the victimization rate for criminal homicide in the general population outside."[9]

Someone who was sentenced to real life imprisonment and has no hope for being released will become incapable of being treated. No matter what he does, it may not aggravate his punishment, as he has got only one life that he has to go through in prison either way, and this will directly result in the efforts of the convict to escape in the most brutal ways, even at the cost of killing wardens, since he may not be sentenced to a punishment that is more severe than the one he is already serving.

For instance, Magda Marinko, an assassin sentenced in Hungary and in Serbia for premeditated homicide, attacked a warden escorting him in December 2003 in the special security ward of the Sátoraljaújhely prison (i.e., in Hungary's safest and strictest prison ward) and pulled him to the ground. It took four other wardens to rescue him. The motivation of Marinko is unknown, but he could have broken the neck of the warden, as he was a skilled fighter as a former foreign legionnaire. Marinko made "death lists" about those arresting, convicting, and guarding him and, due to the potentially dangerous situations he could establish, he had to be transferred two times (first from Sátoraljaújhely to Sopronkőhida, then to "Csillag" in Szeged). Nevertheless, he will not have the chance to kill those on the death lists, because even if he is released on parole in Hungary, he has to start serving his life imprisonment in Serbia.

János Székely also quotes a prime example for that eventuality from the back number of August 18, 1987 of the daily *Népszabadság*.[10] An article was published in the daily newspaper on the second page regarding the prison riot in Elba Island, which rebellion was successfully stamped out, but the authorities could do nothing with the leader of the riot, Mario Tuti. Tuti had been sentenced to life imprisonment three times by then and he openly communicated that he had not been worried about the riot; he had reason to believe that if it failed he would be sentenced to life imprisonment for the fourth time at best. The advocates of capital punishment think that an additional punishment is at all events necessary; if at first only life imprisonment is used, we must also be able to threaten with punishment recidivism and similar crimes committed in prison, so that there should be something that criminals may lose even if they have got nothing left other than their bare lives.

Abolitionists disagree with the latter item (we mean that only the bare lives that criminals condemned to life imprisonment have got left, and that they have nothing to lose other than their lives). They think that such convicts can be threatened not only by taking their lives, but with things that relate to their comfort and facilities in prison. For example, it matters for the convict if he can write or receive letters, talk to his family members from time to time, receive visitors, do sports, or educate himself. In short, by withdrawing these possibilities one can be punished even inside prison—without threatening a convict with taking his life. To refute this, György Pálinkás puts forward, as an instance in Hungary, the case of Richárd Richter[11] who killed three wardens and one of his fellow prisoners during his attempt to escape, since withholding rewards provided in prison had not been threatening enough to him. According to retentionists, this is not true only for Richter; the temptation of the hope for freedom is much greater than the threat of debarring the right to visiting hours.

Real life imprisonment does not even suffice, because it does not permanently exclude the possibility for a criminal to harm another member of society. We have already talked about crimes committed *during* escape from prison that cannot be punished additionally, but potential crimes are more important than those which convicts commit *as a result of* their escape from prison. Prisoners do not have to kill in order to escape; it is just as dangerous if they escape by stealth, not harming anyone, since after getting free they will be just as dangerous to society as they used to be before being caught. As there is no prison from where it would be impossible to escape and unforeseeable and unexpected events may happen at any time (such as fire, earthquake, prison rebellion), which can be used by convicts to escape, so the advocates of capital punishment think that it is only this punishment that can protect society at all events from a murderer killing again. In addition, a person that got out or escaped this way may not find employment (as he is a wanted criminal), but still needs money. Consequently,he will rob others, and if caught he could not expect more to go wrong than the trouble he was in before escaping, and he is likely to do anything indeed in order not to get back into prison. For instance, he even could kill the person he has robbed so that no witness remains alive. It is obvious that where capital punishment does not exist such an escapee does not have anything to lose. He may rob freely or kill his victims, because after being caught he will carry on serving his previous sentence, but with the homicide (with the extermination of the witness) he tries to prevent this. We may say that killing the robbed person is in his interests, because where there is no capital punishment he cannot receive more than real life imprisonment, which means that he would be in the same situation as before his escape and the murder. Not to mention that "[l]ife imprisonment is not necessarily lifelong; life imprisonment without parole still allows governors to pardon prisoners."[12]

Finally, closing this issue, we must mention the concept of continuous decline in the general dissuasive effect of imprisonment.[13] The advocates of capital punishment think that imprisonment has a sufficient deterrent effect (and, therefore, capital punishment may be unnecessary) as long as there is a significant difference in the quality of between "outside" and "in-house" life. While going to prison implies a substantial drop in living standards, it presents a significant dissuasive power for potential criminals. However, as this difference starts to fall (and today we are witnesses to detention centers being modernized) dissuasive force becomes weaker and weaker. In fact, in extreme cases prognostication may become positive: heated prison cells, three meals a day, the possibility of washing, education, and sports and so on, can be more attractive for homeless and outcast people than railway stations, subway underpasses, and everyday begging. Thus, in these cases, you cannot say in any event that threatening criminals with imprisonment suffices and there is no need to hold out the prospect of capital punishment. Liberty is not a value for such persons as they do not know what to do with it; they are unable to use the opportunities associated with freedom and, therefore, losing it does not present as much of a fear for them than if it was about their own lives. Abolitionists on the other hand rebut this argument that theft is a typical crime committed by outcast and homeless people, and that these unfortunate persons many times commit minor offences of such a degree that they can live through the winter in a penitentiary or prison after being sentenced for it. They consider liberty (as their own "property") as a value, since most of them are not even prepared to obey the fixed in-house regulations of homeless shelters either; they prefer to sleep in the street in the cold weather instead; and if this is so (and it is so) then how much more of a threat can prison present for them as compared to the latter?

Notes

1. This topic is also connected to the issue of the goal of punishment. This goal (or the effect of the penalty of death) can be incapacitation as well. (For the incapacitation effect, see e.g.: Jack P. Gibbs: Preventive Effect of Capital Punishment other than Deterrence, pp. 106–108. In: Hugo Adam Bedau: *The Death Penalty in America*. Oxford University Press, 1982, pp. 103–116. Gibbs himself enumerates several other effects of the criminal penalty that I do not deal with now.
2. As it has been seen this statement does not prevent Beccaria from suggesting lifelong forced labor as an alternative punishment, even though it causes extreme suffering.
3. Cesare Beccaria: *An Essay On Crimes and Punishments* [1764]. E-book. Liberty Fund, Indianapolis, Indiana, 2011, p. 99.

4. Ibid.,51.
5. Ibid.,p. 52.
6. Ibid.
7. Anthony G. Amsterdam: Capital Punishment, p. 357. In: Hugo Adam Bedau (ed.): *The Death Penalty in America*. Oxford University Press, 1982, pp. 353–354.
8. For the Hungarian regulation of real life imprisonment, see e.g.: Balázs Gellér: A tényleges életfogytig tartó szabadságvesztés—büntetőjog-elméleti meggondolások tükrében. (The actual life imprisonment—in the light of criminal law considerations.) In: Miklós Hollán and Tünde A.Barabás: A negyedik magyar büntetőkódex. (*The Fourth Hungarian Penal Code*.) MTA TK–OKRI, Budapest, 2017, pp. 87–108. For the review of the European scene, see: Ferenc Nagy: Gondolatok az életfogytig tartó szabadságvesztésről. (Thoughts on real life imprisonment.) In: *Magyar Jog*, 2013/5. szám, pp. 265–271.
9. Wendy Phillips Wolfson: The Deterrent Effect of the Death Penalty upon Prison Murder, p. 160. In: Hugo Adam Bedau: *The Death Penalty in America*. Oxford University Press, 1982, pp. 159–173.
10. János Székely: A halálbüntetés. (The death penalty.) In: *Magyar Jog*, 1990/3, p. 257, citation 16.
11. See: György Pálinkás: Requiem for a Legal Institution (Requiem egy jogintézményért), p. 72. In: *Belügyi Szemle*, 2001/6.
12. Ernest Van den Haag: Capital Punishment Should Be Retained, p. 145. In: Mary E. Williams (ed.): *Capital Punishment: Current Controversies*. Greenhaven Press, 2005, pp. 145–147.
13. See: Székely: op. cit., pp. 249–250.

5

Miscarriage of Justice

The main concern of abolitionists is that in cases of a mistake capital punishment is irreversible. Even though time cannot be turned back in cases of imprisonment applied mistakenly, and years spent behind bars for non-committed crimes cannot be returned, there is still a chance to carry on with life after the realization of the mistake. The wrongly applied death penalty, however, terminates life permanently and irreversibly. Humans are not perfect, nor are judges; they may convict persons who did not commit the crime they have been charged with. Judicial mistakes are not limited to simpler cases, they may appear in any case. There are more and more cases in which capital punishment is applied wrongly, as there have been cases in the past years in which courts convicted persons upon questionable or disputed evidence and today, mainly with DNA tests and other modern forensic techniques it may be concluded without doubt that these persons did not commit the crime.[1] The number of such cases exceeds one hundred in the United States only[2] and the victims of the miscarriage of justice were mainly colored people. It could be stated that such problems cannot occur today, but this would not be true. When humans judge humans the possibility of making mistakes remains and not only judges, but other participants of the procedure may make

Z. J. Toth, *Changing Attitudes Towards the Death Penalty*,
https://doi.org/10.1007/978-3-030-47557-4_5

mistakes. András László Pap, for example, stresses the influence of wrong expert opinions on judicial decisions. In order to support his statement he cites the case of James Grigson of Texas, who concluded 80 percent of judicial requests with considering the accused permanently dangerous to society and his expert opinions led to judicial decisions ordering capital punishment in the given cases, despite the fact that the American Psychological Association found two-third of these opinions ill-founded and Grigson unsuitable for expert work.[3] Still, the attorney generals of Texas kept appointing him as expert in similar cases for preparing opinions about the personalities of accused persons.

In Hungary, the well-known case of a young woman called "Zsanett" was a good example of the possibility that even an objective, knowledge-based expert opinion may be wrong. Of the two well-known and acknowledged psychologist experts appointed in the case of the alleged rape of E. Zsanett one gave an opinion according to which E. Zsanett presented her statements naturally and shows signs which may be shown only by those who suffered the shocking events. According to the other expert the presentation of the alleged victim was unreal and only the product of her fantasy. Obviously, the author of this work cannot know what happened, but based on formal logic it may be stated that *one* of the acknowledged experts' opinions is wrong, as a statement and its opposite cannot be right *at the same time*.

The misjudgment of the expert may not be the only thing to lead to sending a mentally ill or innocent person to death row: there are several procedural phases in which there is a chance for making mistakes (or for conscious manipulation), which may also affect the judicial decision. In the United States, for example, 70 percent of judgments ordering capital punishment between 1973 and 1995 were changed by the appellate court, mainly because the lower court made a serious procedural mistake.[4] These procedural irregularities ranged from the biased judicial information provided to jury members, and the employment of informers interested in conviction, to the neglecting of mitigating evidence by the prosecution (or to keeping them secret from the defense lawyer and the accused).

It is rather common, for example, that convicts of murders are put into cells in which there is a cellmate who is charged with less serious crimes or has been sentenced for such crimes. The attorney general offers a guilty plea, which means that it drops charges against the accused or charges with less serious crimes, or proposes for the court to release the rest of the punishment, or—if he hasn't been convicted yet—to change preliminary detention to house arrest, in return for which he expects the cellmate to give proof that the person charged with murder actually did commit the crime. In such cases the cellmate is interested in providing the evidence, and there have been several cases in which the—innocent—convict was sentenced upon the incriminating statement of the cellmate; for example this latter one stated that the accused had confessed about the murder.

Besides this, in many cases the total incompetence of the defense lawyer is the reason why the accused is sentenced to death (e.g., the lawyer sleeps through the hearings). Some judges like working with such defense lawyers, because they do not bother with "unnecessary" cross examination, evidence proposals, or other remarks. It should be noted that this characteristic of appointed defense lawyers is not an American specialty. In any country, if defense lawyers receive low amounts of pay, and it depends on the judge whether they are appointed again, the lawyers will be interested in spending the lowest amount of time on the cases, allowing some time for the next one and in not bothering the judge too much in conducting quick hearings, because otherwise they might not be appointed again.

Based on his experiences gained in four US states[5] Stephen B. Bright arrives to the same conclusions; in one-third/one-fourth of procedures conducted for the most serious crimes the defense lawyer had been excluded from the chamber, but then readmitted, or his operation had been suspended, or he had been convicted for committing a crime. For example, in Illinois four accused persons, who were eventually sentenced to death were assisted by the same defense lawyer, who was famous for being the only lawyer in Illinois who had been excluded from the chamber twice. He managed the first two cases after his readmission following the first exclusion, but before his second exclusion; he was readmitted even though he was emotionally unstable and a drunk.[6] Finally, the partiality of jury members toward the accused may result in capital punishment. This latter phenomenon is so apparent in the USA that it does not even require any explanation; significantly more black people are sentenced to death if the jury mainly consists of white people than if its members are mainly black. Moreover: often the decision about guilt depends on the color of the accused and of the majority of jury members, as it was proven in the procedure of O. J. Simpson.

Abolitionists believe that in addition to the already revealed cases there have been many cases of miscarriage of justice and only some will be revealed in the future. Many of them are not revealed (or will not be revealed in the future) because it is useless to deal with a case which has been closed by an execution; the consequences of the judgment cannot be undone, the dead convict cannot be revived, thus compensation is impossible; authorities are not interested in pointing out their own mistakes and publishing their miscarriages of injustice. Earlier mistakes were revealed mainly because the perpetrator was caught in relation to another crime and he admitted the perpetration of crimes with which someone else had been charged (and for which someone else had been convicted) and mentioned some circumstances in his confession which could be known only by the perpetrator; otherwise cases which ended with execution were never reopened. (Obviously, if authorities convicted and executed somebody they were not interested in revealing their mistake.) The situation has not changed much today; old, disputed cases are reopened only if there are serious reasons for it and mainly upon the strict claims of the relatives of the executed convict. This means, therefore, that the majority of miscarriages of justice made in the past will never be revealed, even though with the modern DNA tests the majority of disputed cases could be verified.

Abolitionists, therefore, believe that judicial mistakes have and will always exist and miscarriage of justice may be eliminated only if capital punishment is abolished; however, the advocates of capital punishment claim that mistake is not a necessary element of justice, and it usually happens in less relevant cases. In those cases in which capital punishment may be applied, the introduction and extension of procedural guarantees may avoid the possibility of wrongful capital punishment. Such procedural guarantees might be if capital punishment could be applied only with the unanimous decision of bench members; if the number of bench members was increased to seven or nine and each member had to give his consent to capital punishment; or if the bench could consider the application of this punishment only based on the separate proposals of two or three attorneys, etc.

The advocates of capital punishment state that mistakes should not be corrected by applying life imprisonment or in imprisonment for a definite period of time, but in such cases conviction as such should be avoided. This means that any punishment (including fines) should be applied only if the court is convinced beyond doubt that the accused is guilty, otherwise (if there is the slightest doubt about guilt) the accused should be acquitted, no matter if the case concerns capital punishment or not. József Földvári wrote: "I firmly believe that in such cases it is not the capital punishment which should be avoided, but conviction, as such. … Conviction, and the application of any kind of punishment could be applied only if there is no doubt at all that it was the accused who committed the crime he was charged with."[7] Alexander Deak shares this view; if there is a possibility of mistake, capital punishment should not be applied, but the possibility of applying it should not be excluded in *each* case (even in the most obvious ones). If we concentrated on mistakes, we should not do anything, should abolish justice as a whole, not to make any more mistakes. Obviously, this is a very straightforward opinion which cannot be right in this form, because it is unquestionable that even if there are mistakes made during the course of justice, they are at a different quality if the case involves capital punishment.

Some scholars deny the possibility of miscarriage of justice. Hungarian György Pálinkás believes that the rules of evidence make mistakes impossible, as there has never been such a case in Hungary—at least regarding common crimes.[8] Regarding executions based on wrong judicial decisions, as far as information is available (not considering those executed after summary show trials, as they were victims rather of political murders, not of capital punishment) no such case happened in Hungary in the decades preceding the abolition of capital punishment in 1990 (and obviously were impossible afterwards). At the same time it did happen that the convict had not committed the crime for which he would be eventually sentenced to death (but the sentence was not executed). So, while there is indeed no knowledge of innocent people executed in Hungary, with, certainly, the exception of the political show trials following the revolution of 1956, we do know of two persons who were sentenced to death before the political transition of 1989–1990 without their having committed the crimes of which they were accused, but their innocence was proved before the death sentence could be carried out. Two such persons were the "sex criminal of Martfű"[9] and Simon Ébnert.[10]

Nevertheless, wrongful convictions occurred even after 1990, which proves that there is no such infallible criminal procedure law system where only appropriate and solid judgments are made. The most famous example for this is the so-called Mor bank robbery. Mor is a small town one of whose banks was robbed in May 2002 by several gunmen who murdered all the eight people who were on the premises. The suspects, Ede Kaiser and László Hajdú, were apprehended shortly after the crime, while a third alleged perpetrator was supposed by the police to be still on the loose. The court adjudged Kaiser guilty of aggravated murder as a coactor and sentenced him to life without parole, whereas Hajdu was condemned to fifteen years of prison as an accomplice. The appellate court later annulled Hajdu's sentence, ordered the court of first instance for the retrial of the case but, as a final decision, upheld Kaiser's punishment. Only when the real offenders had been arrested did it become apparent that they had nothing to do with the slaughter. Many a lawyer is confident that if capital punishment had been in effect in Hungary at that time, Kaiser would have already been executed by the time the real perpetrators were apprehended. Obviously, Kaiser is only legally innocent, otherwise he made a living from robberies, but he did not commit murder which he was charged with and convicted of.

Obvious irregularities led to the conviction of Attila Szántai who received thirteen years imprisonment in a high security prison for "attempting to intentionally kill more than one person" (killing one and attempting to kill another) and spent six years and nine months in prison when the execution of his sentence was suspended, because it had been proven that he acted in self-defense. The Metropolitan Court of Budapest, as court of first instance, held, and the Appellate Court of Budapest, as court of second instance confirmed, based on an originally very unlikely statement of facts that on January 6, 2001 Szántai wanted to kill two members of the mafia organization called "black army." He killed József Vajda and injured Attila Szűcs. According to the court decisions he did this after initiating fights with the two "victims" and others in the usual pub of the criminal organization located close to Szántai's hotel. He was hit on the jaw twice, then he dropped his clothes and ran towards his hotel while shouting for help. According to the judicial reasoning Vajda and Szűcs went to the hotel to return the clothes and when they left Szántai started shooting at them in his hotel without any reason. (The clothes were not found in or around the hotel.) Szántai was lucky because the alleged leader of the "black army," Róbert Magyar, was caught and was later sentenced to life imprisonment together with some members of the "black army," among them Attila Szűcs, who survived the events of January 2001 and as the nineteenth person accused of the case he was sentenced to twelve years imprisonment in a high security prison. The facts about the case relating to Szántai resembled the ones which were presented by Szántai during his procedure. According to this in the real course of events he was introduced to Szűcs by a policeman in 2000 (this policeman was later also convicted, and the statement of facts of the case confirmed those said by Szántai) and Szűcs immediately wanted to force Szántai to pay protection money. He resisted, therefore, on January 6, 2001 he was extorted and threatened in the bar belonging to the criminal organization, moreover, he was beaten. He lost his clothes during the fight, tried to escape and shout for help, then he threatened Vajda and Szűcs, who followed him to his hotel, with his licensed weapon, and fired warning shots. Vajda tried to take the gun from him but if fired, giving Vajda a deadly injury; this was considered an accident both by the Metropolitan Court of Budapest, as court of first instance held, and the Appellate Court of Budapest, as court of second instance which acted in the reopened procedure (contrary to the proposal of the defense for self-defense). After this Szűcs tried to escape, but changed his mind and attacked Szántai who rendered him unable to fight with a deliberate shot. This act was considered self-defense by both courts. The final decision about the innocence of Szántai was delivered in March 2012.

It is important to take discrimination into consideration when inspecting faulty judicial decisions as it is not a rare occurrence that the judge is also imbued with social prejudices and who, as a result, makes a—sometimes wrong—decision on the basis of his own biases. This is a universal attitude of humankind rather than an American peculiarity, which led to wrongful convictions in Hungary as well and will always do as long as adjudication is performed by humans. That is why it makes a huge difference whether there is a possibility for the infliction of irreversible sentences in a particular legal system or not. The case of Dénes Pusoma is an excellent example showing that mistakes and errors can take place at any time. We are not talking about a capital case here because Pusoma was not accused of murder and not even of homicide, but was charged with battery causing death. Nonetheless, the procedural errors in question could well occur in any homicide or murder case.

Pusoma was an extremely poor Roma (gipsy) man who earned a living by doing odd jobs. An elderly woman was killed in a small Hungarian village on the evening of March 16, 1994 and Pusoma was shortly charged with this crime. Pusoma did indeed visit the house at noon on that day where the witnesses saw him quarrel with the woman and leave upset afterwards. The mentally disabled brother of the victim's neighbor testified that at the time of the crime, that is, in the evening, he had seen Pusoma entering the house and reappearing later with his clothes covered in blood. The court-appointed forensic expert said that the testimony was realistic and probably true. Later in the investigation, another person in pre-trial detention, with whom he shared a cell and who wished to be put under house arrest (for this reason he promised the public prosecutor to find evidence for Pusoma's guilt if he was going to be granted his request), handed a letter over to the authorities. This latter, according to the informer, had been written by Pusoma and which he opened out of curiosity. The letter contained a confession in Pusoma's handwriting, as attested by an expert. The circumstances of the composition of the letter are still not known to date, but the intellectually handicapped person admitted to the crime. There was an additional piece of evidence against his innocence: the scent sample supposedly originating from the crime scene (from the room of the victim) was identified to be the same as Pusoma's by two dogs on five different occasions, while a match with other persons' scents was deemed implausible. However, it was not documented either in the pictures taken by the police or in the onsite investigation report that the scent sample had truly come from the crime scene, the lady's bedroom. In other words, there was no proof that the scent sample (which undoubtedly was Pusoma's) had been taken in the bedroom and not in the kitchen where Pusoma had demonstrably and actually been. At the same time, the police had been disregarding any fact interfering with their theory all along the investigation, even though several witnesses stated that they had seen two strange men near the house of the victim at the presumed time of the crime.

In the end, after the judgment of the court of first instance had come into effect and Pusoma had already been serving his prison term against which he did not lodge an appeal (to be more precise, his incoherent request was not regarded as an appeal), it turned out by a stroke of luck (the real perpetrators were apprehended) that the crime had been committed by those two men who had been seen near the crime scene. That is, in these proceedings, a number of mistakes led to the conviction of an innocent person—mistakes made by the police; by the public prosecutor, who did not instruct the police to conduct a more thorough investigation and to inspect other possible scenarios as well and who accepted the offer of a police informant, giving credits unconditionally to the evidence supplied by him; by the court which failed to give a careful consideration to the aforementioned errors and which based the credibility of the evidence only on one of the contradictory experts' opinions on the reliability of the mentally disabled eyewitness; and by the assigned counsel, who did not warn his defendant about the consequences of an overdue appeal, moreover, although it should have been his ethical obligation as an attorney to do so, he did not even file an appeal in his own name.

Sadly, the story of Dénes Pusoma did not end well. After it had been found out that he had been falsely imprisoned, his prison term was suspended and he was exonerated. However, when he claimed for compensation from the state for nonmaterial damages, his case was dismissed because the Hungarian law requires the defendant to lodge an appeal against the first-instance sentence in order to be entitled for compensation. Not much later, Pusoma committed suicide.

The cases of Mór, Szántai, and Pusoma are only three random instances of wrongful convictions. However, numerous erroneous judicial decisions that were not learned of are highly likely to have happened besides the known ones, even in capital cases, and only a few of them will be discovered even in the future. Therefore, simply the fact that there is no knowledge of ill-founded death sentences and executions in Hungary or in any country does not necessarily mean that such incidents have not happened. Plenty of judicial murders (wrongful imposition of the death penalty) have not been—and most of them will never be—discovered because the re-examination of a case concluded with capital punishment is useless. The consequences of the sentence are irreversible as the person cannot be revived, their death cannot be redressed, and pointing out mistakes and drawing attention to them is not in the authorities' interest. Mostly, such errors were and still at present are, discovered only if the perpetrator had been apprehended on account of another investigation and, among others, they confessed to that particular crime as well, of which somebody else was accused (as well as convicted) previously and mentioned circumstances in their statement only they could know. Otherwise, cases concluded with execution were not further inspected. Evidently, once the authorities have convicted somebody and executed them, they do not attempt to reveal a possible slip.[11] The situation has essentially remained the same up to this day; the closed, but debatable cases are re-opened only for strong reasons—and ordinarily only when the convict's relatives demand it. Hence, although most of the old cases of debatable nature could be cleared up, it is very plausible that the vast majority of the past judicial murders will never come to light. That is, wrongful judicial decisions were, are, and will always be made[12] and the abolitionists are right in that the easiest and most risk-free way of avoiding judicial murders is to keep away from the application of capital punishment. It is of course possible that by introducing increased procedural guarantees (e.g., independent indictments from two or three public prosecutors should be necessary for a death warrant, or the judicial council should only be able to inflict the death penalty when they are unanimous in their decision), the number of ill-founded death-sentences could be reduced in those legal systems in which this punishment is still in use, but the complete elimination of possible errors could still not be accomplished.

From those mentioned above it follows that not knowing about something does not mean it did not happen, therefore, it cannot be stated for sure that no one was hung innocently in Hungary, as (just like everywhere else) authorities are not interested in reopening old cases in order to reveal their mistakes and rehabilitate a dead person. Some others (mainly Americans) reason that even if there were few cases in the past, today they could not happen due to procedural guarantees and modern evidence procedures which lead to undoubtedly correct results. Abolitionists believe, however, that in addition to the fact that there are no perfect methods, it is possible to make mistakes even today. For example, in the United States accused persons of certain crimes causing public outrage are convicted based on insufficient evidence, partly because judges give in to the pressure coming from the public and partly because investigation authorities want to show quick results. They wish to prove their competence and to prevent public outrage which might occur if the investigation remained unsuccessful for a longer time, therefore the first possible suspect is arrested and brought to court quickly, even if the evidence is not clear. If the person is black, the court and the jury is white, it may happen despite the (obviously imperfect) modern procedural guarantees that an innocent man is sentenced to death.

In noncapital cases it may happen that the accused is convicted upon the report (statement) of the alleged victim, without any specific evidence. This happened to Brian Banks who was only sixteen at the time of the report (in 2002) and was charged with rape and against whom the only evidence was the statement of the alleged victim; however, Banks provided evidence against himself when during plea bargaining he admitted to have been the perpetrator of the alleged rape, due to which he received five years imprisonment—otherwise he could have received up to forty years from the jury. Finally, ten years after the conviction, in May 2012 he was proven to be innocent. Banks met his alleged victim and recorded the meeting on tape, including the admission by the woman stating that she had made up the whole story in order to sue the school, the security personnel, and security system which was unable to prevent such crime. (The school paid 1.5 million USD to the victim for her suffering.) This, in addition to the case of Dénes Pusoma, is a good example that even confessions do not mean certainty, and that the guilty plea (and the intention of state attorneys to increase their figures to 100% percent) is sometimes not only dysfunctional, but also counterproductive and contributes to wrong judgments and jury verdicts.

All in all, despite procedural guarantees and modern forensic tests there is only one perfect way to avoid the miscarriage of justice: to restrain from applying capital punishment.

Notes

1. Attila Badó and János Bóka raise attention to this danger. In their book they analyzed twelve cases in which it turned out later, through DNA tests that the originally convicted persons were innocent. See: Attila Badó and János Bóka: Ártatlanul halálra ítéltek. (Az amerikai igazságszolgáltatás tévedései) (Innocent people sentenced to death. [Mistakes in American justice]) *Nyitott Könyv Kiadó*, 2003. For further descriptive examples see: Stephen B. Bright: Why the United States Will Join the Rest of the World in Abandoning Capital Punishment, pp. 158–165. In: Hugo Adam Bedau and Paul G.Cassell (eds.): *Debating the Death Penalty*. Oxford University Press, Oxford/New York, 2004, pp. 152–182.
2. Up till September 2012 140 people were released in the past forty years who had been sentenced to death innocently based on false evidence and/or insufficient defense lawyer activities. They were acquitted after the realization of the mistake (most were in Florida and Illinois, 23 and 20; 71 of the 140 were black, 55 white, 12 Latino and 2 other). (Cf.: DPIC Fact Sheet /September 7, 2012/, p. 2. http://www.deathpenalty-info.org/documents/FactSheet.pdf).
3. See: András László Pap: Pénz, politika, jogbiztonság – halálbüntetés az Egyesült Államokban (Money, politics, legal certainty – the death penalty in the United States), p. 76. In: *Belügyi Szemle*, 2001/6, pp. 74–83.
4. Pap: op. cit., p. 80.
5. Illinois, Kentucky, Tennessee, Texas.
6. Stephen B. Bright: op. cit., p. 169. For other cases of incompetent defense lawyers proceeding in capital cases see for example: Ira Mickenberg: Drunk, Sleeping and Incompetent Lawyers: Is It Possible to Keep Innocent People Off Death Row? *University of Dayton Law Review*, Vol. 29, 2003–2004, pp. 319–327.
7. József Földvári: Kriminálpolitika (Crime politics). KJK, Budapest, p. 133.
8. See: György Pálinkás: Requiem for a Legal Institution [Requiem egy jogintézményért], p. 67. In: *Belügyi Szemle*, 2001/6.
9. Cf.: András Sajó: A halálbüntetés alkotmányossága. Szakvélemény. (The constitutionality of the death penalty. Expert opinion.) In: Tibor Horváth (ed.): A halálbüntetés megszüntetése Magyarországon. Dokumentumgyűjtemény. (The abolition of capital punishment in Hungary. Document collection.) Halálbüntetést Ellenzők Ligája (Anti-Death Penalty League), Miskolc, 1991, p. 93.

10. Cf.: P. Gál Judit: Ördögök ügyvédei 2—Gyilkosságból felmentve (Devil's Lawyers 2—acquitted of murder). BABUSZ Bt., Budapest, 2007, pp. 81–84.
11. That is why, for example, the Hungarian police deserve praise, which re-opened the case of the Mór bank robbery claiming the life of eight people despite the alleged perpetrator having been convicted with binding force.
12. For other, non-Hungarian examples, see: Stephen B. Bright: Why the United States Will Join the Rest of the World in Abandoning Capital Punishment, pp. 158–165. In: Hugo Adam Bedau and Paul G.Cassell (eds.): *Debating the Death Penalty.* Oxford University Press, Oxford/New York, 2004, pp. 152–182; as for, specifically, the possible lack of effective representation, see: Ellen Kreitzberg: Death Without Justice. *Santa Clara Law Review,* Vol. 35, 1994–1995, pp. 485–518; Ira Mickenberg: Drunk, Sleeping, and Incompetent Lawyers: Is It Possible to Keep Innocent People Off Death Row? *University of Dayton Law Review*, Vol. 29, No. 2, 2003–2004, pp. 319–327.

6

The Goal of Punishment

The cases discussed in the previous chapters provide sufficient ground for debate on capital punishment, but we could get closer to the truth if we examined the problem in light of the goals of punishment. In Hungary, article 79 of the Penal Code (act C of 2012) declares the goal of punishment as: "for the protection of society the goal of punishment is to prevent the commission of crime either by the perpetrator or by anyone else." Hence, punishment has a final goal, the protection of society, and there are two direct (or partial) goals in order to reach it. The first one is the prevention of any further criminal behavior of the perpetrator himself (special prevention); the second one is the prevention of anyone else from conducting behavior in the future which is against criminal law (general prevention). In addition to these, there is a further goal which appears in the literature from time to time: retribution and, in relation to this, the restoration of the legal order which has been violated by the commission of the crime. Other relating aims can be the enforcement of the principles of justice against the perpetrators, the reinforcement of the rule of law, the reassurance of the public and thus the restoration of public order and trust, and the compensation of the victim's family. (These goals may be called repression.)

Z. J. Toth, *Changing Attitudes Towards the Death Penalty*,
https://doi.org/10.1007/978-3-030-47557-4_6

The advocates of capital punishment believe that the goal of punishment is just retribution. This means that the application of capital punishment is necessary, because this is the only punishment which is proportionate to the crime, therefore, it is able to meet the public's need for justice. Abolitionists deny that the life of a person (even if he is a murderer) may be taken away to calm down the public and satisfy the need for justice (based on this the obligation to pay tax could be abolished as a whole, because the majority of society would probably support it). Those who oppose capital punishment believe that only goals defined in the Penal Code should be considered and these should be kept in mind when murderers are sentenced.

The main goal, therefore, is the protection of society, which may be achieved by realizing the two partial goals. One of these partial goals is general prevention, the other one is special prevention. In theory the latter one may be realized in three ways: first, by improving the behavior of the perpetrator, the final goal of which is to resocialize the offender, to lead him back to society after successful moral education, which means that the perpetrator regrets his actions for internal, psychological reasons, condemn his previous self, and becomes a law abiding citizen, and a useful member of society. Second, this goal may be realized in a way that the perpetrator does not regret his actions and does not believe that committing crime is morally wrong, but his fear of punishment and state sanctioning prevents him from acting this way in the future. This method is deterrence or legal education, through which society may be protected even if the tendency of the perpetrator to commit crime remains, because it introduces fear from punishment (instead of moral beliefs) as a criminal law barrier. This is less ideal than the previous solution, of course, but it still facilitates the protection of society. The third method is to make the perpetrator harmless, which (if the first two methods prove to be unsuccessful) still serves the achievement of the final goal (protection of society) properly, but it is too drastic and thus should not be applied frequently.

It is obvious that in the case of capital punishment the resocialization of the perpetrator is impossible. The situation is the same with legal education, because after execution the deterrent effect is uninterpretable (at least regarding the executed person); there is no need to deter a dead person. Some abolitionists trust the success of these methods even in case of perpetrators committing the most serious crimes, therefore, they reject capital punishment because it prevents the achievement of resocialization. The advocates of capital punishment believe that murderers should not be resocialized at all; in the case of a person who took another's life the correction effect is doubtful, therefore, the safety of society should not be put at risk by trying to resocialize murderers. They argue that the lives of innocent, decent people should not be risked in favor of murderers who *have already proven* to be unworthy of the trust of society.

This leads to the conclusion that the advocates of capital punishment only consider the third method acceptable, the elimination of perpetrators, and in an extreme way by physically eliminating the perpetrator. The majority of capital punishment's opposers also support elimination, but its milder form, namely separation from other, decent members of society. The main difference between the two groups, therefore, is in relation to the special preventive goal. Abolitionists believe that it is enough to apply life imprisonment for reaching the goal, the advocates of capital punishment warn about early release (not life imprisonment without parole, presidential pardon) and about the always existing threat of escape. In these cases, the perpetrator will (or may) be free again one day, therefore, elimination is not realized. Furthermore, the advocates of capital punishment completely reject the beliefs of abolitionists according to which even murderers may be corrected and resocialized.[1] In the opinion of László Gábor Hajnal the majority of examples prove that "the correction of the perpetrator is merely an idea from the age of fifteen, even though there are exceptions."[2] It is a question, of course, whether due to these few exceptions it is wise to put society at risk with the resocialization of perpetrators. The advocates of capital punishment obviously answer negatively, because special prevention may be *completely realized* only if the perpetrator is eliminated for good, because in every other case there is a chance for repeating the crime.[3]

Another direct goal of punishment serving the protection of society (next to special prevention) is general prevention, namely the prevention of any member of society who has not committed any crime to start doing so in the future. This may be achieved by establishing sanctions (threatening with punishment), by applying the sanctions to the crimes of other criminals, and mainly by executing these sanctions in reality. It shall not be forgotten that the use of these methods has one common ground: deterrence. It has a role also in "legal education" described at special prevention, but it is even more important for general prevention. Here it is not enough to deter one person (the perpetrator) from the commission of another crime, but all members of society (i.e., many potential criminals), which means that the enforcement of the goal of punishment appears in a new dimension and gets extremely high importance. In this latter case, however, punishing the individual (the perpetrator of the crime) becomes a mere tool; it is necessary only to teach a lesson to others. This is the reason why abolitionists deny the application of capital punishment for the goals of general prevention, because this logic leads to the result that the perpetrator dies only in order to deter others from committing a crime, even though they might have never thought of committing one. Furthermore, they believe that capital punishment is not suitable for deterrence.[4] The advocates of capital punishment do not only focus on general prevention, as the goal of punishment, but also stress the idea of special prevention resulting in the final elimination of the perpetrator and of just retribution. Moreover, they state that if capital punishment did not have a deterring-incapacitation effect for society no other forms of punishment would have it, in which case general prevention as such could be deleted from the goals of punishment.

Regarding this issue it is worth mentioning Beccaria, who believes that the main goal of punishment is to be just.[5] In addition to this he considers the protection of society and general prevention important goals, but (contrary to the present Hungarian regulation) he does not view these in the relationship of the final and direct goals, but coordinate, equal goals. If these goals of punishment are in harmony with the principles of justness, they may provide reason for the use of capital punishment. (He considers this necessary if even lifelong forced labor is insufficient for deterring people from committing crime.) "The death of a citizen cannot be necessary, but in one case: when, though deprived of his liberty, he has such power and connections as may endanger the security of the nation; when his existence may produce a dangerous revolution in the established form of government ..."[6] This is where Beccaria states that capital punishment may be applied if it is *for the protection of society*. Then he declares the possibility to use capital punishment for the purposes of general prevention: "I do not believe that it is necessary to kill a citizen except if his death is the only real deterring force from committing crime: this is the other reason why the application of capital punishment may be considered just and necessary."[7]

Finally, we close the chapter on the goals of punishment with the thoughts of József Földvári, who believes that the existence or abolition of capital punishment is "a political issue."[8] Goals of punishment may reason both the existence and the abolition of capital punishment. "Goal of punishment proving the unnecessity of capital punishment may be found easily, but obviously we may find goals which ground the existence of this form of punishment,"[9] therefore, the need for the existence or abolition of capital punishment cannot be decided merely upon the examination of the goals of punishment, it is necessary to consider other (political, sociological, criminology, and statistical) reasons too.

Notes

1. It should be noted that in cases of real-life imprisonment supported by some abolitionists (instead of capital punishment) the resocialization of the perpetrator is excluded as well.
2. Hajnal László Gábor: Bitófa nélkül. Töprengések, monológok a halálbüntetésről (Without gallows. Reflections, monologues about the death penalty). In: *Börtönügyi Szemle*, 1997/3, p. 97.
3. Between 1997–2011 the number of recidivists for homicide was between three and fourteen, of special recidivists was between one and eight, and of multiple recidivists was between four and twenty-three in Hungary. (For details about this issue see Chap. 2 on the deterrent effect.)
4. For details about this issue see Chap. 2 on the deterrent effect.
5. "*For a punishment to be just* (highlighted by me—T.J.Z.), it should be at a degree which is just necessary to deter people from committing crime ..." Cesare Beccaria: *An Essay On Crimes and Punishments* [1764]. E-book. Liberty Fund, Indianapolis, Indiana, 2011, p. 89.
6. Ibid., p. 87.
7. Ibid.,p. 88.
8. József Földvári: Kriminálpolitika (Crime politics). KJK, Budapest, p. 131.
9. Op. cit.

7

Economic Considerations

Right at the beginning of the chapter it shall be stated that a human life is not a matter of money. Financial considerations cannot reason life or death, as capital punishment may be proven cheaper or more expensive than life imprisonment. Even if those are right who say that applying capital punishment to a murderer is cheaper than keeping, guarding, feeding, etc. him in prison till he dies, this simply cannot be a reason in favor of capital punishment. The sick and the old are not exterminated either, based on the fact that keeping them alive costs more to society than their death. Therefore, even the issue of capital punishment applicable for a criminal cannot be solved merely upon financial considerations. Nevertheless, pro and contra reasons about the financial issues of capital punishment are brought up quite often in the literature, hence, if we aim at thoroughly examining the issue of capital punishment, we cannot neglect this aspect.

Just like in cases of the other issues, there are two opinions regarding financial questions. The advocates of capital punishment argue that sentencing murderers to death and executing the punishment is cheaper than keeping them until they die. They have two reasons. First, if a murderer is executed, there won't be any more related costs for the state, while

Z. J. Toth, *Changing Attitudes Towards the Death Penalty*,
https://doi.org/10.1007/978-3-030-47557-4_7

if he is sentenced to life imprisonment he has to be fed, guarded for decades, his cell should be heated and lit, etc., which means that keeping the convict alive puts an extra burden on society and the convict costs much more to the state than if he was executed.

The other approach has an economic-legal theoretical starting point. The basic idea of economic approach to criminal law (criminal law and economics, economic analyses of criminal law) is that the costs emerged in relation to the crime and the criminal process do not only include costs of the execution of punishment, but also the material and immaterial damage, disadvantage, negatives, as well as all lost material and immaterial advantage, benefit and positives which were caused by the perpetrator by *committing* the crime. If, therefore, the commission of crimes results in material and immaterial disadvantages for society (and mainly for the victim), the costs of society may be reduced not only by choosing the cheaper solution in the dilemma of capital punishment or life imprisonment (either of these two), but social disadvantages may be reduced also (mainly) by preventing as many crimes as possible. Putting it in simple words: the less crimes are committed, the lower the disadvantage of society is in relation to criminal activity.

The aim, therefore, is to prevent potential criminals from committing crimes. Criminals are generally considered to be rational beings who weigh the expected benefits of their actions, as well as the negative consequences, therefore, the best way of deterrence (and or reducing criminal activities) is to make these negative consequences as severe for criminals as possible. The economic theory of law states that the price of crime is punishment. The bigger the crime, the bigger the punishment, obviously and the bigger the punishment is, the more people are deterred from paying this "price," from committing that specific crime, therefore, the higher the price, the lower the net benefit is, hence the number of those who are satisfied with this low benefit will drop (in consideration of income resulting from law abiding activities).

Obviously, this price is highest in the case of capital punishment, which means that the possible net benefit resulting from homicide will be the lowest by using capital punishment. Capital punishment is the penalty which is mostly able to deter rationally thinking people from committing homicide, thus the costs to society will be lowest if capital punishment is applied. Although some murderers do not think and act rationally and there will be always some who are not held back by the high "price" of committing a crime, in a realistic approach not only the abolition of homicides would be a step forward, but also a drop in their number.

The other group of arguments denies both the law and economics approach (which is a fiction, according to abolitionists) and that the application of capital punishment would be cheaper for the state than life imprisonment. These arguments reject the latter statement for two reasons. First, they believe that imprisonment is more economic because the work-force of the convict may be utilized. Second, they prove with facts and data that a procedure conducted in a legal system which enforces rule of law guarantees through the right to fair procedure and trial, in which capital punishment may be ordered, is way more expensive than a procedure in which this punishment cannot be applied.

This means, therefore, that the first reason that abolitionists state that capital punishment is less "profitable," is because we lose a person who could have been involved in the production of social goods. A reason why Beccaria favored lifelong forced labor (in addition to considering the goal and necessity of punishment) was that this way the labor force of the convict could be utilized (and also because he believed that this punishment is more frightening than death). Nowadays, naturally, there is no eternal slavery, but the abilities, knowledge, and skills of the convict may be used even today. If murderers are convicted to life imprisonment instead of capital punishment, there is the possibility to make them work during the whole term of the punishment (till the end of their life) and earn the costs of their imprisonment, and as convicts do not have much to do in prison, they usually decide by themselves to work in the prison factory to avoid boredom, by this earning some money to spend on cigarettes, coffee, or anything else in the prison shop. Moreover, convicts may be requested to do heavy or dangerous physical work which could not be performed by free men or only in a much more expensive way.

The second reason is that abolitionists argue that the existence of capital punishment in a legal system results in more costs than if the legal system did not recognize capital punishment at all. It is possible (moreover, very likely) that *one* procedure resulting in execution is cheaper than life imprisonment, but regarding all procedures conducted in cases of crimes punishable with capital punishment (in which increased procedural guarantees shall be enforced due to the possibility of capital punishment, even in those rather frequently emerging cases in which capital punishment is not applied eventually)[1] the costs are much higher than in those procedures in which the most severe punishment cannot be applied (because in these cases less procedural guarantees are enforced).

The costs of procedures involving capital punishment are increased by more detailed, lengthy evidence procedures; appeals which are very likely to be resorted to (or sometimes are obligatory) in cases where capital punishment was ordered at first instance; higher frequency of repeated first instance procedures; often applied revision and pardon procedures; costs of appointed defense lawyers; obligatory checking mechanisms (more witnesses, more experts, and so on).

In addition to this, keeping and guarding the prisoner till the day of execution is more expensive, because special security measures are necessary both on the death row and at the execution. Subsequent acquittals are more frequent in capital punishment cases than otherwise (judges are less willing to take the risks of sentencing an innocent person, because the mistake would be final and irreparable), but in these cases extremely high compensation claims should be expected due to the years of imprisonment.[2]

András László Pap mentions some examples from the United States in order to prove the high costs of capital punishment procedures. According to the figures he cited "the costs of procedures concerning capital punishment are four times of the ones in which capital punishment cannot be applied." In California procedures related to capital punishment cost 1 billion USD between 1993 and 1997, even though only two executions were performed in the state in this time period. Executions cost on average 44 million USD in Florida, which is much more than sentencing to life imprisonment and enforcing it.[3] According to Raymond Paternoster's calculations, procedures which may result in capital punishment are also more expensive than life imprisonment. The trial of a capital case may be three times longer than in the same case without the possibility of capital punishment; the attorneys' costs in repeated procedures and appeals filed to federal level (in 1991) cost average 160–170 thousand USD; while the costs of judges and defense lawyers could have been even higher. The value of the time spent and other expenses reach a total of 1 million USD, while building and operating prisons suitable for executing life imprisonment cost (including amortization) only 750 thousand USD, calculating with thirty years of imprisonment.[4]

Spangenberg and Walsh present even more stunning figures; they believe guarding the convict for his whole life costs 600 thousand USD, delivering and executing capital punishment costs 1.4–3.2 million USD.[5] In addition to this, on March 8, 1992 the *Dallas Morning News* reported that capital trials in Texas cost about three times more (2.3 million USD) per accused than keeping them in the highest security cells for forty years. The research of Duke University shows that at the beginning of the 1990s in North Carolina the costs of capital cases were 2,160,000 USD more than in noncapital cases. In Indiana, capital cases cost 38 percent more, in Kansas 70 percent more than noncapital cases (adding that in Kansas no execution has been performed since 1976, when capital punishment was reintroduced). In Florida, upholding capital punishment resulted in 51, in California 114 million USD extra expenses annually (in 2000 and 2005, respectively), compared to the cases if all perpetrators punishable with capital punishment were sentenced to life imprisonment.[6,7]

Notes

1. According to one of the most famous living abolitionists, Hugo Adam Bedau in the United States only 10 percent of criminals punishable with capital punishment are sentenced to death and only some of these are executed finally. (Cf.: Hugo Adam Bedau: An Abolitionist's Survey of the Death Penalty in America Today, p. 27. In: Hugo Adam Bedau and Paul G. Cassell (eds.): *Debating the Death Penalty.* Oxford University Press, Oxford/New York, 2004, pp. 15–50.)
2. For the detailed comparison of the costs of capital and noncapital cases and the features of the two procedures see: Barry Nakell: The Cost of the Death Penalty. In: *The Death Penalty in America* (ed. Helen Prejean), 1982, pp. 241–246.
3. See in details: András László,: Pénz, politika, jogbiztonság—halálbüntetés az Egyesült Államokban. In: *Belügyi Szemle,* 2001/6, pp. 77–78.

4. For the details of the calculation of costs, and for the comparison of the prices of capital punishment and life imprisonment see: Raymond Paternoster: *Capital Punishment in America*. Lexington Books, New York, 1991, pp. 187–216.
5. See: Robert L. Spangenberg and Elizabeth R.Walsh: Capital Punishment or Life Imprisonment: Some Cost Considerations. In: *Loyola of Los Angeles Law Review,* Volume 23:45, 1989–1990, pp. 49–50, and 52–58.
6. Cf.: Death Penalty Information Center. Criminal Justice Project of the NAACP Legal Defense and Educational Fund, Inc.: Fact Sheet, 4. p In: http://www.deathpenaltyinfo.org/FactSheet.pdf.
7. There are further figures about the pecuniary costs of capital punishment in the following studies: Richard C. Dieter,: Millions Misspent: What Politicians Don't Say About the High Costs of the Death Penalty. In: http://www.deathpenaltyinfo.org/article.php?scid=45&did=385; Ronald J. Tabak and J. Mark Lane:, The Execution of Injustice: A Cost and Lack-of-Benefit Analysis of the Death Penalty. In: *Loyola of Los Angeles Law Review*, Volume 23:59, 1989–1990, pp. 133–138.; and the cited works of Paternoster, and Spangenberg and Walsh.

8

Other Reasons for and Against Capital Punishment

The examination of the reasons for, and the pros and cons of capital punishment and their rebuttal, should be started with aspects related to human rights and the scope of the state's punitive power. Abolitionists agree that the state's punitive power does not allow taking lives and that there are fundamental human rights of which no one can be deprived, not even a killer, so that the right to life belongs to them. Regarding the nature of these limitations reasons differ. Some argue that "the state … does not have more right over the natural person than which was intentionally waived by the natural person."[1] This, however, is obviously incorrect, because based on this criminals could not be put into jail, because they did not voluntarily give up their right to liberty. Others argue that the state is not allowed to kill a murderer with capital punishment because it would be simple homicide and by this the state would lower to the moral level where the murderer is.

According to Van den Haag the difference between the crime and the punishment is not physical but legal. The unlawful crime and the legal punishment ordered in a lawful procedure fall under different moral and rational considerations. Describing the essence of this with Hungarian examples: no one considers the imprisonment ordered for the crime

Z. J. Toth, *Changing Attitudes Towards the Death Penalty*,
https://doi.org/10.1007/978-3-030-47557-4_8

"violating personal freedom" unlawful, even though their methods of execution are similar (limitation of the freedom of movement). Furthermore, no one believes that fines ordered for extortion are unlawful, even though in case of failed payment it has to transform into imprisonment. In this latter case the state threatens the offender who fails to pay with the same kind of disadvantage as the extorter did. There is quality (moral and legal) difference between the criminal act and the state's response, despite the physical similarities of the two actions.

Furthermore, the advocates of capital punishment refuse the abolitionist idea according to which murderers have the same rights as anyone else. According to Van den Haag not everyone has inherent rights: the victim has more right to life than the murderer.[2] The best example may be the regulation of self-defense: unlawful attack against one's life may be avoided even by killing the attacker without getting any criminal law punishment for it. The legislator does not force the victim to sacrifice his life; from the lives of the unlawful attacker and the victim it favors the latter one. The application of capital punishment is practically the same, the difference is that in this case the law does not protect one specific life, but the lives of all potential victims, due to general prevention. Furthermore, from the comparison of the rights of the murderer and his (actual or potential) victims it seems that if capital punishment was not allowed, the right of the murderer to life would be more valued than of the victim, because the innocent victim dies, but the murderer lives. In other words: anyone could take anyone's life without having to fear the same.

The main difference between the opinions of the two groups regarding capital punishment is whether they focus on the protection of the rights of the murderer or the victim. While abolitionists stress that criminals have the same rights as any other members of society, the advocates of capital punishment do not give much attention to the rights of the murderer and rather consider the victim's rights important and protectable. In this relation they try to restore the balance which is shaken by abolitionist literature which (they believe) deals too much with the murderer and his rights and less with the victim and his rights.[3] They try to repress this one-sided approach, as they view it and make it clear that not only murderers, but also victims have rights; moreover, the victims should have rights in reality, not criminals.

The advocates of capital punishment believe that there should be a change in approach regarding this punishment. The murderer is not sentenced to death by the state, but by himself, and the court only declares the death penalty when it finds the perpetrator guilty (or does not declare it and applies another kind of punishment). If there was an act according to which perpetrators of certain crimes may be punished with capital punishment, those committing such crimes (e.g., homicide) would implicitly agree to the death sentence (by committing the given crime), because they decided freely that he wanted to commit the crime and they also took the chance being aware of capital punishment. Criminals are not forced to commit crimes punishable with capital punishment, they freely decide to take the risks of being sentenced to death. "Let the gentlemen who do the murders take the first step!"—said Alphonse Karr[4] in the nineteenth century, and this statement has been a guideline for abolitionists ever since. Their starting point is that if someone does not kill, he does not have to fear capital punishment; if someone respects the life of others, the state will respect his. If someone does not commit serious crimes—he does not have to fear anything. Those who do not violate the rights of others do not have to worry about theirs being violated. It is always the murderer who decides whether to risk capital punishment or not.

But in arguments related to capital punishment not only the perpetrator–victim relationship is featured (in one way or the other), but also the rights and obligations of other people; therefore, abolitionists stress that conviction and the execution brings about tremendous psychological effects for several groups of people. First of all, the family members of the convict suffer from the judgment with which their relative was sentenced to death for a crime for which they are not responsible. They have to suffer because of the thought of losing their loved one, then they have to live through the time when their relative's life actually ends at a previously defined time. (On the other hand, the advocates of capital punishment focus on the psychological health of the convict's family members who are usually relieved by the execution and regarding the relatives they mention that imprisonment for decades or for life is a bigger burden for the family on the long run, because they will probably never see their loved one again, but they cannot let him go either. The negative attitude of the environment does not change, because it is a permanent situation and probably the partner will not be able to start a new life, because the relationship has not ended permanently.) However, abolitionists believe that capital punishment does not only make the relatives of the convict suffer psychologically, but others are affected as well. For example: judges or the jury, who have to declare that someone has to die; the wardens, who have to guard the convict and prevent him from any danger; the official witnesses, who have to follow the death battle of a man, then have to certify the execution and its lawful process; the official persons who have to process the execution out of their duty, who actually have to end a person's life; the members of the discriminated group; and all those whose moral standing is not compatible with the thought of living in a state which executes people "on the behalf of them."

In addition to relatives the effect made on doctors is the most important; usually they have to participate actively at executions, even though according to the Hippocratic Oath their task is curing, not killing. The fact that doctors have to prepare the poison and examine whether the convict is physically ready for the execution; that usually they have to inject the lethal poison or otherwise manage the execution; that they have to supervise the execution process, examine the convict and declare him dead or on the contrary they have to give orders to continue the execution; this may led to internal division, caused by the thought that they acted (had to act) contrary to their own morals and oath.

The next reason for abolitionists to be against capital punishment is that capital punishment may be abused. According to this argument dictators may use capital punishment for political cleansing, for the liquidation of their enemies, and may get rid of their political enemies by executing death sentences ordered in summary show trials. As opposed to this, the advocates of capital punishment state that capital punishment should not be used in political cases (except for crimes including homicide which are considered common crimes in most states anyway, regardless of their motive and goal). They also argue that in dictatorships, where summary show trials are conducted, political enemies are not safe, regardless of capital punishment. In dictatorship assassinations, political killings, encouragement for lynching are common, no matter whether capital punishment exists or not. This means that even if this type of sanction exists in a totalitarian state, it does not mean that capital punishment is abused, but it means that political murders are executed as if they were death sentences. The essence is this: the execution of political enemies after "summary show trials" has nothing to do with capital punishment; simply a feature of the dictatorship is that the regime's enemies are liquidated, regardless of the institution of capital punishment. A dictator will not be hampered by the lack of legal capital punishment, mainly because the dictatorship's feature is that there is no legality (this is why it is dictatorship). This means, therefore, that lawful capital punishment should be distinguished from the political murders of totalitarian systems, even if the latter ones appear in the form of allegedly legal capital punishment.

The advocates of capital punishment warn that if the system of punishment is not in line with the sense of justice of society, informal, non-state justice may take over. This means that if, in a certain country, murderers receive low punishment, "accidents" happening to them may spread. A good example for this is headhunters operating in the USA (those men who live from catching wanted criminals and getting the reward money for it, live from rewards of catchers) often create situations in which they make wanted criminals use their gun in order to prevent their arrest and thus headhunters get into a self-defense situation and "in protection of their lives" they may shoot the wanted criminal without any consequence.[5] Or in Brazil, where criminality is extremely high,[6] but there is no capital punishment for common crimes, lynching of criminals caught in flagrante delicto or held in prison, directly or indirectly supported by authorities often happens, because the outraged masses do not trust justice and, therefore, believes that this is the only way criminals get really punished for their crimes.[7] (It should be added, though, that in addition to the leniency of judgments it often happens due to the high level of corruption that those persons skip punishment whose guilt could be proven otherwise.) Furthermore, often "execution groups" or "death brigades" are formed with police or former police members, and the members of military police[8] are especially active in this form of arbitrary "justice."[9] These death brigades usually perform targeted actions the aim of which is to liquidate certain criminals, and even though sometimes innocent passers-by also become victims of these actions and street gun fights, the majority of the population who otherwise fear criminals and are unable to do anything against them still support these illegal assassinations.[10] For example, these death brigades killed 104 people in 1995 and 107 in the first half of 1997 without judicial verdict;[11] the number of people killed by the (military) police in action was 330 in São Paulo in 1999 and 449 in Rio de Janeiro in the first half of 2000.[12] These figures led some advocates of capital punishment to warn that punishments which do not serve the people's sense of justice may easily lead to the arbitrary actions of people and investigation authorities, which is worse and scarier than capital punishment ordered in a well-grounded process after proper consideration in a criminal procedure based on the principle of the presumption of innocence and other procedural guarantees.

Abolitionists believe that one of the main arguments against capital punishment is its discriminative nature. For example, in the United States, up to May 10, 2018 1475 people had been executed since 1976, that is, since the reintroduction of capital punishment[13] (practically for homicide or other crimes including intentional murder) and only sixteen of the convicts were women[14] even though every seventh homicide is committed by women and the brutality of these crimes is not lower at all than of the ones committed by men. Regarding race there is further disproportionality,[15] not concerning the convicts, but the victims of homicides; 507 of the 1475 convicts were black, which is 34.37 percent. The rate of African-Americans in society is only 12 percent, while the number of executed white people in the same period was 820 (55.59 percent), and of other (Latino, Asian, Indian, etc.) the number of executed convicts was 148 (10.03 percent).[16] If we consider that about half of all murders are committed by black people,[17] it becomes obvious that based on the skin color of those sentenced to death and then executed there is no institutional, state-level discrimination (which obviously does not mean that black or perpetrators with other handicaps could not be discriminated against in certain procedures). In the judicial and jury practice of the past years and decades discrimination mainly appears in relation with victims: perpetrators of homicides with white victims are more likely to be sentenced to death (regardless of having white or colored skin), that murderers killing colored people (again, regardless of the perpetrators' race); this is shown well by the fact that among the 1475 convicts executed in the past forty-two years 1153 people killed Caucasian victims, while only 220 murderers killed African-American victims.[18,19]

In general, without specific figures it may be concluded that the death sentence is more often delivered against disadvantaged groups (colored skin, poor, members of religious groups, lone murderers, homeless, immigrants) and it is more often executed than against people coming from upper classes of society.[20] The reasons for this are as follows. First, disadvantaged people do not have connections which they could use at courts (even informally). Second, the poor cannot hire as good lawyers as rich people in similar cases and the activities of the appointed lawyer (in lack of financial motivation) is not even close to the efficiency of a hired defense lawyer. Third, judges, attorney generals, and often jury members reflect the same negative social attitude which is shown by the majority of society towards these minority groups. This is why it may happen that the official participants of the procedure are more tolerant towards people in higher positions (e.g., doctor, civil servants, high school teacher), even if they commit similarly serious crimes, which is contrary to the constitutional requirement of an equal and fair trial.

In addition to this it is also discriminative that the place of procedure is important in relation with capital punishment. From the USA's fifty-one state level administrative units twenty-nine recognize and twenty-two do not recognize capital punishment, and it is unfair that while perpetrators of crimes committed in one state cannot be sentenced to death, perpetrators of similar crimes committed in another state may be sentenced to death.[21] It does matter, therefore, where the perpetrator commits the crime (in a state which recognizes capital punishment or in one which does not) and it also matters whether it is in the South or in the North (capital punishment is more frequent in the Southern states), or whether the given state has Democrat or Republican governor (conservative Republican governors reject pardon petitions more often), which is discriminative, that is,unfair.

According to Camus, capital punishment is discriminative also if there is a jury (for example in the USA), because it is affected by irrational factors. Even though judges are humans and are affected by factors beyond law, this is even more threatening in case of lay and often less educated jury members. Jury members are affected by irrelevant factors in making their decision about the issue of guilt or innocence, such as the outlook, social situation, education, moral standing (e.g., if adulterer), way of talk, style, etc. of the accused and they often consider these when they decide whether the accused is guilty or not, and if yes, whether the punishment should be the death sentence or imprisonment. As "there are no two similar juries, the executed person could even stay alive"[22] in front of another jury. It is the same the other way around, of course; if one jury convicted the perpetrator to imprisonment, he could have been sentenced to death by another jury, based on the same facts.

The advocates of capital punishment can only repeat that the discriminative nature of capital punishment should not be solved by abolishing this form of punishment, but by terminating discrimination.[23] Obviously, until the human factor is not excluded from the procedure of justice (which will probably never happen), subjectivism will always be present in one way or another, but according to Van den Haag unequal justice is also justice; guilty people will not be innocent or deserve death (or any other punishment) less, even if others escape it. (The police do not reveal every crime, but some perpetrators are caught and they cannot reason with discrimination stating that there are some who committed the same act but are still at large.) He believes that discrimination should be abolished in a way that those also should be sentenced to death who could have escaped it earlier due to money, influence, or position in society.[24] It is obvious that discrimination should be abolished, because a life should not depend on where the horrific act is committed or who the judges are.

The advocates of capital punishment often argue that capital punishment is needed in order to satisfy people's sense of justice and to calm public outrage. They believe that the majority of people clearly favor capital punishment, therefore, this institution should not be abolished. There are frequent surveys conducted about this in the USA and they always show that people support capital punishment and that they need this sanction in order to feel safe, and the situation is very similar in Hungary.[25] Abolitionists oppose this idea with three arguments. (1) The abolition, maintenance, or restoration of capital punishment is a professional issue and as "everyday people" who are not competent in certain issues do not get the chance to decide about certain questions (even though they express their opinion), it should be the same with capital punishment. (2) The results of surveys often depend on the formulation of questions, thus with deliberate wording (or simply with ad hoc questions which are not considered carefully in advance) different results may be reached. (3) These surveys are usually conducted in countries which recognize capital punishment and in which it was abolished not long ago, therefore, (the usually conservative) public opinion still holds on to the old patterns. In countries where capital punishment has not existed for decades it is a strange thing for people, just like ordeal, torture, blows, pillory, or stocks would be for us, therefore, according to abolitionists public opinion does not support capital punishment, it supports the maintenance of traditions; hence, where citizens have got used to having capital punishment they will object to abolishing it and on the contrary, its restoration would be objected to in countries where they did not have it for long.

Finally, abolitionists mention several significant reasons in support of their opinion about the abolition of capital punishment which are difficult to deny. Among them we primarily focus on the brutalization effect of capital punishment. Beccaria stated long ago: "The punishment of death is harmful to society from the example of cruelty it presents."[26]

The next argument of abolitionists is that this sanction cannot be individualized. While in cases of imprisonment or fines the features of the crime, and its circumstances may be taken into account to the fullest, as well as the personality, motive, purpose, and criminality of the perpetrator, his dangerousness to society—this is impossible in the case of capital punishment. Capital punishment cannot be applied in a more or less severe way, the judge cannot apply this sanction individually and everyone, the simple murderer, the multiple, brutal child killer and the serial sex criminal receive the same punishment. Individualization would be necessary if cruel death was reintroduced, but this barbarian, inhumane method obviously does not have any room in the criminal justice of the twenty-first century.

Abolitionists also stress something which those in favor of capital punishment often forget, namely *that the existence of murders is a problem of society*. The possibility of applying the most serious sanction (and its actual application) makes society believe that crimes against life are managed well, therefore, capital punishment diverts attention away from prevention, the abolition of conditions (alcoholism, poverty, lack of education, etc.) leading to homicides. Capital punishment makes people focus on false priorities; not on the abolition of the reasons leading to criminality, such as social disease, but on the surface treatment of it.

Finally, we have to mention one of the biggest dangers of the reactivation of capital punishment, namely that if such a process starts, it does not necessarily stop by sanctioning homicide (slippery slope). If we restore capital punishment even if for the most serious crimes, it may be slowly extended to further, less serious crimes. The great step would be its restoration; this would be most debated by society but if it was reintroduced eventually, its extension would not be debated so much. Changing the scope of crimes subject to capital punishment is not as significant as the restoration of the institution, therefore, the extension of the scope of capital punishment "in secret" would be a real threat.

* * *

As a closing remark we wish to repeat that this part of our book is not propaganda for or against capital punishment. Its goal is merely to present those possible reasons for the Reader which frequently appear in the arguments of the two sides and those rebuttals with which both the advocates of capital punishment and abolitionists try to shed light on the (real or putative) mistakes of the other side. We tried to present the possible pro and contra reasons at the widest possible scale and tried to confront them with each other. Everyone shall consider their own values and preferences in order to decide which ones he favors and opposes, which are more important and more necessary to put into practice. Arguments are equal and the Reader has the right to choose; however, everyone should admit, regardless of personal preference, that the representatives of the other side are not "immoral" or "savage" just because they communicate their own beliefs, because they fight for their opinion based on their best intentions, and consciously try to enforce those values which they themselves believe to be the most important.

Notes

1. When the state kills..., p. 98. Amnesty International Publications, 1989 In: Ágnes Sebes (ed.): A halálbüntetésről. [On capital punishment.] Magvető, Budapest, 1990, pp. 95–218.
2. "*Abolitionists are wrong when they insist that we all have an equally inalienable right to live our natural term ... if the victim died, the murderer does not deserve to live.*" Ernest Van den Haag: Capital Punishment Should Be Retained, p. 332. In: Mary E. Williams (ed.): *Capital Punishment: Current Controversies*. Greenhaven Press, 2005.
3. The "victim-centered" or victim-oriented criminal policy approach which started in the USA in the 1980s and has spread across most developed Western countries tries to correct the balance (but rather regarding less serious crimes).
4. Cited by, for example: Imre Szabó: A halálbüntetésről. (On capital punishment) In: *Valóság*, 1980/12, p. 75; Albert Camus: Thoughts on capital punishment, p. 64. In: Ágnes Sebes (ed.): A halálbüntetésről. [On capital punishment.] Magvető, Budapest, 1990, pp. 7–74.
5. As headhunters receive the reward money anyway, this is practically no different from the *"dead or alive"* searches of the second part of the nineteenth century.
6. For example, in 1997 40,000 homicides happened in the country of 146 million, which means more than twenty-five murders per 100,000 inhabitants, but regarding the average homicides per year between 1994 and 1997 the rate of homicides is twenty-four, which is extremely high if compared with the period's European figures (1997) or the situation in the USA. (At the same time in Germany this rate was 1.44, in the UK 1.49, in France 1.60, in Italy 1.61, in Spain 2.60, but it did not exceed eight even in the violent USA (it was 7.34). (See: Paulo Sergio Pinheiro: The Paradox of Democracy in Brazil. In: *The Brown Journal of World Affairs*, 2001–2002, Volume VIII, Issue 1, p. 115.)
7. Cf.: Pinheiro: op. cit., pp. 116–117.
8. The police organization is divided into two in Brazil: there is "civil" police which investigates crimes, and military police that should prevent crimes and restore order if necessary. Military police usually act violently against the population, their acceptance by the population is low, and majority of people have bad feelings about them. (Cf.: Eduardo Paes-Machado and Ceci Vilar Noronha: Policing the Brazilian Poor: Resistance

to and Acceptance of Police Brutality in Urban Popular Classes (Salvador, Brazil). In: *International Criminal Justice Review*, Volume 12, 2002, pp. 64–65.)

9. See: Paes-Machado: op. cit., p. 66; Pinheiro: op. cit., pp. 117–118.
10. Cf.: Paes-Machado: op. cit., pp. 70–72.
11. Paes-Machado: op. cit., p. 72.
12. See: Pinheiro: op. cit., p. 118.
13. Source of the following statistical data: NAACP's Death Penalty Information Center, Searchable Execution Database (http://www.deathpenaltyinfo.org/views-executions).
14. It is interesting that from the sixteen women six were executed in Texas.
15. Famous American defense lawyer Bryan Stevenson published the shocking figure according to which in the USA one-third of black people between the ages 18–35 are in high security or ordinary prison, or due to a crime are under supervision, or are on parole. (Cf.: Bryan Stevenson: Close to Death: Reflections on Race and Capital Punishment in America, p. 85. In: Hugo Adam Bedau and Paul G. Cassell (eds.): *Debating the Death Penalty*. Oxford University Press, Oxford/New York, 2004, pp. 76–116.)
16. Not the same, though similar rates are observable regarding the race of those awaiting execution. On April 1, 2012 3170 people were sitting at the death row in the USA. Among them 1325 were black (41.80 percent), 1371 were white (43.25 percent), 474 belonged to another race (14.95 percent). (Cf.: NAACP Legal Defense and Educational Fund, Death Row USA, Spring 2012 [Aa of April 1, 2012], http://www.deathpenaltyinfo.org/documents/DRUSASpring2012.pdf, p. 1.)
17. For example, in 2002 7005 murders and nonnegligent manslaughters were committed which involved one perpetrator and one victim. From these 7005 perpetrators 3386 were black (48.37 percent), 3309 were white (47.24 percent), 180 other colored people and 130 unknown. (Source of figures: US Department of Justice, Federal Bureau of Investigation, Crime in the United States, 2002 /Washington, DC: USGPO, 2003/, p. 22, chart 2.8 /Murders and nonnegligent manslaughters known to police by race and sex of victim and offender, United States, 2002/. In: http://www.fbi.gov/ucr/cius_02/xl/02tbl2-8.xls).
18. An indirect effect of this is that among executed convicts who perpetrated "interracial murders" there are only eighteen white people who killed African-American victim(s), while there are 225 black people

whose victims belonged to the "Caucasian" race; however, at the same time it should be stressed that white people usually kill white people, while blacks kill blacks: in 2002 from 3309 murders involving one perpetrator and one victim, committed by white people 3000 had white victims (90.7 percent) and only 227 had black victims (6.9 percent). From 3386 lone black killers 2853 (84.3 percent) killed another African-American, while 483 (14.3 percent) killed a white victim. (For the sources of figures see the previous footnote.)

19. Source of data: Death Penalty Information Center: Death Penalty Fact Sheet (http://www.deathpenaltyinfo.org/FactSheet.pdf).
20. For further reasons and examples about the discriminative nature of capital punishment see: William O. Hochkammer, Jr.: The Capital Punishment Controversy, pp. 68–69. In: James A. McCafferty (ed.): *Capital Punishment.* Aldine, Atherton, Inc., Chicago and New York, pp. 65–87; Amnesty International: op. cit., pp. 135–137; Victor H. Evjen: Let's Abolish Capital Punishment, p. 221. In: James A. McCafferty (ed.): *Capital Punishment.* Aldine, Atherton, Inc., Chicago and New York, pp. 218–224; Van den Haag: op. cit., p. 368.
21. It should be noted that in addition to crimes defined by states as punishable by capital punishment certain federal or military crimes also allow the use of capital punishment—now in both jurisdictions lethal injection is the only accepted method.
22. Camus: op. cit., p. 52.
23. See: Hochkammer: op. cit., p. 69.
24. See: Van den Haag: op. cit., pp. 323–324.
25. See this in detail in the last chapter.
26. Cesare Beccaria: *An Essay On Crimes and Punishments* [1764]. E-book. Liberty Fund, Indianapolis, Indiana, 2011, p. 91.

Part II

A Case Study of Capital Punishment in Hungary in the Twentieth Century

In Hungary, the death penalty was an ordinary punishment from the foundation of the state (in AD 1000) until the abolition of the death penalty in 1990. However, the annulment of the capital punishment was imminent many times (e.g., the draft of the Criminal Code of 1843, finally not sanctioned by the king, did not include the death penalty as a punishment applicable for common offences, and no death sentence was executed for years in the late nineteenth century); due to the wars, revolutions and dictatorships in the twentieth century, the annulment did not occur eventually (on the contrary, the application of death penalty was extended several times). The criminal sentences of the martial law proceedings during World Wars I and II and of the other exceptional proceedings during the era of Communism (State socialism) caused the death of the most of the convicted perons, which judgments often were based expressly on political grounds. The opportunity to deliver a politically motivated death sentence was eliminated only in 1989 when Act XVI of 1989 abolished the death penalty as punishment for offences against the state; while in case of other offences it was abolished by an early decision (23/1990. (X. 31.) AB) of the newly established Constitutional Court of Hungary.

In most of the history of Hungary, the death penalty used to be a regular punishment (*poena ordinaria*) that could be imposed for various crimes against life, limb, state, religion, and even property, mostly on the grounds of customary law or under the rules of local statutory regulations. The Middle Ages and the early modern age may be considered as the "classical" era of the extensive use of the capital sanction, however, even in those times it was not the death penalty but the various types of corporal punishment that were most commonly used. Under the enlightened absolutist rulers the actual application of the most severe penalty decreased significantly (for a short time it was even formally abolished by Joseph II in respect of common delicts)[1] and in the Reform Era the death penalty was rarely sentenced and more rarely carried out even on the grounds of customary law. Apart from the retaliation following the 1848/49 Revolution and War of Independence[2] the capital sanction increasingly became an exceptional punishment in the nineteenth century, as evidenced by the first Hungarian Criminal Code Act V. of 1878, the so-called Code of Csemegi. The Code of Csemegi made the death penalty only applicable (but never obligatory) for the most serious forms of treason, such as the murder or intentional killing of the king or the attempt thereof (Article 126, Point 1.)[3] and murder (Article 278),[4] provided that the perpetrator of the offense was at least twenty years old at the time when the crime was committed (Article 87). Partly due to this and partly due to the changed conception of criminal law, at this time the death penalty was rarely applied actually (even compared to other contemporary countries) and even if it was, it was sentenced exclusively for murder. Between 1881 and 1898 a total of 223 (twelve per year on average) death penalties were imposed by courts of first instance, however, in only thirty-four cases were these approved by the Curia (this meant, on average, two executions per year during this period). Moreover, there was a short period (between 1895 and 1899) when no death sentence was approved by the Curia, and between 1896 and 1900 no executions were carried out in Hungary.[5]

This peaceful era ended in the years during World War I and shortly afterwards. This time the threat of war, then the war itself and, later, the "necessity" for protection of the results of the revolution, extraordinary criminal norms were introduced, to a lesser extent by Acts, mostly by decrees delegated by these Acts. These regulations made capital punishment applicable (in state of siege even compulsory) for more and more offences. The first in line of these norms were three Acts, adopted before World War I.: the parallel or twin Acts XXXII. and XXXIII. of 1912 on Military Criminal Procedure for the Joint Forces and the Army and Act LXIII. of 1912 on Exceptional Measures in the Event of War. These were followed by, under the delegated power of Article 31. of the latter Act, the Decrees No. 12.002. of 1914 I.M.E., and 5.487., 5.488. and 5.491. of 1914 M.E. of the Government on accelerated procedure and martial law, then additionally the Decrees No. 5.735., 5.488.and 6.082. of 1914 and 2.060. and 9.550. M.E. of 1915, as well as Act XIX of 1915. Lastly, during the Hungarian Soviet Republic, in addition to the regular criminal tribunals, the so-called revolutionary tribunals were allowed to impose the death penalty under Decree No. IV. of the Revolutionary Governing Council.[6] Under Decree No. XLV., the summary courts that were set up again were also allowed to impose death sentences "in case of urgent need" for any other delicts, and, later, under Decree No. XCIV. also for felonies most threatening to the established order.[7]

Against this background, we get to August 1919, when, with the collapse of the Soviet Republic of Hungary, a new political order emerged and the Horthy era began. This period of the history of Hungary on the one hand consolidated the legal (including criminal) conditions by restricting again the use of capital punishment in respect of common offenses, on the other hand continued the practice of previous years, the answer of which for the extraordinary situations was the creation and enforcement of extraordinary rules on a regulatory level. These all ultimately culminated in the martial law regulations of World War II.

Notes

1. This was done by *Sanctio Criminalis Josephina 1787*, that was nevertheless revoked before his death in 1790 and this status (that is, inter alia the *de iure* reintroduction of the death penalty) was sanctioned by Act XL of 1790/91 of Leopold II. (Cf: Lajos Hajdu, II. József büntetőtörvénykönyve Magyarországon (Joseph II's Criminal Code in Hungary). In: *Jogtudományi Közlöny*, 1974/1–2., pp. 48–55; Barna Mezey (ed.): *A magyar jogtörténet forrásai* (Sources of the Hungarian legal history). Osiris, Budapest, 2001, p. 243.)
2. Based on his archival research, Károly Kecskeméti speaks about approx. 150 executed political and military leaders, while Barna Mezey writes about not quite 120 executions, however, they both recognize that the number of those killed by imperial soldiers in resistance to their arrest or in order to prevent their escape may be a multiple of this. (Cf. Károly Kecskeméti: A halálbüntetés eltörlésének ügye az országgyűlésen. (The issue of the abolition of capital punishment in the Dieta of Hungary.) In: Klára Kerezsi (ed.): *Kriminológiai Közlemények* 53. Magyar Kriminológiai Társaság, Budapest, 1996, pp. 84–104; and Barna Mezey: Az 1849. évi megtorlások történetéhez (To the history of retaliation in 1849). In: *Jogtudományi Közlöny*, 1999/11., pp. 457–466)
3. "Any person who murders or intentionally kills the king or attempts to accomplish any of these crimes is guilty of a felony of high treason..." (Article 126. 1.) "High treason in case of Article 126. 1. is punishable ... by death." (Article 128)
4. "Any person who, with premeditated intentions, kills another person, is guilty of murder and is punishable by death." (Article 278.)
5. These numbers do not include the crime statistics of Croatia.
6. Crimes punishable by death are listed in Decrees No. I., V., XX., XXIII., XXIV., XXXIII., XLII., LVII., LVIII., LXXIV., XCIV. and CIX.

7. For exhaustive information on the regulation of the capital sanction in these few years, see: Zoltán J. Tóth: Rendkívüli büntetőjog és halálbüntetés az 1910-es évek Magyarországán. (Extraordinary criminal law and the death penalty in Hungary in the 1910s.) *Themis*, June 2007, pp. 49–62.

9

Statutory Regulation of Capital Punishment in Hungary during the Horthy Era and World War II

After the fall of the Soviet Republic of 1919 just three weeks were needed for the new government to restore (at least declaratively) the former legal status: this was done by Government Decrees No. 4.038 and No. 4.039., adopted on August 19, 1919, promulgated and entered into force the next day. The former stated that all criminal proceedings conducted by the bodies of the Soviet Republic and every decision and judgment taken by them were invalid[1] and that for the future, the laws originated before the foundation of the Soviet Republic were considered normative.[2] The latter ordered to punish all those who had exerted any such activity to the Soviet Republic, which was contrary to the previous legislation.

According to Article 1 of Government Decree No. 4.039, "[t]he Tribunal adjudicates, according to the rules of accelerated criminal procedure, regulated by this Decree: 1. over the bodies, officials and agents of the Soviet Republic, who, by usurping and pretending to act with official powers, committed acts in violation of the criminal laws; 2. over the armed bodies of the Soviet Republic or the persons not mentioned in Point 1. who committed crimes in order to establish, maintain or restore the Soviet Republic, regardless of whether the act was committed before or after the enactment of this Decree." For this, the Decree ordered the

Z. J. Toth, *Changing Attitudes Towards the Death Penalty*,
https://doi.org/10.1007/978-3-030-47557-4_9

creation of separate councils consisting of five judges (presiding judge and four members) in each criminal tribunal, for the procedure thereof it ordered the application of the rules of accelerated criminal procedure, regulated by the same Decree. Some of these rules were the same as in Decree No. 9.550. of 1915 I.M.E.[3,4] while others rather approximated the accelerated procedure to martial law. These included, for example, that while Article 18 of Decree No. 9.550. of 1915 I.M.E. provided the opportunity for one level of appeal, according to Article 11 Para. (1) of Decree No. 4.039. of 1919 M.E. there were places for appeals against the decisions of the court. Furthermore, the 1919 regulation held that the process, from beginning to end, shall be held before the court sitting together and, whenever possible, going down without interruption.[5] If the defendant was sentenced to death, the court shall decide immediately whether or not to propose the convicted for amnesty. If the court did not find the convicted eligible for amnesty, then, after passing the judgment, if possible and desired by the convicted, they are to provide a clergyman beside the convicted and after an appropriate deadline given for the convicted for the preparation for death, the death penalty shall be implemented. If the court found the convicted eligible to be proposed for amnesty, the criminal records, together with the possibly submitted petition for amnesty and the opinion of state prosecutor's office and the court, shall be filed immediately to the Curia of Hungary, which shall, in a closed council meeting, without justification, finally decide on the amnesty within twenty-four hours. If the condemned did not receive amnesty, after the promulgation of the decision thereof, the death penalty shall be carried out according to Article 11. All these provisions clearly lend a martial law nature to the so-called "accelerated procedure."

Furthermore, Government Decree No. 4.039 also governed martial law specifically,[6] which it made applicable for crimes listed in Article 12, Point 4 of Act LXIII. of 1912,[7] exclusively in case of prior promulgation, for subsequently committed delicts, regardless of whether these acts—according to the same decree (due to their realization in the interest of the Soviet Republic)—fell under the milder accelerated procedure. (In this case, therefore, the more stringent martial law had primacy.) However, for the state of siege, the government decree—in contrast to the accelerated procedure—did not impose any specific rules, but ordered the application of Chapter II. of Decree No. 9.550. of 1915 I.M.E.

The possibility of the imposition of martial law became allowed by the government in the next year also by law, in cases of high treason and in respect of certain violent crimes against authorities or individuals. All this was done by Act XXXVIII. of 1920 on the extension of martial law offenses, which in turn dealt with martial law on similar delicts committed by soldiers as well. Finally, the criminal aspects of the transition period were closed by Act III of 1921 on the protection of public and social order. This statute, clearly in response to the events of the Soviet Republic, ordered the death penalty to those who committed an offense against the state, that is, who committed a crime in conjunction with and for the objectives of an organization or a movement, the purpose of which was the violent subversion or destruction of the legal order of the state and society, especially the violent establishment of the exclusive reign of a social class. It also ordered the death penalty to those who initiated or led such an organization or movement, if the law established the death penalty for the crime committed.[8] This meant, that if any laws (such as the Criminal Code) made it *possible* to impose the death penalty on a perpetrator of a delict, then any such perpetrator who committed that delict with an anti-state intent, was to be *mandatorily* punished by death.

The use of martial law regulations in the period between the two world wars culminated twice thereafter: in the early twenties and in 1931/32; however, only the latter had a practical significance. As regards the former, with Decree No. 28.123 of 1921 I.M.E, above all, riot and arson were brought under martial proceedings. This was supplemented with certain crimes[9] by Decree No. 29.307 of 1923 I.M.E, however, this supplement was repealed after only four days[10] by the Ministry of Justice Decree No. 30.004 of 1923. Finally, Decree No. 135 of 1924 I.M.E, in addition to riot and arson, ordered the application of martial law for "murder and intentional homicide committed with the use of a blasting agent or any kind of explosive," the attempt thereof and "the alliance created for such crimes," and this Decree remained in force until 1932.

Martial law only had an actual role from 1931, when due to the blowing up of the viaduct of Biatorbágy at dawn on September 13,[11] six days after the assassination, on September 19, this was extended by Decree

No. 10.479 of the then Minister of Justice Tibor Zsitvay to actions against authority,[12] collective violence against private persons,[13] murder and intentional homicide committed with the use of firearms, crimes against public health by causing death, crimes of the causation of public hazard on iron tracks or ships, crimes directed towards the subversion or destruction of the legal order of the state and the society as defined in Act III of 1921,[14] as well as the attempts of the above delicts. The assassin of Biatorbágy, Szilveszter Matuska (who was captured in Vienna for crimes committed there) could not be executed as the Austrians extradited him to Hungary[15] only on the condition that no such sanction (namely the capital sanction) was to be imposed which did not exist in Austria. Hence, Horthy was forced to transform by grace to the penalty to life imprisonment. However, several other people were not only sentenced to death under the thus enabled martial proceedings but were actually executed too. Among them, the most famous were Imre Sallai and Sándor Fürst, illegal communist leaders, who, as victims of the anti-communist hysteria, were arrested, sentenced to death and executed in July 1932 for anti-state crimes, specifically for initiating and leading an organization and movement directed for the violent establishment of the exclusive reign of the working class. The hysteria and the application of martial law ended more than one year later, on October 10, 1932, when Andor Lázár, appointed to replace Zsitvay, released Decree No. 9.900 of 1932 I.M., which abolished martial law—promulgated by the decrees of 1931 and also the decrees of 1921 and 1924 that were still in force—throughout the country.

In the 1920s and 1930s in Hungary, in addition to the introduction, extension, restriction, and abolition of martial law regulations, as well as the executions[16] on judgments of martial (and, of course, "regular") courts, until 1939 only two (interrelated) legislative event occurred that were relevant to capital punishment: the creation and entry into force of Act II of 1930 on the Military Penal Code and Act III of 1930 on the promulgation of the Military Penal Code and on the related amendments and extensions of certain provisions of ordinary criminal law.[17] The former ordered or allowed the death penalty for six different military crimes that were to be carried out by hanging or shooting. The punishment of virtually all delicts was death by shooting, only the desertion to the enemy, as the most severe crime was sanctioned by hanging. The Military Penal Code, however, was not allowed to impose capital punishment on offenders who had not reached their twentieth year when committing the crime; such persons were to be sanctioned by ten to fifteen years imprisonment.

For riot[18] all those had to be punished by death who took part in a riot in which they or any of their partners committed violence against their superior; those who committed battery, intentional homicide or the attempt thereof or attempted murder against a member of the counterforce seconded to restore order and obedience, or against a person seconded or embarked to defend the superior; the instigator and the leader if they continued to participate in the riot after the appearance of the counterforce seconded to restore order and obedience; and finally all those who "by denial of service against the enemy" frustrated or caused serious disadvantage to such service.[19] For crime against a military guard, i.e., violence or dangerous threat against a military guard,[20] also those were punishable by death, who, during the implementation of this crime committed murder, intentional homicide or the attempt thereof, as well as those who, in time of war, "by force or dangerous threat deliberately prevented the guard from carrying out his lawful duties or forced him to take action," if the act resulted in serious disadvantage (Article 89). Perpetrators of desertion[21] received the most severe sanction if at the time of war they deserted from guard stations, or other such service, the leaving of which could result in serious disadvantage; or if the desertion was committed by three or more persons in mutual agreement, as well as if the perpetrator had already been punished twice for desertion; furthermore if the perpetrator deserted or attempted to desert to the enemy,[22] provided that he did not check in voluntarily for thirty days. For guard duty crime,[23] those guards (being simple guard, set up guard, patrol guard, or commander guard) were punishable by death, who committed the act at the time of war and caused serious disadvantage, as well as those guards or guard members, who were intended to guard a prisoner, and who intentionally abducted the prisoner, and therefore great disadvantage occurred. For the delict "cowardice" also the most serious legal consequence had to be imposed against the person, who as commander fearing for his personal safety did not set out the necessary resistance against the enemy and, therefore, gave up his post, let himself or his team captured, who hid or fled during combat operations and those who, by discouraging his comrades, caused their desertion, surrender or diffidence.[24] Finally, for "felony committed in the line of duty" those commanders were punishable by shooting who in time of war intentionally violated one of the ten types of duty,[25] if this violation caused great disadvantage in military operations.

Act III of 1930 brought two important measures in respect of our subject: on the one hand, it redefined the facts of treachery from that of the Criminal Code (Code of Csemegi); on the other hand it changed the list of crimes that could be brought under, as well as the conditions for the imposition of martial law. Regarding the former: from the number of instances of treachery, the law ordered those to be punished by death who in the time of war deliberately sought to weaken the fighting ability of the Hungarian army, if serious consequences were derived therefrom, as well as those who in time of war spied for the enemy or provided assistance thereto. The latter measure identified three groups of offenses which could fall under martial procedure. The first group includes the most serious crimes, which could be assigned to martial procedure without the prior promulgation of martial law, provided that "the restoration of disturbed discipline requires the giving of a deterrent example,"[26] the second group included those delicts which could be assigned to martial procedure without the prior promulgation of martial law only in time of war (ergo not at any time);[27] perpetrators of the crimes included in the third group could only be held accountable under martial procedure in case of prior promulgation of martial law (nevertheless this could be done also in time of peace or war). This was possible in a wide range of crimes: these included the military offenses "against the order and discipline" (the plundering of the civilian population, battlefield looting: looting from the dead, injured or sick remaining in the battlefield);[28] the felonies of incitement, desertion and mutiny, delicts mentioned in Act XXXVIII of 1920; crimes listed in Article 12, Point 4 of Act LXIII of 1912 (treachery, riot, murder, intentional homicide, crime against public health by causing death, robbery, arson, crime of the causation of water flooding, crimes of the causation of public hazard on iron tracks, telegraphs (telephone) or ships); all new forms of treachery re-regulated by this Act (not only those that were punishable by death); crimes against the state according to Act III of 1921 on the protection of public and social order; and the crimes committed with the use of explosive or blasting agent.[29] Finally, as a result of another new measure in martial proceedings capital punishment could also be imposed also on attempt, complicity, and failed incitement, according to the law.

The nearly two decades of relative tranquility[30] ended in 1939; starting this year new legislation appeared every so often, which allowed the imposition of capital punishment on more and more crimes and subsequently the use of the martial proceedings. The first of these was Act II of 1939 on national defense that deserves attention in respect of the death penalty for three reasons. First, the Act as a continuation to Act II of 1930, created the facts of new crimes (which could be committed not only by soldiers) of which four were also punishable by death. Thus, according to the Defense Act capital punishment was to be imposed on those who in time of or in imminent danger of an air raid violated the regulatory provision issued in order to prevent the attack or its impact, with the intention of the occurrence of someone's death or serious prejudice to the interests of the state, if this outcome as a consequence of the offender's conduct actually occurred.[31] The same penalty had to be imposed on public officials, who intentionally committed any of the offenses defined in Sections 7–8 of Act XIX of 1915 on shipments of war (official corruption, practically), if "the act resulted in someone's death and it was foreseeable by the perpetrator,"[32] or if "the act resulted in serious prejudice to the interests of defense in time of war";[33] on those who committed "vandalism endangering national defense interests," if it caused one or more deaths and this result was foreseeable;[34] as well as those who damaged aircrafts or their accessories in time of war[35] if "the act caused more than one deaths or serious disadvantage to the operations for the protection or the security of the country, or caused the destruction of large quantities of war material."[36]

The second significant feature of the Act was that it authorized the government to extend the scope of any wartime legislation or criminal provision to the times when imminent danger of war was threatening the country and even this (i.e., what constitutes imminent danger of war and how long) could be determined by the government itself by means of a regulation.[37] Finally, it could be considered as the third important measure of the Defense Act, that it provided almost unlimited opportunity to the government for the implementation of martial law[38] in both civilian and military criminal proceedings, which, by regulation, could either be introduced to the whole or part of the territory of the country (or of the military criminal justice), in respect of any crime and even the rules of procedure could be determined by the government (the "Ministry").

These mandates were also used by the government. As regards the former, Decree No. 2.730 of 1941 M.E on the starting day and territorial scope of the application of specific provisions of criminal law in time of war, which ordered these specific wartime norms to be applied throughout the whole territory of the country and of the military criminal justice, from April 12, 1941 until regulated otherwise, was issued by the Bárdossy government on April 9, 1941, following the attack on Yugoslavia. As the Kingdom of Hungary had not yet declared a state of war,[39] therefore, wartime legislation could not be entered into force only under the Act itself, which is why it was necessary to adopt the government regulation based on the Defense Act. Not much later, on June 30, 1941, general rules were created by the Ministry that defined the time from which wartime legislation had to be applied (and the same decree brought the persons otherwise subject to civil criminal jurisdiction under military criminal jurisdiction for certain crimes). According to this decree (Decree No. 4.850 of 1941 M.E.) these rules had to be applied in the case of general mobilization from the date of promulgation throughout the whole territory of military criminal jurisdiction. In the case of partial mobilization (where there is no such promulgation) this had to be applied from the first day of mobilization at the mobilized army groups and in the case of the country's entry into war from the date of the publication of the official statement thereof, also throughout the whole territory of military criminal jurisdiction. (The wartime particular material criminal provisions have only been abolished by Decree No. 7.300 of 1945 M.E.,[40] adopted by the new interim national government which formed as representative of the democratic power; while the application of the provisions of wartime military criminal procedure has been abolished by Decree No. 1.740 of 1946 M.E.)

More important was, however, the government's regulation of martial law (at least regarding our subject, the death penalty), as not only quantitatively many more norms were created on the basis of this mandate, but the importance of these decrees were also far superior to that of Government Decrees No. 2.730 of 1941 and No. 4.850 of 1941. The procedural rules of civilian martial law were promulgated and entered into force by the government on August 28, 1939, based on the right included in Article 221 of the Defense Act (Decree No. 8.020 of 1939 M.E. of the Royal Hungarian Ministry) The same regarding a subfield of military martial law, namely the martial law applicable to the mobilized army, was done by Decree No. 1.420 of 1944 M.E. (by Sections 38 and 39 which covered this case specifically) on May 1, 1944.[41] The latter did not differ in any essential element from those set out in Act XXXIII of 1912 (due to its much more superficial and interleaved regulations it was not even applicable without this)[42] and with one notable exception (regarding Decree No. 9.550 of 1915 I.M.E.) the same could be said about Government Decree No. 8.020 of 1939.[43] Thus, while under the 1915 regulations of the Minister of Justice, under the 1939 decree the government was mandated to the promulgation of martial law, to the determination of the areas and crimes affected by martial law as well as to the abolition of the state of siege. This could also be seen from the legislation on the actual application of martial law, while before the entry into force of Decree No. 8.020 of 1939 M.E., that is, August 28, 1939, the promulgation, abolition, extension, or restriction of martial law was regulated by decrees of the Minister of Justice, the subsequent legal norms with similar content appeared in the form of government decrees.

Long before the entry into force of the ominous Government Decree No. 8.020 of 1939 (and the outbreak of World War II), three regulations (decrees of the Minister of Justice) were adopted which were about the practical applicability of martial law. Decree No. 3.431 of 1939 I.M.E. dated on February 4 ordered the promulgation of martial law regarding certain crimes throughout the country (but only in respect of the civil criminal jurisdiction and not that of the military). The number of these crimes was reduced by Decree No. 12.727. of 1939 I.M.E. on the restriction of martial law.[44] Then, against the perpetrators of the same delicts the extension of martial law was ordered by Decree No. 24.168. of 1939 I.M.E.[45] "in the Transcarpathian region returned to the Hungarian Holy Crown." The scope of martial law was further extended in 1940 by one and in 1941 by two regulations (government decrees).[46] Finally, with regard to the escalation of the war and the increase of internal tensions in 1943 and 1944 the promulgation of martial law was ordered by another four government decrees for new delicts ("of course" along with the earlier crimes), in respect of both civil and military criminal jurisdiction, throughout the whole territory of the country and of military criminal jurisdiction.[47] Subsequently, after the country's borders becoming overrun by the enemy, the failed breakaway attempt, and especially after the Arrow Cross taking power (as a consequence of the breakaway attempt) the internal state of Hungary and the battlefield situation became so chaotic that its management by means of legislation would have been totally pointless, and the reign of terror of the Arrow Cross had expressly not requested it. As they did not need any normative background (no matter how formal) for the realization of the practical consequences of their inhuman ideology (in fact that would have only just been hindering them and while the number of extinguished human lives within a given time reached an unprecedented level), yet, these executions carried out by those in power had nothing to do with the death penalty, as it no longer had anything to do with the law either.

Notes

1. Article 2 and Article 10 para. (2).
2. Article 1 para. (1).
3. In 1915, with Decree No. 2.060. of 1915 M.E. the government amended and supplemented Decree No. 12.002. of 1914 I.M.E. on accelerated procedure and martial law and with this a new, uniform code was introduced, which was officially named then as Decree No. 9.550. of 1915 I.M.E.

4. Such as, for example, the prohibition of the formal investigative process, or the regulation of the defendant's right to defense.
5. Article 7 para. (2).
6. Articles 17–18.
7. Treachery, riot, murder, intentional homicide, crime against public health by causing death, robbery, arson, crime of the causation of water flooding, crimes of the causation of public hazard on iron tracks, telegraphs (telephone) or ships.
8. Article 2.
9. These were the following: treachery, riot, murder, intentional homicide, crime against public health by causing death, all of the acts that may be subject to martial law, named by Act XXXVIII of 1920, furthermore, crimes directed for the subversion or destruction of the legal order of the state and the society (Act III of 1921, Articles 1–2)
10. Ministry of Justice Decree No. 29.307 of 1923 was promulgated and entered into force on August 2, 1923, while No. 30.004 of 1923 on August 6.
11. The assassination happened exactly at 0:20 am.
12. At that time, these were defined by Act XXXVIII of 1920 and Act XL of 1914.
13. These were rugulated by Act V of 1878 in Articles 175–176.
14. Articles 1–2.
15. Before the extradition, Matuska served a six-year prison sentence imposed by Austrian criminal courts.
16. Between 1923 and 1939 a total of twenty-five death sentences were carried out for common and political crimes and for delicts that fell under martial procedure (not including the military crimes).
17. These repealed (from February 1, 1931) the previous, in many ways outdated, Military Penal Code that was forced by the Austrians on January 15, 1855.
18. Article 77.
19. Article 78, paras. 1–4.
20. Article 87.
21. Article 93.
22. In this case only (in case of desertion or attempted desertion to the enemy)—as mentioned before—the method of execution of soldiers was hanging.

23. Article 102, para. (1).
24. Article 107.
25. Article 133, para. (1).
26. Article 42 para. (1) These included the offense of insubordination, mutiny and all those felonies against a military guard, that were punishable by death according to the Military Penal Code (as well as a few, similarly dangerous cases of the above); murder if committed in conducting or in order to conduct the past three military crimes, and the delict of cowardice.
27. This group included only one felony: espionage which was punishable by death as a form of treachery (Military Penal Code, Articles 60–63).
28. Military Penal Code, Articles 113–115.
29. As of Article 1, para. (3) of Act XV of 1924.
30. This "tranquility" obviously did not apply to the years 1931 and 1932; therefore, is considered to be only "relative."
31. Article 190.
32. Article 191, para. (2).
33. Article 191, para. (3).
34. Article 204, para. (2).
35. The somewhat archaic literal title of this crime was "damaging aeroplanes and objects associated therewith."
36. Article 209, para. (4).
37. Article 219.
38. The same (the implementation of martial law) was also made possible by another act from this period, Act XVI of 1931 on the development, direction and supply of electricity [cf. Article 61, para. (2)].
39. Hungary officially entered into war only on June 26, 1941.
40. The adoption of which happened on August 16, 1945, while it was promulgated and entered into force on September 6.
41. The adoption and promulgation of the decree itself happened on March 29.
42. Of course, the martial procedures not applicable to the mobilized army were exclusively based on Act XXXIII of 1912 and Act III of 1930, thus their scope was not affected by Government Decree No. 1.420 of 1944.
43. With the entry into force of Decree No. 8.020 of 1939 M.E., the Decree No. 9.550 of 1915 was repealed.
44. Promulgated and entered into force on May 9, 1939.

45. Promulgated and entered into force on August 25, 1939.
46. Decrees No 5.850 of 1940, No. 2770 of 1941 and No. 4.870 of 1941 M.E.
47. Decrees No. 1.020 of 1943, No. 3.940 of 1943, No. 1.130 of 1944 and No. 1.250 of 1944 M.E Decree No. 1.130 of 1944. was adopted by the Sztójay government immediately after the German invasion on March 27, 1944; it was promulgated and entered into force the next day.

10

The Death Penalty in the Years after Liberation from Nazi Occupation and During the Establishment of the Soviet Dictatorship

With the gradual liberation of Hungary from the German and Arrow Cross rule (which also meant the occupation of Hungary by the Soviets), law came to the fore again.[1] On December 21, 1944, the Provisional National Assembly convened in Debrecen. Next day, on December 22, they elected the Provisional National Government[2] and authorized it to take the necessary measures to stabilize the situation, to re-organize public administration, to provide supplies, to restore public safety and public order, and to arrest and prosecute war criminals and those who had committed crimes against the people. On the basis of this authorization, as one of its first measures, the government issued the Government Decree[3] of the People's Jurisdiction no. 81 of 1945 of January 25, 1945,[4] no. 1400 of April 27, 1945,[5] and no. 5900 of August 1, 1945,which contained war crimes and crimes against the people, as well as the procedural rules governing the perpetrators of such acts. This decree entered into force on August 5, 1945 and it only regulated the procedure against the absent accused. Accordingly, such an accused could be prosecuted and the death penalty could be imposed on him/her. If such a person was caught, he/she had to be interrogated at a public hearing and based on the outcome of this, the sentence (including death sentence) of the previous main trial

Z. J. Toth, *Changing Attitudes Towards the Death Penalty*,
https://doi.org/10.1007/978-3-030-47557-4_10

(the one held in the absence of the convict) could be approved (without holding a separate trial), or a new main trial could be ordered. Finally, all of these laws (as well as Government Decree no. 6750 of 1945 on the enhancement of the work discipline of public officials) were signed into law by Law no. 7 of 1945 that was published and entered into force on September 15, 1945. These norms are particularly important because they resulted in the prosecution of thousands of people for war crimes and crimes against the people and many of the "main culprits" were executed.

The people's tribunals started their operation in February 1945 and the most active people's tribunal (the one from Budapest) had already imposed several death sentences. A total of about 60,000 people (not only those accused of war crimes) stood before the people's tribunals, the majority of whom were convicted and many were executed; the death sentence was executed on 189 people.[6] It should be noted that since statistical data was not available between 1945 and 1951, these data are not entirely reliable. This is also shown by the fact that, according to Tibor Lukács, the number of those sentenced to death in the proceedings of the people's tribunal and actually executed is 180, while according to Ákos Major, the president of NOT (National Council of People's Tribunal) at that time, this number is 194 or 197.[7] The most famous war criminals and people accused of crimes against the people who were sentenced to death by people's tribunals were the "leader of the nation" Ferenc Szálasi, and former prime ministers László Bárdossy, Béla Imrédy, and Döme Sztójay.

Based on Government Decree no. 81 of 1945, the war criminals who could be sentenced to death[8] in the first place, were those who helped Hungary join the war, had prevented entering into an armistice agreement, had a leading role in the Arrow Cross movement, and brutalized, executed, or tortured without cause the population of the occupied and reclaimed territories, as well as prisoners of war. According to the original text, the Decree punished by death criminals who facilitated the escalation of the war of 1939 to Hungary or the involvement to a greater extent of Hungary in the war by their activity or behavior in a leading position;[9] who tried to prevent entering into an armistice agreement by force or by making use of their influence;[10] who, by their leading conduct, helped the Arrow Cross movement in their rebellion for gaining more power and keeping power, or who assumed a leadership position within the Arrow Cross government, public administration, or national defense after obtaining such power without being forced by threats on their lives (a leadership position refers to the positions of minister, state secretary, count, lord mayor, army commander, commanding officer, or positions with similar importance);[11] and who seriously violated international laws on war regarding the treatment of the population from the occupied territories and prisoners of war, or tortured the population of the reclaimed territories by abusing their authority, or who was usually the instigator, offender, or participant in the illicit execution or torture of people.[12] They were the main culprits of the war, but in addition, the common people not holding a leading role could also face this sanction[13] if they joined the German army or security police (SS, Gestapo, etc.) in spite of being Hungarian citizens[14] if these acts or their service within these bodies resulted in the death of Hungarian citizen(s), if they fought against the Hungarian Defense Forces or prevented the surrender of certain persons or troops to the Red Army; as well as the people who regularly or in exchange for a reward, provided data that constituted an "offence affecting the Hungarian interests" to a German group, or served as an informer to them.[15]

Regarding the procedural rules, the judgment of these crimes, under the terms of Article 20 of the Decree, belonged to the jurisdiction of the people's tribunals as special tribunals, including the procedures against juvenile offenders (the death sentence could not be imposed on juvenile offenders). Furthermore, according to the same article, people's tribunals had jurisdiction over crimes aiming at the subversion or destruction of state and social order, punishable even by death in some cases (Act no. 3 of 1921 Articles 1–5), military disloyalty also punishable by death (causing disadvantage for the army and advantage for the enemy—Articles 58–59 of 1930), rebellion (Act no. 5 of 1878 Articles 152–162), incitement against authorities [Act no. 5 of 1878 Article 172 para (1)] and the adjudication of other crimes committed in this context. This list was later supplemented by Law no. 47 of 1948 on the jurisdiction provisions on disloyalty regarding military confidentiality, which allocated jurisdiction to the people's tribunal in cases of military disloyalty, even punishable by death, such as espionage related to military confidentiality (Act no. 3 of 1930 Articles 60–64, 66 and 68 and Act no. 18 of 1934 Articles 2–4) and all crimes that were committed in relation to these. These rules of jurisdiction are important because in addition to war crimes, people's tribunals were able to hand out death sentences in show trials; the most famous of these lawsuits (that was based on the abovementioned provisions of jurisdiction before the Special Council of the People's Tribunal of Budapest) was the Rajk trial.[16]

The people's tribunal had a body and functioned as distinct from the ordinary court, and special rules applied to its procedure; however, this was not the only body authorized to impose capital punishment during this period; besides the people's tribunals, summary courts, court-martials, and usury courts constituting of workers' judges also functioned as extraordinary courts. According to the Decree, the people's tribunal also had the right to prosecute those who committed state crimes against state and social order,[17] crimes of espionage and disloyalty,[18] rebellion,[19] "incitement against the constitution, the law, the authorities or the officials,"[20] or any other crimes related to these delinquents (crimes abusing or endangering life, health, physical integrity or personal freedom, causing vandalism, arson or flood, damaging railways, ships or telegraph offices or other acts threatening the public), but in the latter case only "if the act is of political nature and the head of the competent prosecutor's office of Budapest allows the presentation of the case to the people's tribunal by the head of the people's prosecutor's office."[21] Later, other laws allocated other offences to the people's tribunal.

At the headquarters of each tribunal there was a people's tribunal (sometimes with several councils), which sat in a council of five. In each council, there was one delegate[22] of one of the (five) parties of the Hungarian National Independence Front founded in Szeged, in December 1944; however, in order to ensure professionalism, in addition to them a professional judge also participated in the procedure as a "chief judge"—but without a right to vote. The five parties were the following: Social Democratic Party; Independent Smallholders' Party; Civic Democratic Party; National Peasant Party; Hungarian Communist Party. Later, Government Decree no. 1400 of 1945 expanded the people's tribunal to six members to grant the National Trade Union Council the right to delegate a member in the councils of the people's tribunal. Each party could propose five people in each council, of whom the count appointed a regular and an alternate member based on the proposal made by the local national committee. Interestingly, accepting the assignment was mandatory, it could not be refused, but after three months of operation as people's judge, they could resign from their position.

All members participated with equal right in the judgment, but it consisted of two separate stages: in the first one (by simple majority vote), they made a decision regarding the question of guilt (and the crime itself if the accused was found guilty); in the second one (by simple majority vote as well), they decided on the legal consequences that were to be applied if the accused was found guilty. The task of the chief judge in this regard was that he had to formulate an opinion first about the probable crime based on the factual situation established and then (if there was such a crime) about the nature and level of the punishment imposed for the crime determined by the people's judges. The chief judge was entitled to vote in one case; if for some reason there were no three unanimous opinions (votes), the chief judge could join the unanimous opinion of any of the two judges. Finally, the chief judge also had the role of guarding legality; because if they considered that the people's tribunal delivered an unlawful judgment and there was no possibility for an appeal (thus it did not apply to cases of the death penalty), then they could turn to the National Council of People's Tribunal for remedy. Interestingly, according to the Decree, voting was compulsory, beginning with the eldest judge of the people's tribunal and finishing with its youngest member.

In the case of a death sentence, the Decree allowed for appeal. According to Government Decree no. 81 of 1945, making an appeal was possible only in the case of certain sentences; thus, in addition to the imposition of the death penalty, there were sentences of complete confiscation of property, loss of employment, imprisonment of at least three years, or a fine of more than 20,000 Hungarian pengős. The appeal was adjudicated by the National Council of People's Tribunal (or one of its judging councils) acting at the current headquarters of the government.[23] These councils were also constituted of five members delegated by the above parties (basing their judgments rather as laymen, considering political aspects over legal ones). With all these provisions, the new practitioners of power "successfully" ensured that the tribunals judging those accused of war crimes were biased in every aspect and their members could (and did) freely enforce their political prejudices against the accused persons. This, of course, does not mean that the sentences would not have been substantiated in many of the cases; there were, however, a number of cases that were conceptual.

Government Decree no. 1400 of 1945, on the one hand, extended the scope of war crimes to be punishable by death,[24] while on the other hand it amended and supplemented the procedural rules that applied for the procedures of people's tribunals. Among substantive laws, it was possible to apply this sanction also in the case of war criminals who did not try to prevent Hungary from falling into war, even though they could have done so, or who contributed to the adoption of a decision that led to the expansion of war in Hungary. According to this, the following persons were punishable by death as well: those who facilitated the escalation of the war of 1939 to Hungary or the involvement to a greater extent of Hungary in the war by their activity or behavior in a leading position and did not strive to prevent it, although they had an opportunity to do so due to their position at a public office or their roles as political, economic, or public figures;[25] and who, as a member of the parliament or a public servant in a leading position, was the initiator or participated in, although they could foresee the consequences, of making a decision that forced the Hungarian people into World War II in 1939.[26] Furthermore, Government Decree no. 1400 of 1945 Article 6 introduced a new, sixth point in the enumeration of Government Decree no. 81 of 1945 Article 11; according to this new regulation, in addition to the above, apart from a committing war crimes, a person could be sanctioned by death if they, in a printed form (in any multiplied document), in a speech recited in front of a gathering or through radio, engaged in permanent and continuous activities in order to make the country join the war and continue the war with a greater involvement, by influencing significantly public opinion and by pointing the country in the wrong direction. The "simple" war criminals could have already been punished by death if they publicly instigated others for war; if they assisted soldiers in violent acts; and if, although not as leaders, they took part in the Arrow Cross movement or engaged in war propaganda. According to Government Decree no. 1400 of 1945, a "simple" war criminal could be subjected to capital punishment if the person incited the continuation of the war to a greater extent in a printed form (in any multiplied document), in a speech recited in front of a gathering or through radio; helped a certain military unit in committing violent acts against a person or property; helped, by their non-leading conduct, the Arrow Cross movement in gaining or keeping power, or, after obtaining such power, voluntarily assumed an important position within the Arrow Cross public administration or national defense; and performed significant intellectual work in the service of war publicity.[27] In addition, Government Decree no. 1400 of 1945 Article 8 para. (2) introduced, as point 7, a new factual situation in Government Decree 81 of 1945 Article 13. According to this, the person who engaged in or promoted activities that were capable of complicating or breaking the peace of collaboration of the people after war, or by inducing international disputes is considered a war criminal (and as such is punishable by death). With this, Government Decree no. 1400 of 1945 extended the possibility of the death penalty to all war crimes, which was regulated only by Government Decree 81 of 1945. (Other legislation did not make provisions regarding war crimes.)[28]

Among procedural rules, the most important amendment to the Decree of April 27 was that it narrowed the possibility for appeal by depriving this right from all those who were condemned as main culprits by the people's tribunal for any crime defined in Article 11 of Government Decree no. 81 of 1945 (namely, any penalty, including the death penalty). If the sentence was death, then the people's tribunal (if the convict or the defense counsel filed a petition for mercy) would have to express their position on whether the sentenced person was worthy of mercy. According to Article 2 of the Decree, the death sentence could be imposed only if the death penalty was the only punishment consistent with the gravity of the crime and the subjective culpability of the defendant. Of course, this provision did not restrict the people's tribunals in any way in imposing this sanction, as this "rubber regulation" could include any conduct considered punishable by the Decree. The petition for mercy could be presented exclusively by the convict or the defense counsel (the people's prosecutor or any other person were not entitled to present it, including even the people's tribunal as an ex officio intervention) and filing it was only possible in the case of the death penalty. If they considered that the person deserved mercy, they would present the case files and the proposal for mercy to the High National Council as the temporary collective head of the state body (after it stopped operating, to the President of the Republic), which made a decision without justifying it; but if the people's tribunal did not find the defendant worthy of mercy, the death sentence had to be executed immediately (possibly within two hours) after imposing it. (This was the case when the High National Council rejected the petition for mercy. Here, of course, the two-hour deadline did not refer to the period after imposing the sentence, but the period after publishing the decision rejecting the petition for mercy, that is, announcement of the decision.)

The High National Council as a temporary head of the state body of three members, however, was established on January 26, 1945 by the Provisional National Government. Initially, the members of the body were the Prime Minister, the President of the Provisional National Assembly, and an elected (communist) representative of the Provisional National Assembly's Political Committee, and from December 1945, its members were the President of the Provisional National Assembly and two elected representatives. The operation of the body stopped with the election of the President of the Republic, on February 1, 1946. If the High National Council (or later the President of the Republic) pardoned the convict, the Decree modified the death penalty to forced labor for life and in case of physical unfitness, to life imprisonment. Finally, the Decree also made provisions regarding the method of the execution; the death sentence had to be executed "by bullet or rope in a closed space, but without the absence of the public."[29] Act no. 34 of 1947 on certain provisions related to the People's Jurisdiction made some minor changes to those described above. On the one hand, for example, it stated regarding execution that the death penalty should be primarily executed by rope, or "if the execution by rope met obstacles, by bullet,"[30] thus, it limited the prosecutor (people's prosecutor) in choosing between the two permissible ways of execution and it set out the primacy of the method of hanging. On the other hand, it excluded the public from the execution, although it allowed the people's prosecution to authorize any adult person (with a specified and justified reason) to be present at the execution. Although the law still did not allow the appeal, it provided an opportunity for the accused to submit a complaint of nullity as a remedy in the event of an infringement, which was judged by the NCPT (National Council of People's Tribunal).[31] Finally, Article 30 para. (1) set out that the President of the Republic is entitled to judge petitions for mercy and to grant individual (procedural and executive) mercy based on the proposal of the Minister of Justice (but without such a proposal).

The authorization given to the government by the Provisional National Assembly on December 22, 1944, did not, of course, include only formulating of the rules necessary for the prosecution of war criminals and those who had committed crimes against the people, but also took other extraordinary measures, such as new penalty provisions or defining the punishment for certain offences (strengthening them as well). The first such legislation of criminal law imposing the death penalty was Government Decree no. 6730 of 1945 published and enforced on August 18, 1945, on strengthening the punishment for price gouging abuse, that set out the death penalty as an absolute sanction against the perpetrator of price gouging abuse (Act no. 15 of 1920 Article 1),[32] provided that the crime was committed as a recidivist,[33] involved a significant value (based on the original provision, more than 20,000 Hungarian pengős, which in this case was much higher due to inflation)[34] or was committed commercially, if by doing so, the offender jeopardized public supplies.[35]

On October 19, as a second legal norm of this type, Government Decree no. 9480 of 1945 of the Provisional National Government on the punishment of export without authorization of items of public need, was published and entered into force.[36] Although this act was also punishable with death based on Government Decree no. 6730 of 1945—as we have seen—due to the shortage of items of public need and the relative gravity of the act resulting from this, the legislator considered that there was a need for a special regulation that states *expressis verbis* that these acts were sanctioned by the death penalty. According to the Decree, a capital sanction was imposed for the export of items of public need without a ministerial authorization (in quantities exceeding the personal needs during travel),[37] if the act seriously violated or endangered the interest of public supplies, and in the case of commercializing.[38] Also on the basis of the authorization from December 22, 1944, Government Decree no. 60 of

1946 of the Government ordered the death penalty for the cases of trafficking stolen property that were committed in relation to goods acquired from the property or the detaining of a public transport company, or from robbery.[39] Finally, Government Decree no. 1750 of 1946, in relation to non-military crimes set out that if the execution of the death penalty by rope met obstacles, it should be executed by bullet,[40] and for this, in the first place, the guarding personnel of the local arresting institute, in the second place, the local guarding personnel of the state police and as a last resort, the local corps of the military should be mobilized (who are, of course, obliged to comply with this request made by the public prosecutor or the people's prosecutor).

The National Assembly formed as a result of the National Assembly elections held on November 4, 1945, now granted new statutory authorizations to the government for issuing various regulations, in the area of criminal law as well. The first authorization of this type was included in Law no. 6 of 1946, which set out that "the Ministry may, in order to ensure the economic, financial and administrative order of the state, by Decree, make any other provision of private, criminal, administrative law and others under legislative competence, and thus it may, with the exception of the laws of the National Assembly, set out provisions different from the existing laws." The mandate was valid with effect until July 31, 1946,[41] but it was first extended by Law no. 16 of 1946 until October 31, 1946, and then by Law no. 28 of 1946 until February 28, 1947. Based on the authorization of these two latter laws, "the Ministry may, in order to ensure the order of economic life, the balance of the national budget and the undisturbed operation of public administration, make any other provision by Decree under legislative competence and thus it may set out provisions different from the existing laws."[42] At the same time, "provisions different from the laws of the National Assembly and of public law could not be set out, the organization of public administration could not be modified, new crimes could not be defined and a more severe punishment for a crime than the one set out by law could not be ordered, except for those aiming to restore the balance of the national budget and to ensure public supplies."[43] These stipulations, however, restoring the balance of the national budget and ensuring public supplies, still provided a great opportunity for action for the government to regulate criminal law, while the government did take advantage of it.

Based on these authorizations, the government also published Government Decree no. 8800 of 1946 regarding the protection of economic order by criminal law. This Government Decree, on the one hand, re-regulated the different types of price gouging abuse set out in Government Decree no. 6730 of 1945, while on the other hand, it listed and defined the crimes endangering the interest of public supplying. The Decree imposed the death sentence for five types of price gouging abuse[44] (price exceeding, usury of goods, price gouging profiteering, withdrawal of goods, deceit of price gouging)[45] if one of these acts was committed by a person with criminal record, commercially or for a significant value[46] and the offender caused a serious violation to the economic order.[47] Under the same conditions (on the one hand, the criminal record, the commercializing nature or the significant value of the act, on the other hand, the serious violation of economic order), a person was punishable by death[48] if he/she committed an "act endangering the interest of public supplying."[49] These included the breach of statutory production obligation (if a person did not produce the crop and product specified in the legislation, or if they did not take into account the prescribed quantity and procedure); the withdrawal of the stock of products or crops;[50] the failure to notify the authorities regarding them, or making a false or incomplete statement about them; the withdrawal of the stock of products or crops sequestrated for public supplies or material management;[51] withholding such stock against a legislation setting out its marketing, as well as its marketing in an inappropriate manner, quantity, or for inadequate purposes; the failure to comply with the statutory obligation to deliver the product or crop; the purchase of a product or crop by exceeding the maximum price set out by the authority (even without the intention of resale); the false notification regarding the right to purchase, deliver, or use a product or crop by the non-disclosure of the truth or by any other fraud, as well as any illicit profiteering with this right. Finally, Article 20 para. (2) of the Decree allowed usury courts,[52] too, to proceed in such cases against the offenders, who, with different financial offences,[53] seriously violated the interest related to the stability of the new legal tender, the Hungarian currency "forint" introduced simultaneously with the entry into force of the Decree.[54]

The mandate of this later provision, based on Article 20, was effective until December 31, 1946, but this deadline was first extended by Government Decree no. 24650 of 1946 until June 30, 1947 and then by Government Decree no. 8000 of 1947[55] for the period after July 1, 1947 (according to the latter created Government Decree no. 15340 of 1947[56] until July 31, 1948). Government Decree no. 5450 of 1948 extended the possibility of the death penalty, in addition to the crimes enlisted in Government Decree no. 8800 of 1946 Article 20 (under the conditions mentioned therein), to the "crime and the offense of counterfeiting committed in relation to banknotes and coins denominating values of forint"[57] as well, and assigned the jurisdiction of procedures of such offences to the usury court. Finally, the mandates of both Government Decree no. 8800 of 1946 Article 20 and the newly created[58] Government Decree no. 5450 of 1948 were extended by Government Decree no. 7920 of 1948[59] for the period after August 1, 1948 (according to Government Decree no. 12590 of 1948[60] until December 31, 1949).

Regarding the usury courts mentioned in the previous paragraphs, they were not the invention of the republican legislation, as they were created at the beginning of the Horthy era, by Government Decree no. 5950 of 1920 published for the implementation of Act no. 15 of 1920 on price gouging abuses. These special courts, initially, did not (and based on the provisions of Act no. 15 of 1920, they could not) have the right to impose death sentences, only the legislations after World War II allowed them to do so. In the Horthy era, they operated within the royal court or bigger district courts, in separate councils of three, the president and one member being professional judges, while the other member, as lay magistrate, was the representative ("professional man") of primary production, industry, or commerce.

This organization remained active for a while after 1945 and the criminal proceedings assigned to the jurisdiction of the usury court were judged by councils of similar composition (most of them being professional judges), however, in 1947, the National Assembly adopted Act no. 23 of 1947 on the panels of usury courts, which ordered the establishment of one (or more) "panels of usury court" at the usury courts operating at the seats of Regional Courts of Appeal, which had a function distinct from the tasks of usury courts (moreover, its composition significantly differed from its "mother organization"). The panels of usury courts, however, were bodies of five members and only their president was a professional judge (appointed by the Minister of Justice), the members (and the two alternate members) were non-professional "workers' judges." The latter were admitted to their offices after a two-round process: in the first one, the bigger industrial and mining plants (of at least 2000 people in Budapest and 500 people in other areas) nominated one worker doing physical labor after every one hundred workers to the nomenclature of the Trade Union Council, from which they chose by lot the workers' judges for the panels of usury courts.[61] Thus, according to the law, the jurisdiction of the panels included the judgment of the price gouging abuses set out in Government Decree no. 8800 of 1946 and the "acts endangering the interest of public supplying,"[62] even if, based on qualifying circumstances, the imposed sanction for the offence was the death penalty and the crime of exporting items of public need without a ministerial authorization (Government Decree no. 948 of 1945), and if the act was committed commercially but other, subsequent legislations disposed of the assignment of criminal proceeding regarding certain offences to the panels of usury courts. Government Decree no. 680 of 1948, no. 3350 of 1948, and no. 4940 of 1948 allowed panels of usury courts to impose capital punishment, but the most important of these other legislations was Government Decree no. 2140 of 1948, which assigned certain crimes endangering the implementation of the economic plan (regulated by Government Decree no. 14200 of 1947) to the jurisdiction of the panels of usury courts.

Usury courts, panels of usury courts, and summary courts as a form of special court along with people's tribunals, continued to exist. The procedural rules of summary jurisdiction did not change compared to the Horthy era (i.e., the regulation from 1912); although, Government Decree no. 11800 of 1945 adopted on December 5, 1945, published and entered into force on December 13, modified the procedural regulations of martial law, it did not make many substantive changes.[63] With regard to substantive norms, there were not many changes in their nature as compared to the regulation from a few years earlier (except for the fact that the provisions connected to the war [for instance, crimes committed during or in relation to air raid alerts, blackouts, air strikes, etc., crimes related to postal packets sent to operational areas, etc.] were implicitly missing in this era from the offences that could be subjected to martial law).

The re-introduction of summary jurisdiction after the war was made by the Provisional National Government on October 18, 1945.[64] This was when Government Decree no. 9600 of 1945 was published, which ordered the martial law for the entire territory of the country both for civil and military jurisdiction for the specific cases of murder, intentional killing, robbery and burglary,[65] as well as for any crime committed by fabricating, purchasing, possessing and using explosives and explosive substances,[66] for the attempts in this regard and for alliances made for committing murder. The subsequent Government Decrees had gradually expanded this circle to more and more offences, both in civil and military criminal justice and not just to the crime itself, but to attempts at them, and not only to offenders, but to partners as well. This included Government Decree no. 50 of 1946[67] published and entered into force on January 2, 1946, Government Decree no. 1830 of 1946 of February 22, 1946,[68] Government Decree no. 6330 of 1946 of June 4, 1946,[69] Government Decree no. 7200 of 1946 of June 22, 1946,[70] and Government Decree no. 23700 of 1946 of November 30, 1946[71] (however, Government Decree no. 9700 of 1948 published and entered into force on September 29, 1948, limited procedures of martial law compared to the previous ones).[72]

According to Government Decree no. 1830 of 1946 of February 22, 1946, the following were subjects to summary procedures: crimes of causing flooding;[73] crimes of public endangerment carried out by vandalizing any artwork, installation, material, equipment, etc. used for flood protection and the protection of inland waters,[74] as well as thefts in this regard;[75] crimes of public endangerment carried out by vandalizing or stealing object, installations, etc. used for rail transport and road traffic;[76] offenses of public endangerment carried out by vandalizing or stealing objects, etc. used for postal, telephonic or telegraphic installations;[77] crimes of public endangerment carried out by vandalizing vessels, aircraft and objects connected to them;[78] the crime of public endangerment carried out by vandalizing the installations and accessories of generating, conducting, and distributing electricity, by interrupting or impeding their usability;[79] crimes of theft on or near the scene of a flooding.

The fourth type of special court entitled to impose the death penalty (in addition to the people's tribunal, usury court, and summary court) was the court-martial. Government Decree no. 7290 of 1945, published and entered into force on September 6, 1945, provided the establishment of court-martials. According to the decree, the president of the court-martial was a military judge and the two assessors were two individuals of the military personnel. One of the latter was always an officer, while the other one, depending on the military rank of the defendant, was either an officer (if the defendant was an officer), or a warrant officer (if the accused was one as well), or a member of the enlisted personnel (if the person under investigation was an enlisted man or a civilian). It is important that a person with a lower military rank than the rank of the defendant, can not be involved in the court-martial (for example, in the case of a major, a captain should not assist). Government Decree no. 7290 of 1945 set out that regarding military criminal jurisdiction, namely the judgment of military crimes and non-military offences committed by soldiers, court-martials of three members should be established, which have the jurisdiction to carry out both ordinary and summary procedures The procedure was carried out in accordance with the rules set out in Act no. 33 of 1912 (Military Criminal Procedure Code), although Government Decree no. 1740 of 1946 made some small changes in this regard.[80] One of these provisions set out that if the sentence of the death penalty could not be executed with rope, the convict should be shot.[81] Another provision supplemented the Military Criminal Procedure Code in relation to summary jurisdiction[82] with the same detail that was set out in Government Decree no. 11800 of 1945 in relation to summary jurisdiction, namely that a person can be declared guilty and thus sentenced to death only unanimously, but on the issue of qualification and punishment it was sufficient to reach a decision by majority vote.[83]

The recast of the substantive part of military criminal law was set out within a short time; the National Assembly carried it out by Law no. 62 of 1948 on the Military Criminal Code,[84] which imposed the death penalty as the sanction of fourteen different crimes. According to Article 7 of the Military Criminal Code based on the main principle, the death penalty should be executed by a firing squad; execution by rope was only allowed, if Act no. 62 of 1948 made provisions in this regard (it did so only in the case of absconding to the enemy), but even then, the execution was to be carried out by bullet, if the execution of hanging was not possible (for example, in the absence of a professional hangman). After the entry into force of the new Military Criminal Code, the instigators and leaders of mutiny could be sentenced to death,[85] as well as those who called for mutiny, if, as a result, the mutiny did take place. (According Article 33: "The soldier who calls for committing mutiny or mediates such a call…if…as a result of the call, mutiny takes place, the inciter should be punished in accordance with Article 30 para. (2).") The offender of "cowardly conduct" was also punishable by death,[86] if he, as a commander, allowed his unit to be captured or abandoned them, or if he demonstrated a cowardly conduct in battle and this implied the cowardly conduct of others as well.[87] The offence of "absconding"[88] was punishable by capital sanction in one case; if the soldier deserted or attempted to desert to the enemy. In this case (as the only crime in the Military Criminal Code), the execution was to be carried out by hanging representing a shameful and humiliating method for soldiers.[89] The crime of evading to perform military service was also punishable by death (by bullet) if the act was carried out by a commander during the war and, as a result foreseeable by the offender, one or more people lost their lives, or a large amount of war material was destroyed, or if the act imposed a great disadvantage to military operations.[90]

The same sanction was imposed for the abuse or other form of violence against chiefs or superiors if those were committed while the person was serving in a time of war; for "the intentional murder of a chief or superior"[91] (in all cases without exception); for insubordination to a service command if the explicit denial of the order during the war was related to the abuse of the superior, or to other violent or dangerous threat, or if the soldier committed the act during the war and, as a result foreseeable by the offender, one or more people lost their lives, or a large amount of war material was destroyed, the act being a disadvantage for military operations;[92] and for "the violation of a general order"[93] if the act was deliberately committed during the war by the commander and, as a result foreseeable by the offender, one or more people lost their lives, or a large amount of war material was destroyed, the act being a big disadvantage for military operations.[94] The death penalty was imposed on the offenders of the crimes committed against the military guard[95] (as of Chap. 6) if the soldier intentionally killed the guard,[96] and in some cases[97] if the soldier did not obey the instructions of the guard on service;[98] on those carrying out crimes related to service (as of Chap. 10) if the military guard, who violated the general or special instruction of the guard[99] committed this act during the war and it resulted in a big disadvantage, and when the offender could foresee it;[100] and on those who committed crimes against the population of the occupied territory (as of Chap. 17) if the offenders carried out serious "crimes of sexual assault"[101] and intentional killing.[102]

Notes

1. For capital punishment and martial law before 1944, see: Zoltán J. Tóth: Statutory Regulation of Capital Punishment in Hungary during the Horthy Era and World War II. *Journal on European History of Law*, Vol. 6, 2015, No. 2, pp. 23–28.
2. At the same time, the Provisional National Assembly declared itself "the exclusive representative of the Hungarian state sovereignty" and then, by founding its own legitimacy, it changed into law the decree by Law no. 1 of 1945.
3. These laws had a retroactive effect; thus, they were also applicable for the crimes that were committed before their entry in force.
4. Date of entry into force: February 5, 1945.
5. Date of entry into force: May 1, 1945.
6. Source of data: Tibor Szincsák: Történelmi kronológia (Historic chronology). *Tóth Könyvkereskedés és Kiadó Kft.*, Debrecen, 1998, p. 436.
7. See the latter references in: Tibor Horváth (ed.): A halálbüntetés megszüntetése Magyarországon. (The abolition of capital punishment in Hungary). Halálbüntetést Ellenzők Ligája, Miskolc, 1991, p. 42.
8. See Article 12.
9. Article 11 para. (1).
10. Article 11 para. (3).
11. Article 11 para. (4).

12. Article 11 para. (5).
13. Article 14 paras. (3)–(4).
14. Article 12 para. (4).
15. Article 12 para. (5).
16. Cf.: Gábor Paizs: Rajk-per (Rajk's trial). Ötlet, Budapest, 1989; István Soltész (ed.): Rajk-dosszié (Rajk's file). Láng Kiadó, Budapest, 1989. In this case, former foreign and interior minister László Rajk, as well as Tibor Szőnyi and András Szalai were sentenced to death on September 24, 1949 and then executed on October 15.
17. As of Act no. 3 of 1921 Articles 1–5.
18. As of Act no. 3 of 1930 Articles 58–59.
19. As of Act no. 5 of 1878 Article 152–162.
20. As of Act no. 5 of 1878 Article 172 para. (1).
21. Article 21 of the Decree.
22. These judges—being lay people—were not even bound by the normative and established standards of the legal profession; their judgments can rather be considered as political statements and only to a minor extent as "true" judgments.
23. Until April 1945, Debrecen filled in this status, followed by Budapest.
24. Article 7.
25. Government Decree no. 81 of 1945 Article 11 paras. (1)–(2).
26. Government Decree no. 81 of 1945 Article 11 para. (2).
27. Government Decree no. 81 of 1945 Article 13 paras. (1), (2), (3), and (6).
28. For the practical activity of people's criminal court, see. e.g.: Attila Papp: Volt egyszer egy népbíróság… (Once upon a time, there was a people's criminal court…), *Nagykanizsa,* 2017; Frigyes Kahler: Joghalál Magyarországon 1945–1989 (*Justizmord* in Hungary 1945–1989), Zrínyi Könyvkiadó, Budapest, 1993; Tibor Zinner: XX. századi politikai perek (Political trials in the twentieth century), Rejtjel Kiadó, Budapest, 1999.
29. Government Decree no. 1400 of 1945 Article 1 para. (3).
30. Article 1 para. (1).
31. Article 19.
32. Based on Act no. 15 of 1920, the types of price gouging abuse are the following: sale at a price higher than the official (limited) price (price exceeding); setting a price of unjust profit (usury of goods); setting an unjust wage by taking advantage of the oppressed position of the other

party (either the employee or the employer) (usury of wage); setting a disproportionate remuneration for mediation related to the marketing of an item of public need (price gouging profiteering); the unauthorized withdrawal from public supplies of a stock of items of public need ordered for marketing with price gouging methods for profit purposes (withdrawal of goods); the unauthorized foreign trade of items of public need with restricted distribution (smuggling of goods); refusal of the sale of items of public need ordered for marketing for the reason that the buyer reported the seller to the authorities for any of the above acts (Article 1 paras. (1)–(7)).

33. Based on the application of this provision, a recidivist is someone, who, for a similar crime, "has already been punished, and the period between that punishment and committing the newest act was shorter than five years" (Act no. 6 of 1944 Article 3 para. (1)).
34. Act no. 6 of 1944 Article 3 para. (2).
35. Government Decree no. 6730 of 1945 Article 1.
36. Article 3 of the Decree assigned the proceeding to the competence of usury courts (see later).
37. In addition, in accordance with the last sentence of Article 2 para. (2), as in the case of many similar legislations of the following years, full confiscation should also be set out.
38. Article 1 para. (2).
39. … the crime of trafficking stolen property is punishable by death, if the person 1. acquires or hides such a stolen thing or assists in selling such a stolen thing about which he/she knows that the thief stole it from the property or detaining, transport equipment, railway station, premise of area belonging to a public transport company, ordered for railway tracks and public transport; 2. acquires, hides or assists in selling a thing about which he/she knows that its owner or detainer obtained by committing robbery. (Article 1)
40. Article 1.
41. If a general change of government had taken place prior to that date, the validity of the mandate would have ended. (The same will be true for the following two similar laws.)
42. Act no. 16 of 1946 Article 1 para. (1).
43. Act no. 16 of 1946 Article 1 para. (2).
44. Government Decree 8800 of 1946 Article 1 paras. (1)–(5).

45. As it can be seen, the crimes listed in Act no. 15 of 1920 Article 1 para. (1) and punishable by the death penalty according to Government Decree no. 6730 of 1945 did not include usury of wage (point 3), smuggling of goods (point 6), and the refusal of the sale of items of public need (point 7), however, a new factual situation was added, the deceit of price gouging. According to Article 1 para. (5), this is committed by someone, who, in order to mislead or deceive the authorities regarding a significant condition in determining the price, consciously provides false information to the authorities.
46. These qualifying conditions were basically the same as the previous regulations, namely, the provision set out in Act no. 6 of 1944 Article 3 paras. (1)–(3).
47. Government Decree no. 8800 of 1946 Article 9 para. (4).
48. See the previous footnote.
49. Government Decree 8800 of 1946 Article 7 paras. (1)–(6) and Article 8 paras. (1)–(2).
50. This included their use, consumption, destruction and rendering them unusable.
51. Such a "withdrawal" was the concealment, hiding, disposal of this stock, or the failure to perform the obligation of transferring or transporting them.
52. For the statutory provisions and the judical practice of usury adjudication in Hungary, see: László Major: Az uzsorabírósági eljárás (The usury courts' procedure). Grill, Budapest, 1947.
53. The issuing by the public official of a mandatory payment order including impermissible loan transfers violating legal provisions relating to state accounting, that of additional expenses and payment without appropriation pursuant to the budget credit or the total amount of credit provided by the Ministry of Finance as well as the intentional breach of other obligations of public officials under the legal provisions relating to state accounting during the issuing of such mandatory payment orders (Government Decree no. 8800 of 1946 Article 19); tax fraud; excise violation; profiteering with international and domestic payment instruments (Act no. 36 of 1922 Article 1 para. (1)]) non-declaration or the deliberate declaration of false information regarding international payment instruments and accounts receivable (Act no. 32 of 1931 Article 1 para. (1) and Article 2 para. (1)); exceeding salaries or other allowances set out in a collective agreement (Government Decree

no. 490 of 1956 Article 13); misuse of loans or advances granted for the purpose of primary production, industry, commerce or transportation (Government Decree no. 8990 of 1945 Article 3).

54. August 1, 1946.
55. The publication and entry into force of this Decree took place shortly before the end of the mandate, on July 28, 1947.
56. Published on: December 23, 1947.
57. Government Decree no. 5450 of 1948 Article 1 para. (1).
58. Government Decree no. 5450 of 1948 was published and entered into force on May 12, 1948.
59. Date of publication and entry into force: July 27, 1948.
60. Published on: December 15, 1948.
61. For the detailed regulation of this, see Decree no. 70000 of 1947 of the Ministry of Justice regarding the implementation of Act no. 23 of 1947, basically, on election procedure of workers' judges.
62. This also meant that financial crimes regulated (and in some cases, punishable by death) by Government Decree no. 8800 of 1946 Article 20, did not belong to the jurisdiction of the panels of usury courts; in that regard, the procedure (according to Article 22 of the above Decree) continued to be carried out by the "ordinary" usury courts.
63. The most important substantive change was the one that set out that, although sentencing to death would require the unanimous vote of the members of the court, but "regarding the issue of qualification and punishment, it is sufficient if the decision is reached by majority vote" (Article 2 para. (2)).
64. Summary jurisdiction disappeared only in 1953, to be reintroduced in 1956.
65. According to the Decree, the procedure of the summary court was ordered when the theft committed in a building, fenced area, or ship, by breaking in, climbing in, or breaking the lock or other device serving for protection, was carried out during the night, being armed or collectively (by several people together).
66. As of Act no. 15 of 1924 Article 1.
67. Government Decree no. 50 of 1956 extended summary jurisdiction to stealing assets related in any way to public transport companies.
68. According to the Decree, the following are subjects to summary procedures: crime of causing flooding; crime of public endangerment carried

out by damaging public utility objects or stealing parts thereof; crime of theft on or near the scene of a flooding.

69. It ordered martial law for the crimes of arson and alliances for committing arson.
70. The Government Decree imposed summary procedure for those who, by the violation or circumvention of legislative regulations, acquired, held, delivered, or circulated firearms or ammunition and who did not comply with their obligations to report or to surrender (Government Decree no. 7140 of 1946 Article 2 (1)).
71. Government Decree no. 23700 of 1946 imposed summary jurisdiction for all cases of price gouging abuses and acts endangering the interest of public supplying, which were punishable by death based on Government Decree no. 8800 of 1946 Article 9 para. (4), as well as the crime of exporting items of public need without authorization (Government Decree no. 9480 of 1945). (See the detailed regulations of these previously.)
72. On the one hand, it abrogated Government Decree no. 23700 of 1946, thus, the summary jurisdiction ordered therein could not be applied anymore, on the other hand, it terminated martial law in all cases of burglary, previously falling under this procedure (as set out in Government Decree no. 9600 of 1945).
73. As of Act no. 5 of 1878 Article 429–431.
74. As of Government Decree no. 1820 of 1946 Article 1 and Act no. 2 of 1939 Article 208.
75. As of Government Decree no. 1820 of 1946 Article 2.
76. As of Government Decree no. 3780 of 1945 Article 1 para. (1) and Act no. 5 of 1878 Article 434.
77. As of Government Decree no. 3780 of 1945 Article 1 para. (2).
78. As of Act no. 5 of 1878, Article 434 and 444; and Act no. 2 of 1939 Article 209.
79. As of Act no. 16 of 1931 Article 61 and Act no. 2 of 1939 Article 208.
80. The Decree was published on February 27, 1946 and it entered into force on July 15, 1946 (in accordance with Government Decree no 17494/1946 published based on the authorization granted to the Minister of Defense, set out in Article 21(1) of the current Decree).
81. Article 16 para. (4).
82. The Government later (June 8, 1946) published and entered into force a new regulation (Government Decree no. 6340 of 1946) that furtherly

modified certain rules regarding a few points in military criminal justice; however, as those did not include substantive provisions related to death penalty, we do not discuss them.

83. Article 19.
84. This, of course, implied the abolishment of Act no. 2 of 1930 (Military Criminal Code). Act no. 62 of 1948 was the last separate military criminal code, because the further resolution of military offences was not set out in an independent legislation, but in a chapter of the Criminal Code. (This method was also applied by Law no. 5 of 1961 and Law no. 4 of 1978.)
85. Article 30 para. (2).
86. "Cowardly conduct is demonstrated by the soldier who, fearing his own safety, does not fulfill or fulfills improperly his duties." (Article 37)
87. Article 38 para. (2).
88. "The soldier who, in order to avoid service obligations of any kind, arbitrarily leaves his position and place of destination and remains absent, commits absconding." (Article 40)
89. Article 41 para. (2).
90. Article 47 para. (2).
91. Article 58.
92. Article 59 para. (3).
93. This crime is committed by a soldier "who, either intentionally or out of negligence, violates a general order or prohibition serving to maintain discipline and order" (Article 62 para. [1]).
94. Article 62 para. (2).
95. Based on the provision of Article 63, the soldier who, in accordance with instructions of military service, carries out an activity of military guard.
96. Article 67.
97. "If the act was carried out during the war and, as a result foreseeable by the offender, one or more people lost their lives, or a big amount of war material was destructed, or if the act imposed a great disadvantage to military operations" (Article 70 para. [4]).
98. "Insubordination with guard" (Article 70).
99. "Violation of the instruction of the guard" (Article 88).
100. Article 88 para. (4).
101. The soldier, who committed statutory rape (Article 232 of the Criminal Code) or sexual abuse (Article 233 of the Criminal Code) against a

person who belongs to the population of the territory occupied by the army …in a serious case, is punishable by death. (Article 117)

102. The soldier, who committed the crime of intentional killing defined in Article 279 and 280 of the Criminal Code against a person who belongs to the population of the territory occupied by the army, is punishable by death. (Article 119)

11

Capital Punishment in the First Decade of State Socialism

At the beginning of the 1950s, the elaboration of substantial criminal legislation continued regarding common criminal offenses: a good example of this is Law-Decree no. 4 of 1950 on the criminal law protection of planned economy, as well as Law-Decree no. 24 of 1950 on the criminal law protection of social property. The first legislation sentences to death any action that aims to endanger, threaten, or thwart the national economy plan, if it resulted in a serious offense, or if it was committed several times by the same person. The latter one imposed particularly strict methods, one of them the death penalty, to those who committed crimes against social property as a privileges form of property. Accordingly, "social property as the wealth of the working people…is entitled to great criminal law protection" (Article 1). The person who steals, embezzles, illegally acquires, destroys an asset in social property, or causes damage to wealth in social property by fraud (Article 3), is punishable by death if "the same person repeatedly commits a crime against social property, or if two or more members of a criminal organization participated in carrying out the action," in case that "the crime resulted in a particularly great damage" (Article 5 para. [2]). In addition, based on this Law-Decree, the crimes of setting on fire or blowing up assets in social property, as well as

Z. J. Toth, *Changing Attitudes Towards the Death Penalty*,
https://doi.org/10.1007/978-3-030-47557-4_11

stealing assets in social property that results in a particularly great damage, were punishable by death in every case, without any discretion (Article 6).

The settlement of the general part of substantive criminal law also took place in this period (the beginning of the 1950s), as well as its adaption to the altered (typical for the socialist social-economic order) conditions. For this purpose, the parliament set out Act no. 2 of 1950 on the General Part of the Criminal Code, which replaced the First Part of the Code of Csemegi still in force (though it was modified and supplemented by the legislation created in the meantime in several regards). Although the ministerial preamble of the law acknowledged the need of a complete (including the general and special part) and new Criminal Code, at the same time it stated that this still met obstacles. In the meantime, however, until these obstacles were eliminated, it was necessary to introduce a new general part that adapted to the existing circumstances.

The law created this way continued to recognize the death penalty (in Article 30 para. [1]) among penalties of different nature, in relation to which, the ministerial preamble claimed the following: "As for the death penalty, it is obvious that raising the cultural standard and implementing socialism will render this punishment dispensable, however, this time, we are not at the stage of development that would allow the death penalty to be abolished."[1] The legislator, therefore, declared in principle the future abolition of the most severe sanction, but did not consider it to be feasible under the circumstances here and now. (We will see later that all the criminal codes and criminal novella that were created in the era of socialism, declared the inadequacy and future termination of the death penalty, but never seem to abolish it in the current situation.) The death penalty was not an absolute punishment, it could be reduced to ten years to fifteen years of imprisonment if the imposition of the punishment would have been too strict considering the purpose of the punishment[2] and the aggravating and mitigating circumstances.[3] Article 52 went even further; accordingly "in cases where the present law allows unlimited reduction of the sentence, regardless of the general punishment set out in the law, imprisonment and financial penalty could be imposed; in such cases, imprisonment and financial penalty of the lowest degree…could be applied." The General Part of the Criminal Code also recognized the limitation of the punishable offences as a ground for exemption from punishment: in accordance with Article 25(a), the limitation period was fifteen years in this case. Finally, one of the most important warranty provisions of Act no. 2 of 1950 was that in the case of a person who has reached the age of eighteen, but has not yet turned twenty, for a crime otherwise punishable by death, only life imprisonment could be imposed; the validity of this provision was strongly undermined by the fact that a separate law could provide differently (Article 53).

This latter regulation was clarified and supplemented by Law-Decree no. 39 of 1950 on the entry into force of the General Part of the Criminal Code, which established the longest duration of juvenile imprisonment (detention in accordance with the Law-Decree) as fifteeen years, and also set out that in the case of a juvenile (a person who has not reached the age of eighteen) neither the death penalty, nor life imprisonment can be imposed. (The same Law-Decree regulated the limitation of the enforceability of different penalties, including the death penalty: the latter occurred twenty years later based on Article (1)a). Finally, regarding the method of execution, Article 27 set out that the death penalty should be executed in a closed space, with a rope and if this was not possible, it should be executed by a firing squad. (Four years later Law-Decree no. 17 of 1954 Article 30 regulating the entry in force and execution of Law no. 5 of 1954 on the modification of the Code of Criminal Procedure provided literally the same.) The above rules for juveniles were practically repeated by Law-Decree no. 34 of 1951[4] by defining the concept of juvenile on the one hand,[5] and on the other, that, in accordance with the General Part of the Criminal Code, it did not impose detention but imprisonment and also by allowing (similarly to the General Part of the Criminal Code) a separate law to provide differently than these rules.

After the Hungarian revolution[6] of 1956 against the Soviets, that is, in 1956[7] and the following years, extraordinary jurisdiction gained again an important role partly due to the accelerated procedure, partly to summary jurisdiction, and partly to the re-established people's tribunals (panels of people's tribunal). The accelerated procedure (although it did not yet include this name) was introduced by Law-Decree no. 22 of 1956 published and entered into force on November 12, 1956. This law-decree has only stated that in the case of certain offences[8] "the prosecution may bring the offender in front of the court without an indictment, if the person as caught, or the necessary evidence can be immediately presented to the court" (Article 1 para. [1]),[9] however, this was soon replaced and, thus, overruled, by the more detailed Law-Decree no. 4 of 1957 on the regulation of accelerated criminal procedure,[10] which, in addition to the applicability of the death penalty, had a retroactive effect as well (Article 8 para. [1]). In the case of the crimes set out in the Law-Decree an accelerated procedure could take place if the defendant was in pre-trial detention, the necessary evidences are available, and the prosecutor initiated it. These acts included the offences set out in Law-Decree no. 22 of 1956; as well as the crimes committed with the unauthorized possession or unlawful use of firearms and explosive substances; the intentional disruption of public, transport, military, and other plants of similar importance, incitement of call for such acts, if these were aimed at a massive work stoppage or threatened with great danger otherwise; crimes committed by deliberately endangering transport; the organization and alliance against the people's republic of the people's democratic state order; rebellion; and disloyalty. The regulation of the accelerated procedure itself and its conduct was essentially the same as those set out in Law-Decree no. 22 of 1956.

In order to carry out the procedure, a panel had to be set up at county (capital) courts, the Supreme Court, and military courts, which, in case that one of the above crimes was proven, had to impose the death penalty.[11] The president of the panels in the first instance was a professional judge (assigned by the president of the county/capital or military court) and its two members were people's (at the military court, military) assessors (assigned by the Presidential Council of the Hungarian People's Republic). The president of the panel of the Supreme Court and one of its members were professional judges (assigned by the president of the Supreme Court), while three of its members were people's assessors (assigned by the Presidential Council of the Hungarian People's Republic, as well). Making an appeal was allowed (it was judged by the panel of the Supreme Court), however, the standard deadlines were not valid either in the first instance, or in the appeal procedure (the procedure had to be finalized in the shortest time possible; in practice this meant a few weeks at most). The first imposition of the death sentence within accelerated procedure in the first degree was on February 12, 1957 and on March 19 in the second degree. Law-Decree no. 4 of 1957 on the regulation of the accelerated criminal procedure was abolished on July 3, 1957 by Law-Decree no. 34 of 1957 Article 38 para. (2).

The martial law was published shortly after Law-Decree no. 22 of 1956, on December 11, 1956 by Law-Decree no. 28 of 1956 (Law-Decree's Article 1 indicated the time of the entry into force with an unusual preciseness: December 11, 1956, 6 pm) and on its basis, four days later, in Miskolc, the first death sentence was imposed and executed. The legislation was born in the spirit of resisting the revolution (the "counterrevolution" in official terms) and it set out summary procedures for the crimes of murder, intentional killing, arson, robbery, looting, the intentional vandalizing of plants of public interest and plants serving the basic necessities of the public, for all the attempts to commit such crimes, and the unauthorized possession of firearms, ammunition, explosives or explosive substances (as well as for alliances for committing all these crimes and organizing them).[12] This crime was otherwise committed by the person—thus also subjected to martial law—who knew that another person was possessing such devices and failed to report it to the authorities as soon as possible. Interestingly, most of the statutory procedures following 1956 were carried out in relation to this latter crime, although the death penalty, due to the attenuating provisions, was not imposed in the majority of the cases for this crime. Based on the Law-Decree, the process itself was carried out by military courts as summary courts, however, the Presidential Council of the Hungarian People's Republic could assign other courts with the right of carrying out similar procedures.

The Law-Decree on summary jurisdiction authorized the government both for the publication of the martial law (the right to order the sentence [as well as to terminate it] continued to belong to the Presidential Council of the Hungarian People's Republic] and defining the detailed rules on it; the government fulfilled these tasks by Government Decree no. 6 of 1956 (December 11). This formally overruled Government Decree no. 8020 of 1939 that had been regulating summary procedure, in reality, however, it only introduced a few substantive modifications compared to that. One of these was that the composition of the summary court was changed; the former council of five professional judges was replaced by a council of three members: a professional judge as president and two people's assessors as members. In addition, the rejection of the petition for mercy resulting in the immediate (within two hours) execution of the sentence, could only be pronounced unanimously, so if at least one of the judges supported the petition for mercy, it had to be presented through the Minister of Justice to the Presidential Council of the Hungarian People's Republic. Finally, summary jurisdiction was terminated by Law-Decree no. 62 of 1957 on November 3, 1957; up until this date, in the statuary procedures, a total number of seventy death sentences were imposed.

Finally, the third type of special jurisdiction after the revolution ("counterrevolution") was (in addition to accelerated and summary jurisdiction) the re-established people's jurisdiction. This form of sentence was reintroduced by Law-Decree no. 34 of 1957 on the regulations of councils of people's tribunals and the court organization, as well as on certain issues of criminal procedure; however, in opposition to Government Decree no. 81 of 1945, it did not set up for this purpose an individual juridical organization, but it consigned the duties related to people's jurisdiction to the panels operating within ordinary courts.[13] In the county (capital) courts, the council of the people's tribunal consisted of one professional judge as head of council and two lay people's judges, while in the Supreme Court, in addition to the professional head of council there were four people's judges. People's judges were elected by the Presidential Council of the Hungarian People's Republic for an undetermined period, were Hungarian citizens who had reached the age of thirty and had no criminal record; their right and obligation in jurisdiction were similar to those of the presiding judge of the council. "People's jurisdiction" was introduced in military criminal procedure as well; in this case, the panels formed at military courts and the military college of the Supreme Court were the ones to proceed, and, in addition to the military judge, instead of the lay people's judges, military assessors elected by the Presidential Council of the Hungarian People's Republic (who, similarly, were not trained in law), were the members.[14] The procedure at the councils of county people's tribunals, as well as the councils of the people's tribunal of the Supreme Court was carried out by the rules of the accelerated procedure, regarding the same crimes for which, in accordance with Law-Decree no. 4 of 1957, accelerated procedure could be applied.[15]

The executors of the factual situations set out in the Law-Decree of people's tribunals, based on the main rule of the councils of people's tribunals, had to apply the death sentence, however, there was a possibility to impose instead life imprisonment or imprisonment between five to fifteen years as an act of fairness. The Law-Decree had a retroactive effect (Article 36), but this did include the applicability of the death penalty (this rule was also the same as those set out in Law-Decree no. 4 of 1957 on the regulation of accelerated criminal procedure). The procedure was usually carried out by the county councils of the people's tribunal, but the panel of the people's tribunal of the Supreme Court already acted in the first instance if the president of the Supreme Court brought the case to its jurisdiction, or even when the general prosecutor pressed charges there. Decree no. 5 of 1957 of the Minister of Justice (June 29) on the execution of Law-Decree of the People's Tribunal (which entered into force on July 3, together with the Law-Decree) assigned the right of people's jurisdiction to six courts (with a determined area of competence): the capital court, the court of Pest county and the county courts of Miskolc, Szeged, Pécs, and Győr counties. A condition typical for the "justice system" of that period was that in the case of appeal, there was no aggravating prohibition, as during the appeal the first instance sentence presented to the Supreme Court could be modified in the favor of the convict even if only the convict made an appeal (but not the prosecutor). During the procedures of the people's tribunals, three defendants ended up in the situation where only the defense counsel made an appeal against a decision that did not include the death penalty, however, the Supreme Court modified the sentence in the first instance to the detriment of the convict and imposed the death penalty in the second instance. Furthermore, the president of the Supreme Court could place under the jurisdiction of the people's council of the Supreme Court any case sentenced in the first instance (even by the ordinary courts) if the general prosecutor presented the case to him. The council that imposed the final sentence (similarly to the previous rules of special courts) could have decided itself regarding the recommendation on mercy. However, if it did not recommend the convict for mercy, the sentence was not to be executed immediately (though measures on the subsequent execution of the death penalty had to be taken), furthermore, the simple majority vote of the members of the council was enough to recommend a case for mercy. Compared to the rules of previous decades, which provided for unanimity, this certainly meant a step forward, however, it can be considered a step back compared to the rule set out in Government Decree no. 6 of 1956 (December 11) Article 13 para. (1) on the establishment of the detailed rules on summary jurisdiction, which required the *rejection* of the recommendation for mercy as the condition of unanimity.

The part on the councils of people's tribunals of the Decree was overruled on April 16, 1961 by Law-Decree no. 7 of 1961, but the age of retaliation mainly ended in the Fall of 1958. This did not imply that the councils of people's tribunals would not further treat criminal cases of a "counterrevolutionary" nature, or that they would not impose death sentences or that executions would not take place. For instance, the trial of the famous Blaski case began on October 28, 1958 and the sentence in the first instance was delivered on November 21, 1958. The one in the second instance on March 19, 1959 wasknown as the case in which Péter Mansfeld was sentenced to life imprisonment in the first instance, but in the second instance (waiting for him to reach the age of adulthood), he was sentenced to death, and executed on March 21, 1959.[16,17] Up until that day (October 8, 1958, precisely), the "civil" councils of people's tribunals imposed ninety-three final death sentences,[18] eighty-one of which were actually executed, while the military councils imposed sixty-three of these (sixty-two of the death sentences were executed). The most famous such death sentences were imposed on June 15, 1958 in the case of Imre Nagy, in which, in addition to the former Prime Minister of the revolution, Pál Maléter and Miklós Gimes were also sentenced to death and executed the next day, on June 16. (József Szilágyi's case, due to his hunger strike, was treated by the council of people's tribunal led by Vida Ferenc at the Supreme Court, separately from the case of Imre Nagy and others. The people' tribunal sentenced him to death in the first instance on April 22, 1958; he was executed on April 24. Besides this, Géza Losonczy died under unclear conditions during his pre-trial detention.) If we add these numbers to those sentenced to death by summary courts (only considering those sentenced to death for counterrevolutionary crimes, in this case), we can see that up until this date, precisely 206 death sentences were imposed in such cases, and 169 of the convicts were executed. In addition, during this period (between November 11, 1956 and October 7, 1958) thirty people were sentenced to death for public crimes (twenty of them were sentenced by summary courts, one by a military court, and nine by ordinary courts), and all of them were executed; thus, out of the 236 people on whom the death penalty was finally imposed, 199 convicts were actually executed with the death sentence.[19] The last execution for a case related to 1956 took place on July 15, 1961; this definitively ended the age of terror. In the period between November 4, 1956 and December 31, 1962, 341 people were executed, and 229[20] of them for an offence related to the revolution. (The majority of them, 117 persons, were sentenced to death for acts related to participating in armed struggle.) The total number of those prosecuted because of the revolution was 26,621, and the majority of them were sentenced to a short imprisonment (of a few years).[21]

Notes

1. Preamble Part II/Detailed Preamble/"Regarding Article 31".
2. "The penalty was applied to protect the working people, to discipline and educate the offender and generally to keep the members of the society from crime." (Article 50 para. [1])
3. Article 51 paras. (1) and (2) (a).
4. The complete title of the Law-Decree: Law-Decree no. 34 of 1951 on regulations of criminal law and criminal procedure applicable to juveniles.
5. "Within the application of criminal law, a juvenile is the person who, at the time of the crime, has reached the age of twelve, but has not yet reached the age of eighteen." (Article 1)
6. For the course of the revolution (and, within it, partly for the retribution on revolutioners after crushing it), see: János M. Rainer M: *Az 1956-os magyar forradalom* (The Hungarian Revolution of 1956). Osiris, Budapest, 2016.

7. For the practical aspects of retaliaton against revolutioners of the Hungarian Revolution of 1956, see in detail, e.g.: Tibor Zinner: *A kádári megtorlás rendszere* (System of the retaliation during Kádár}. Hamvas Intézet, Budapest, 2001; Gábor Jobbágyi: *Az 1956 utáni megtorlási eljárások* (Retaliatory procedures after 1956). Jogtudományi Közlöny, 1998/12., pp. 472–480.
8. Murder, intentional killing, arson, robbery, looting (burglary), any crime committed with the use of illegal firearms, as well as all the attempts to commit such crimes.
9. Furthermore: "… the court does assign a day for the hearing of the case and does not issue subpoenas. The prosecution presents the accusation at the hearing. The prosecutor selects witnesses and experts and presents other evidences to the court." [Article 1 para. (2)]
10. Published and entered into force on January 15, 1957.
11. An exception to this was the previously mentioned case when the panel proceeded in the cases of the offences committed before the entry in force of the Law-Decree (January 15, 1957).
12. Two days later (on December 13), Law-Decree no. 32 of 1956 supplemented the discussed legislation by the fact that "if the summary court found the defendant guilty in one of the crimes under summary procedure, the court will impose death penalty" (Law-Decree no. 32 of 1956 Article 1 and Law-Decree no. 28 of 1956 Article 3 para. [3]).
13. For the organizational aspects of the criminal adjudication against revolutioners, see: Zsuzsanna Mikó: A forradalom utáni megtorlás bírósági és ügyészségi szervezete. 1956–1961 (The organization of the judiciary and the public prosecution during the retaliation after the revolution. 1956–1961). *Történelmi Szemle* 2006/1–2., pp. 121–169; Zsuzsanna Mikó: A Legfőbb Ügyészség az 1956. évi forradalomban (The Prosecutor General's Office in the Revolution of 1956). *Levéltári Közlemények*, 2006/2., pp. 189–222.
14. For data about the operation of military courts, see: György Markó: A katonai bíróságok statáriális ítéletei 1956. December 1957. október között (Martial law decisions of military courts between December 1956 and October 1957). *Restauráció*, 1999, pp. 319–326.
15. In fact, the Law-Decree on the councils of the people's tribunals can be considered the "successor," substitute, and replacement of the Law-Decree on the regulation of accelerated criminal procedure (this can be seen from the fact that the latter one was overruled by Law-Decree no.

34 of 1957). Although Law-Decree no. 34 of 1957 entered into force on June 15, 1957, Chap. 1 (Articles 1–26) on the councils of the people's tribunal was only entered into force on July 3, 1957 by Government Decree no. 41 of 1957 (June 29) Article 1.

16. Cf., e.g.: Csaba Kósa: Thirteen minutes: Tizenhárom perc. Mansfeld Péter élete és mártíromsága (The life and martyrdom of Peter Mansfeld). Jel, Budapest, 2008; Gábor Jobbágyi: (A "pesti srácok" pere. Mansfeld Péter és társai elítéltetése (Criminal procedure of the "Pest guys": The condemnation of Peter Mansfeld and his associates). *Valóság*, 1996/10., pp. 35–55.] The statement that "the age of retaliation *mainly* ended in the fall of 1958" merely means that the age of plentiful death sentences and executions was mainly over for this period and not that it never happened again.
17. For the post-revolutiary criminal adjudication, see e.g.: Frigyes Kahler,: A megtorlás történetéhez—a büntetőjog általános részének alkalmazása 1956 után. I. rész (For the history of retaliation: Application of the General Part of Penal Code after 1956. Part I.). *Magyar Jog*, 1991/10., pp. 581–587; Frigyes Kahler,: A megtorlás történetéhez—a büntetőjog különös részének alkalmazása 1956 után. II–III. rész (For the history of retaliation: Application of the Special Part of Penal Code after 1956. Part II and III.). *Magyar Jog*, 1992/1., pp. 1–5. and 1992/2, pp. 76–79; Frigyes Kahler: Megtorlás a forradalom résztvevői ellen—a jogtörténet tükrében (Retaliation against participants of the revolution—in the light of history of law). *Valóság* 1994/10., pp. 80–89.
18. For the criminal procedure against Imre Nagy and others, see e.g.: Sándor Kopácsi: Az 1956-os forradalom és a Nagy Imre per (The revolution of 1956 and the procedure against Imre Nagy). Magyar Öregdiák Szövetség Bessenyei György Kör, New Brunswick, I. H. Printing Company, 1980.
19. Source of data: Ibolya Horváth, et al. (ed.): Iratok az igazságszolgáltatás történetéhez (Files for the history of jurisdiction). First volume. Közgazdasági és Jogi Könyvkiadó, Budapest, 1992, p. 654.
20. The majority of them, 117 persons were sentenced to death for acts related to participating in armed struggle.
21. Source of data: Tibor Zinner: A kádári megtorlás rendszere (The system of retaliation in the Kádár-era). Hamvas Intézet, Budapest, 2001, pp. 421–423 and 436.

12

Capital Punishment in the 1960s and 1970s

The year of 1961 was not only a turning point in the history of criminal law in Hungary because in that year extraordinary jurisdiction was terminated once and for all, but also because after eighty years (following the Code of Csemegi) the second coherent and comprehensive Criminal Code (Act no. 5 of 1961) of Hungary was created, which now (for the first time in the history of Hungary) regulated the full range of crimes including crimes against the state and military crimes. This comprehensive nature also meant that with the entry into force of the new Criminal Code (with one exception)[1] all those legislations were overruled, which pronounced certain conducts punishable in separate laws and also set out criminal sanctions for any act, while after this, with the exception of the Criminal Code, substantive criminal legislation was never again constituted in Hungary.

The new Criminal Code, due to the circumstances of the period, did "naturally" know the death penalty (Article 35 para. [1]), but never ordered it as a mandatory sanction. For every special case that involved the death penalty for its execution, the alternative punishment was imprisonment from ten up to fifteen years. The Criminal Code argued for the justification for the most severe sanction in a very similar method

Z. J. Toth, *Changing Attitudes Towards the Death Penalty*,
https://doi.org/10.1007/978-3-030-47557-4_12

to that of the General Part of the Criminal Code, namely: "Socialist criminal law, for theoretical reasons in perspective, advocates against the death penalty, however, as long as there is a direct and indirect harmful effect of the capitalist environment, a state building socialism cannot lack the most severe tool of criminal law."[2] The same conclusion is drawn in the preamble when it discusses the purposes of punishment. Based on Article 34 of the Criminal Code "the purpose of the punishment is to apply the penalty set out by law for the crime in order to protect society, to improve the behavior of the offender and to prevent the members of society from committing crimes." The ministerial reasoning explains all these as follows: "If the purpose of punishment is not only retaliation, but also correction, the proposal may only apply exceptionally retaliatory punishment...," however, "among the acts endangering society...there are those the abstract danger of which, makes threatening by death penalty justifiable, considering the significance of the legal interest that needs to be protected. These legal interests are the state (our social, political and economic order), the life, the social property, as well as the discipline and fighting capacity of the armed forces therefore, the proposal recognizes death penalty as a form of punishment, however, when imposing the penalty, when it comes determining the degree of danger of the specific crime to society, it sets out for the judge: 'death penalty...can only be imposed if the purpose of punishment cannot be achieved with another punishment' [Article 64 para. (2)]."

The exceptional nature of capital punishment was, in principle, applicable to several levels as well. For example, the regulation of Article 64 urged the judge to ponder the aggravating and attenuating circumstances. It allowed imposing such a sanction only if it was the exclusive way of fulfilling the purpose of the punishment (general prevention and, thus, the protection of society). Moreover, the exceptional nature of capital punishment revealed itself in the formulation of certain specific partial facts that regulated the death penalty as an alternative punishment without exception (alternatively with imprisonment of ten to fifteen years); in the right to modify the death penalty to imprisonment of up to twenty years, as an act of mercy (Article 36 para. [4]); and in the provision that "the death penalty may only be imposed on a person who had reached the age of twenty when the offense was committed" (Article 36 para. [1]).

Finally, we have to mention in the context of the General Part the limitation of the punishability of the crimes punishable by death, as well as the limitation of the enforceability of the imposed death penalty, both of which periods were provided as twenty years (Article 31[a] and Article 58 para. [1] [a]).

The Special Part of the Criminal Code of 1961 set out the death penalty as an imposable punishment for thirty-one crimes: nine of these were crimes against the state, two crimes against humanity, twelve military crimes and eight common crimes. Accordingly, *crimes against the state* (Criminal Code Chap. 9) should be punished by death if those are considered certain cases of conspiracy; the qualified cases of rebellion; damage resulting serious disadvantages, committed during the war (Article 124 para. [2]); destruction resulting in particularly serious disadvantages, committed by endangering the public during the war (Article 125 para. [2]); assassination; high treason with serious consequences, by making use of state service or official mandate, committed during the war (Article 129 para. [2)]; supporting the enemy; the qualified cases of committing espionage; and all these acts even if they were not committed against the Hungarian People's Republic but another socialist state.[3] Those who committed crimes against humanity (Criminal Code Chap. 10) would also have been sentenced to death if they were guilty of the qualified cases of the offences of genocide or war atrocity, however, no such acts were carried out in Hungary, fortunately, neither under the Criminal Code of 1961, nor the current one.

In a detailed way: the initiators and leaders of a conspiracy could be punished with death if they committed another crime in connection with conspiracy, which was punishable by imprisonment of more than eight years if the conspiracy seriously endangered the state, social, and economic order and if the conspiracy was committed armed or during the war (Article 116 para. [3]). The same sanction could have been applied to the participants or supporters of the conspiracy if the offenders committed another crime in connection with conspiracy, which was punished by law with imprisonment of more than eight years (Article 117 para. [3]), rebellion was punishable by death if it led to the serious disturbance of public order and if it was committed armed or during the war (Article 120 para. [2)]. In accordance with Article 124 para. (1), the delict of damage was committed by someone who, in order to undermine or weaken the state, social, and economic order of the Hungarian People's Republic, with their activity related to their official duties, services, or public services, as well as by the failure to comply with or inadequate performance of their obligations, causes a significant disadvantage. Destruction could be committed by the person who, in order to weaken the state, or the social and economic order of the Hungarian People's Republic, destroys, renders unusable or damages public utility, a facility of production, public transport or communication, public building or edifice, stocks of production or crops, war material or other property with the same importance, commits the crime of damage against the state (Article 125 para. [1]). The death penalty can be imposed for assassination on a person "who kills a member of state body, a person in a leading position at a state body or social organization for their activity carried out in the interest of socialism" (Article 126 para. [1]) and who causes lethal bodily injury to one of such people (Article 126 para. [2)].

High treason is committed by the Hungarian citizen who, in order to violate the independence, territorial integrity, political, economic, defense, or other important interest of the Hungarian People's Republic, interacts, forms an alliance, or cooperates with a foreign government or foreign organization, or their agent (Article 129 para. [1]). As for the crime of supporting the enemy, the person who, during the war, in order to weaken the military force of the Hungarian People's Republic, interacts with or helps the enemy, or causes disadvantage to their own armed force or the ones belonging to their allies, can be punished with imprisonment of ten up to fifteen years or the death penalty (Article 130 [1)]. The delict of espionage punishes those who obtain, collect, or disclose data that can be used to the disadvantage of the Hungarian People's Republic, in order to provide them to a foreign government, foreign organization, or the agent of these (Article 131 para. [2]); the death sentence also can be imposed if the perpetrator committed the crime in relation to state secrets, either regularly, or as the member of a spy organization or during the war (Article 131 para. [3]). As for genocide, according to Article 137 para. (1): "The person who, in order to partially or completely exterminate a national, ethnic, racial or religious group, (a) kill the member of the group, (b) forces the group into living conditions that threaten the group or some it members with destruction, (c) takes measures that aim to prevent births within the group, (d) drags away the children of the group to another group, can be punished by imprisonment of ten to fifteen years, or the death penalty." In the end, the offenders of "war atrocities" were those who, during the war, by violating international legislation, treated inhumanly defenseless civilians, refugees, the wounded, the sick, members of the armed forces who had already laid down their arms, as well as prisoners of war (Article 139 para. [1]). This act was punishable by death if the crime caused death (Article 139 [2]).

The Criminal Code provided the death penalty for twelve types of *military crimes* (as of Criminal Code Chap. 17). Such sanctions could be applied for crimes against the obligations of military service if those persons were considered absconding during the war (Article 312 para. [2] [b]), cases of absconding abroad, and the delict of "abdication from performing military service" (Article 315 para. [1]). Among the factual situations of insubordination, certain cases of mutiny could be punished with capital sanction;[4] the offender of "insubordination to order" who disobeyed the war command out of service commands (Article 317 para. [3]); the offender of "violence against the superior and environment of service" who committed this crime in a war situation and who also carried out intentional killing with this act (Article 318 para. [4]). The death penalty was imposed for two "crimes of service": the (deliberate) violation of the instructions of the guard, if that was committed in battle and it resulted in a specifically great disadvantage (Article 326 para. [3]), as well as the (deliberate) violation of the rules of standby duty, under the same conditions (Article 327 para. [3]). Finally, the "crimes threatening fighting capacity" could have also been punishable by death, in the case of "misconduct on behalf of the commander in battle"; the delict of "abdication from performing battle obligations" (that is the factual situation named "cowardice" at the time); the classified cases[5] of endangering of battle stations; and it could be imposed on the offender of violence against a military attaché who killed the military attaché or their accompanying person (Article 338 para. [2]).

These offenses include the following facts in detail. Absconding, according to the Criminal Code of 1961, is committed by the person who in order to abdicate from performing military service, deliberately leaves or stays away from their station (Article 312 para. [1]). As per Article 313 para. (2), the death penalty could be imposed on the person who deserted abroad, armed, together with another soldier, by making use of their actions of service or during the war. According to Article 315 para. (1), the crime of "abdication from performing military service" is committed by the person who, by mutilating their body or damaging their health, make themselves completely incapable of performing due military service and who, in order to abdicate from performing military service, feigns illness or uses other fraud. As per Article 316 para. (1), mutiny is committed by the person who, together with more soldiers, is involved in an open opposition to the service order of their superior, or against a service order or discipline in general. The offense of "violence against the superior and environment of service" can be carried out by someone who uses violence or threatens of doing so, or shows physical resistance against a superior, guard, or other environment of service (Article 318 para. [1]). The violation of the instruction of the guard is committed by the person who violated the general or extraordinary provisions related to the performing of service during guard service (Article 326 para. [1]). Violation of the rules of standby duty, according to Article 327 para. (1), is carried out by someone who violates the provisions relating to response, police, emergency, courier, or other standby services. As to the "misconduct on behalf of the commander in battle," the criminal conduct is as follows: "The person who, by violating their obligations of a commander, (a) surrenders or lets to be captured the armed force under his command, (b) destroys the battle position, equipment, weapon or other war material delegated to him, or surrenders it to the enemy in a usable state, or (c) does not carry out resistance against the enemy to the extent of his possibilities, can be punished by imprisonment of ten to fifteen years or the death penalty" (Article 331).

According to the crime of "abdication from performing battle obligations," "[t]he person who abdicates from performing battle obligations (a) by the arbitrary abandonment, concealment of or running away from their station, (b) by deliberately causing, pretending the incapacity to participate in battle or by other deceit, (c) by losing, destroying or failing to use their weapon, (d) by the arbitrary surrender to the enemy, or (e) by other serious violation of their service obligations, is punishable by imprisonment of ten to fifteen years or the death penalty." (Article 331) In the end, according to Article 334 para. (1), endangering of a battle station is committed by the person who directly endangers the battle station of the force, by neglecting to provide the necessary weaponry, battle equipment, or other war materials, or to preserve these stocks, while violating service obligations, as well as by "unlawfully destroying, rendering unusable or withholding in other way from their purpose objects of weaponry or other battle equipment, or other important war material."

Lastly, we may divide *common criminal offenses* punishable by death into two groups. One of the groups (the smaller one) includes the offences that are directly or indirectly against human life (or the important personal assets/physical integrity, freedom, etc. of others), while the other group includes the actions that primarily attack and endanger social property as a particular form of property in socialism. The previous category may include, on the one hand, murder, the legal subject of which is directly the human life and the classified cases of which[6] may be punishable by death, on the other hand, the classified cases[7] of prison mutiny,[8] the offender of which attacks directly the social interest related to the order of prison and detention (executing the punishment imposed on criminals), while also endanger indirectly life, freedom, and so on.

The other category only includes actions that violate the existing order or property and the socialist form of collective property. The explanation of this particular protection was formulated in the ministerial reasoning of the Criminal Code: "In the process of building socialism, the assets under social property have a special role. The social property of productive assets ensures production without exploitation, socialist accumulation, expanded reproduction and the production of consumer goods in a quantity that allows for the distribution of consumer goods based on the laws of socialism, and later communism; the social property of consumer goods, beyond the distribution of the goods based on the laws of socialism and communism, allows for the proportionate distribution of national income for the construction of socialism."[9] As a result, the Criminal Code of 1961 did not consider threatening with the death penalty serious, because it classified these acts that damage social property as the most dangerous acts given the nature of protected legal interest, by placing them on the same level, from the aspect of their abstract danger, with the crimes against the state, life, and military crimes, as we have seen. Thus, Article 295 para. (3) of the Criminal Code imposed the death penalty as an alternative sanction (in addition to the "regular" imprisonment of ten to fifteen years) on theft (taking away a foreign property from someone else to unlawfully possess it—Article 291), embezzlement (this can be committed by the person who unlawfully takes away or disposes of as his/her own the property entrusted to him/her—Article 292), fraud (using deceit, deception, or trickery for unlawful financial gain and thereby causing damage—Article 293), and misappropriation (being entrusted with the management of foreign property, causing damage to this property by violating obligations resulted from this assignment—Article 294), damaging social property[10] if the offender committed these act within a criminal organization or as a recidivist, causing particularly great damage. Article 299 para. (4) provided the same sanction for robbery,(that is, unlawfully taking away foreign property by using violence against someone, or threatening the life or physical integrity of someone, or placing someone in an unconscious or defenseless state—Article 299 para. [1]),[11] if it caused a particularly great damage to social property. Finally, under the aforementioned condition, the person committing reckless endangerment[12] was also punishable by death (Article 190 para. [2] [b]). (The crime of reckless endangerment is committed by someone who causes public danger by arson, causing a flood, or by producing the effect of explosive, radiant, or other destructive material or energy, and who obstructs the prevention of such a public danger, or the mitigation of its consequences.—Article 190 para. [1])

The substantive regulations of the Criminal Code of 1961 were supplemented by Law-Decree no. 8 of 1962 on the criminal procedure, which, on the one hand, set out the method of execution, enforcing the existing rule that "the death penalty should be executed in a closed space, with a rope or by a firing squad" (Article 309); on the other hand, it provided the regulations of pardon. Among these latter, as the most important warranty provision, it set out that any death penalty can only be executed after the rejection of the petition for mercy and that the procedure of mercy had to be carried out in all cases (even if the convict did not ask for mercy). With regard to the submission of the petition for mercy and the decree on mercy, the Criminal Code of 1962 did not add a lot to the previous regulation, however, its merit was that, by arranging the chaotic state of the previous years and decades, it cleared and summarized the relevant rules in one singe paragraph. According to this (Article 310), after the final judgment, the president of the judges' council asks the defendant whether he/she wants mercy and requests from the defense counsel to file a petition for mercy on behalf of the defendant (even in spite or regardless of his/her will). After obtaining the opinion of the prosecutor, the court making the final judgment will take a position on whether the convict is recommended for mercy and then the Supreme Court (unless they were the ones to make the final judgment) proceeds similarly after asking for the opinion of the general prosecutor, then sends all these recommendations, petitions, and opinions together with the case files to the Minister of Justice in order to present them to the Presidential Council of the Hungarian People's Republic. The decision on mercy (regardless of the above-mentioned opinions) is made by the Presidential Council of the Hungarian People's Republic itself. If the Presidential Council of the Hungarian People's Republic pardons the person sentenced to death, then, in accordance with Act no. 5 of 1961 Article 36 para. (4), the death penalty is modified to imprisonment of up to twenty years (thus, even of a shorter period); but if it does not pardon the convict, the decision in this regard has to be published by the court in the first instance (even if it did not impose the death penalty), in the presence of the defendant, defense counsel, and prosecutor in the first instance and the sentence will be carried out the next day. Another important element of legal certainty was the rule that a decision rejecting mercy could not be communicated to (and the death penalty could not be executed on) a pregnant woman and a mentally ill person prior to their "recovery" and the death penalty imposed on an absent defendant could only be executed on the basis of a final order concluded during the retrial. (With a slightly different wording, but essentially the same provisions this was repeated a decade later by Act no. 1 of 1973 Article 399 on criminal procedure, therefore, since they are in line with the previous provisions, we do not discuss these regulations of the Code of Criminal Procedure.)

The Criminal Code of 1961 started to become obsolete over the years, so in the early 1970s, a comprehensive reform of the socialist Criminal Code was introduced.[13] From the aspect of our subject, the most important measures of Law-Decree no. 28 of 1971 (hereinafter: the Novel) were that the general conditions for the application of the death penalty were changed, as well as the fact that certain factual situations of the general part ceased to be punishable by death (however, new crimes punishable by death were introduced). In regard of the general provisions, perhaps the most important change was that life imprisonment was included among sanctions and it could have been imposed as an alternative punishment when the law, as the punishment for a certain crime, ordered the death penalty or imprisonment of ten to fifteen years (or twenty years in the case of aggregated or cumulative sentences).[14] The ministerial reasoning explained this by the fact that there was an irrationally wide gap between the longest period of imprisonment (fifteen and twenty years, respectively) and the death penalty,[15] therefore, there was a need for an intermediate sanction, which can be imposed on those who seem to be unfit for reintegrating into society, but for whom the possibility of their improvement is not completely excluded, and which can be used as a deterrence beyond individual prevention in order to achieve the general preventive goal of punishment. According to the ministerial reasoning: "The Criminal Code ignored the punishment of life imprisonment, because it argued that if the protection of society does not require the imposition of the death penalty, the educating purpose of the penalty can still be realized. The achievement of the purpose was only possible by imprisonment for a determined period, based on its considerations. The Plan moves beyond this approach…The possibility of a choice between the death penalty and imprisonment for a determined period…caused difficulties for the court; of course, there are significant reasons for the permanent exclusion of the convict from society, but it can still be assumed that there is hope for improving the sentenced person. In such borderline cases, imposing both the death penalty and imprisonment for a determined time, may be problematic and ultimately it jeopardizes achieving the purpose of punishment. The Criminal Code in force only examined the institution of life imprisonment from the aspect of individual education however, the need for general retention must also be considered, which is clearly in favor of the application of this institution. In order to resolve these contradictions within the system of penalties, the Plan introduced life imprisonment. In cases where, considering the purpose of punishment, the permanent exclusion of the offender from the society seems justified, but the possibility of re-education is not completely excluded, only this penalty provides a satisfactory solution. If the hopes related to re-education are fulfilled, the convict can regain freedom by conditional release therefore, in the cases that do require it, the imprisonment does not last until the end of the convict's life."[16] By introducing life imprisonment, the regulation on mercy was obviously changed as well (Article 36 para. [4] of the Criminal Code); accordingly, from that point on, the death penalty could not only be modified to imprisonment of up to twenty years, but also to life imprisonment (depending on the discretion of the Presidential Council of the Hungarian People's Republic). Finally, tightening the penalties applicable for juveniles can also be seen as a substantial modification. In the case of crimes punishable by the death penalty, for a juvenile who had reached the age of sixteen, but not the age of eighteen, the maximum time of imprisonment became fifteen years compared to the previous ten. In the case of juveniles who had reached the age fourteen, but not the age of sixteen, the maximum imposable imprisonment became ten years compared to the previous five. The rule that (with the exception of soldiers) the death penalty could only be applied to those who had reached the age of twenty at the time of committing the crime, did not change.

Among special factual situations (only regarding the death penalty), there were two significant modifications. The most important of these was the fact that the punishability by death of offences committed against social property was abolished and the social property as a legal interest protected (with some justified exceptions) ceased to exist in general. Thus, Article 295 on theft, embezzlement, fraud, and misappropriation damaging social property was completely annulled by the Novel Decree (and, of course, the threat imposed by the death penalty),[17] while it also abolished the cases of robbery that caused serious damage to social property[18] and reckless endangerment.[19] In the ministerial reasoning, all these were explained as follows: "The Plan, in line with the law in force, sustains the death penalty only for the most serious crimes as an exceptional form of penalty. The socialist development of law is undoubtedly moving towards the narrowing and, ultimately, abolishing the application of the death penalty. The Plan recognizes that this form of penalty is no longer needed for the crimes against property…"[20] "In today's socio-economic conditions…sustaining the death penalty as an exceptional form of punishment is no longer justified among the crimes against property."[21] (The same applies for the ministerial reasoning on reckless endangerment.) A new factual situation punishable by death was introduced in Article 192 of the Code: the "seizure of aircraft."[22] Based on the Novel Decree (and on the Criminal Code after January 1, 1972), this is committed by the person who unlawfully gains or practices control over the aircraft by violence, threat, or placing someone in an unconscious or defenseless state onboard the aircraft" (Article 192 para. [1]). This act was punishable by death if the offender caused the death of others with this act (Article 192 para. [2]). With all these modifications, after the entry into force of the Novel Decree, the number of crimes previously punishable by death, namely thirty-one, was reduced to twenty-six.

Notes

1. The only exception was Act no. 7 of 1945, more precisely, PM Decree no. 81 of 1945 (February 5) signed into law, and some of its provisions on war crimes and crimes against the people remained in force with the comment that the original forced labor for life and life imprisonment, would no longer be applicable (Law-Decree no. 10 of 1962 Article 2 para. [3)].
2. Detailed reasoning for Article 36.
3. Crimes against other socialist state (Article 133 of the Criminal Code).
4. The death penalty could be imposed on the initiator, organizer, and leader of mutiny if the resistance had particularly serious consequences (Article 316 para. [3] [a)]; on the participant of mutiny, who, through his acts committed during the mutiny, caused the death of someone or had other particularly serious consequences (Article 316 para. [3] [b]); on any offender of the mutiny during battle (a simple participant as well), and on the initiator, organizer, and leader of mutiny committed

during the war, who, during the mutiny, committed a violent act against a superior or another person opposing the resisting (Article 316 para. [4]).

5. Accordingly, the death penalty could be imposed on someone who endangered the battle station during war or in a situation of battle if the crime caused particularly great disadvantage on service (Article 334 para. [2]).
6. All classified cases of murder are punishable by death if they were committed with particular cruelty, premeditatedly, endangering the lives of many, for profit, for other vile reasons and aims, against an official person during or because of their official procedure, targeting multiple people, or as recidivist (Article 253 para. [2]).
7. Prison mutiny is committed by the prisoner "who, together with others, participates in an open opposition against the order or discipline of the prison" (Article 186 para. [1]).
8. The death penalty can be imposed, in the first place, on the initiator, organizer, and leader of prison mutiny if the opposition had a particularly serious consequence, on the other hand, on the participator of the prison mutiny, whose action during the mutiny caused the death of another person, or had other particularly serious consequence (Article 186 para. [3]).
9. The foundation of this is provided by the following quote (from the ministerial reasoning as well): "The higher ethical principles in the socialist society, the socialist living conditions require members of society to behave differently than the bourgeois society addresses itself to its members. In the criminal evaluation of certain conducts, these changed higher requirements should be taken into account."
10. According to the provision attached to Chap. 16 of the Criminal Code "the increased criminal law protection for social property includes the assets of the state, the cooperatives, the social organizations and the associations, as well as the foreign properties under their use, treatment or disposition, including the social property of other socialist countries that are on the territory of the Hungarian People's Republic" (Article 311 para. [1]).
11. "The person who unlawfully takes away foreign property by using violence against someone, or threatens the life or physical integrity of someone, or places someone in an unconscious or defenseless state…" (Article 299 para. [1]) "It is considered robbery when the thief caught in act, in

order to keep the property, uses violence, or directly threatens life or physical integrity." (Article para. 299 [2])

12. The crime of reckless endangerment is committed by someone "who causes public danger by arson, causing flood, or by producing the effect of explosive, radiant or other destructive material or energy" and "who obstructs the prevention of such a public danger, or the mitigation of its consequences." (Article 190 para. [1])
13. Cf.: Ferenc Nagy: A magyar büntetőjog általános része (Special part of the Hungarian criminal law). Korona, Budapest, 2001, p. 50.
14. Act no. 5 of 1971 Article 91 para. (2).
15. General reasoning 1 (b).
16. Detailed reasoning for Article 5.
17. More precisely, it aggregated it with Article 296. (Law-Decree no. 28 of 1971 Article 67).
18. Law-Decree no. 28 of 1971 Article 70.
19. Law-Decree no. 28 of 1971 Article 42.
20. Detailed reasoning for Article 42.
21. Detailed reasoning for Article 67.
22. Law-Decree no. 28 of 1971 Article 43.

13

The Act No. IV of 1978 on the Criminal Code of Hungary

In 1978 (as the result of a four-year codification work), instead of piecing out the existing code, an entirely new criminal code (Act no. 4 of 1978) was adopted, which significantly changed the legislation on the death penalty. At its entry into force, it set out the death penalty (as an alternative sanction) to twenty-six crimes (Article 38 para. [1]). Nine of these were crimes against the state, four crimes against humanity, ten military crimes, and three common crimes—as listed in Table 13.1. Despite the fact that a relatively large number of factual situations included the most serious legal consequences, the preamble of the law did not defy the traditions of decades of the socialist criminal law ideology, and the constant dichotomy of Marxist-based criminal science, namely, the permanent difference between the vocal theoretical declarations and real praxis was reflected in Act no. 4 of 1978 as well. (In principle, Marx was opposed to the death penalty, although he acknowledged its practical necessity, especially against the enemies of the proletariat and thus, of "progress"; this approach strongly influenced the whole Soviet-Communist criminal law, including in Hungary.) Although the preamble acknowledged to a certain extent that the complete elimination of criminality is impossible even in socialism, therefore, the goal may (and should) be to reduce it; however,

Z. J. Toth, *Changing Attitudes Towards the Death Penalty*,
https://doi.org/10.1007/978-3-030-47557-4_13

Table 13.1 The comparison of the offences punishable by the death penalty (as well) in Act no. 5 of 1961, Law-Decree no. 28 of 1971 and Act no. 4 of 1978

Act no. 5 of 1961 (original)	Act no. 5 of 1961, from January 1, 1972 (Law-Decree no. 28 of 1971)	Act no. 4 of 1978
Crimes against the state	*Crimes against the state*	*Crimes against the state*
Riot (Article 120[2])	Riot (Article 120[2])	Riot (Article 140[4])
Malicious Mischief (Article 124[2])	Malicious Mischief (Article 124[2])	Malicious Mischief (Article 141[3])
Sabotage (Article 125[2])	Sabotage (Article 125[2])	Sabotage (Article 142[2])
Assault (Article 126[1]–[2])	Assault (Article 126[1]–[2])	Assault (Article 143[2])
High treason (Article 129[2])	High treason (Article 129[2])	High treason (Article 144[2])
Aid and comfort to the enemy (Article 130[1])	Aid and comfort to the enemy (Article 130[1])	Aid and comfort to the enemy (Article 146[1])
Espionage (Article 131[3])	Espionage (Article 131[3])	Espionage (Article 147[2])
Crimes against other socialist states (Article 133)	Crimes against other socialist states (Article 133)	Crimes against other socialist states (Article 151)
Crimes against humanity	*Crimes against humanity*	*Crimes against humanity*
Genocide (Article 137)	Genocide (Article 137)	Genocide (Article 155)
War atrocity (Article 139[2])	War atrocity (Article 139[2])	Violence against the civilian population (Article 158[2])
		Criminal warfare (Article 160)
		Violence against a military attaché (Article 163[2])
Ordinary crimes	*Ordinary crimes*	*Ordinary crimes*
Riot of prisoners (Article 186[3])	Riot of prisoners (Article 186[3])	Terrorist offence (Article 261[2])
Endangerment (Article 190[2])	Unlawful seizure of aircraft (Article 192[2])	Seizure of aircraft (Article 262[2])

(continued)

Table 13.1 (continued)

Act no. 5 of 1961 (original)	Act no. 5 of 1961, from January 1, 1972 (Law-Decree no. 28 of 1971)	Act no. 4 of 1978
Murder (Article 253[2])	Murder (Article 253[2])	Murder (Article 166[2])
Theft (Article 291), embezzlement (Article 292), fraud (Article 293), misappropriation (Article 294) damaging social property (Article 295[3])		
Robbery (Article 299[4])		
Military crimes	*Military crimes*	*Military crimes*
Desertion (Article 312[2])	Desertion (Article 312[2])	Desertion (Article 343[4])
Desertion abroad (Article 313[2])	Desertion abroad (Article 313[2])	Refusal of service (Article 347)
Evasion of military service (Article 315[1])	Evasion of military service (Article 315[1])	Evasion of service (Article 346[1])
Mutiny (Article 316[3]–[4])	Mutiny (Article 316[3]–[4])	Mutiny (Article 352[3])
Disobedience (Article 317[3])	Disobedience (Article 317[3])	Disobedience (Article 354[3])
Violence against a superior or a law enforcement officer (Article 318[4])	Violence against a superior or a law enforcement officer (Article 318[4])	Violence against a superior or a law enforcement officer (Article 355[5])
Violation of the instruction of the guard (Article 326[3])	Violation of the instruction of the guard (Article 326[3])	Breach of discipline in the line of duty (Article 348[3])
Commander's breach of duty in a combat situation (Article 331)	Commander's breach of duty in a combat situation (Article 331)	Commander's breach of duty (Article 364)
Evasion of combat obligation (Article 332)	Evasion of combat obligation (Article 332)	Evasion of combat obligation (Article 356)

(*continued*)

Table 13.1 (continued)

Act no. 5 of 1961 (original)	Act no. 5 of 1961, from January 1, 1972 (Law-Decree no. 28 of 1971)	Act no. 4 of 1978
Compromising combat readiness (Article 334[2])	Compromising combat readiness (Article 334[2])	Compromising combat readiness (Article 363[2])
Violence against a war emissary (Article 338[2])	Violence against a war emissary (Article 338[2])	
Violation of the rules of standby duty (Article 327[3])	Violation of the rules of standby duty (Article 327[3])	

the remarks on sustaining the death penalty suggest that the legislator still could not (or did not want or dare to) get rid of the theorem saying that "in communism, criminality will be removed at some point and thus penalties, including the death penalty will not be needed." This is also reflected in Part 3 of the general reasoning by the explanation that "the socialist development of law is moving towards the gradual overshadowing and ultimately, abolishing of the death penalty, however, the removal of the penalty *is currently not timely*"[1]; moreover, the remark for the detailed reasoning of Article 39 highlights the same issue with a less sharp edge. The latter reads as follows: "Sustaining or abolishing the death penalty is one of the most controversial issues of criminal law…The justification of sustaining it, is primarily based on whether it is unavoidable for individual and general prevention. In the cases of the most serious crimes against life, the state and military crimes, the acts of terrorism that are multiplying on an international level, the protection of society *currently*[2] cannot lack the death penalty." Interestingly, in addition to the theoretical disapproval of the death penalty, in order to justify sustaining this sanction, the preamble of the Criminal Code is willing to contradict itself as Part 3 of the general reasoning describes the results and achievements of the socialist criminal law as follows: "In Hungary, the evolution of criminality has been characterized by decreases and increases in the past one and a half decades, but overall and essentially it has not risen, as opposed to the majority of the developed capitalist countries in which there is a large, even rapid, increase in criminality. It is a positive phenomenon that in Hungary, the vast majority of the crimes committed are of little weight and the dangerous forms such as an organized criminal underworld, drug trafficking, terrorism and kidnapping do not occur essentially." Thus, while terrorist acts and similar crimes are unknown in Hungary, yet, among other things, "terrorist acts multiplying on the international level" are the ones to justify the sustaining of the death penalty, based on the ministerial reasoning.

The ministerial reasoning places a special emphasis on the exceptional nature of the the death penalty, with the same arguments as the preamble of Act no. 5 of 1961. The first and most important of these, based on Article 84, is that "the death penalty may be imposed exceptionally and only if, by considering the particular danger of the crime and offender on the society, and the specifically high degree of guilt, the protection of society can only be ensured through the application of this punishment." (This provision was very similar in content to the regulation set out in Act no. 5 of 1961 Article 64 para. (2), according to which "the death penalty... can only be imposed if the purpose of punishment can not be achieved with another punishment.") An additional argument of the Criminal Code of 1978 to the exceptionality of the capital punishment was the "limited number of crimes punishable by the death penalty"[3]; "that in the Special Part the death penalty is always presented as an alternative punishment, along with the lighter punishment of imprisonment"[4]; that "the death penalty can only be imposed on someone who had reached the age of twenty when he/she committed the crime"[5] (with the exception of soldiers; they could still be sentenced to death, based on Article 126, if they had reached the age of eighteen, provided that the crime seriously offended the military interests); and that there is always the opportunity of exercising mercy, in which case the law does not determine the nature and degree of the punishment that will replace the the death penalty, because "there is no need for the Criminal Code to limit the exercise of the right of pardon."[6] Thus, in exercising its right of pardon, the Presidential Council of the Hungarian People's Republic can impose the lightest punishment of the lowest degree instead of the death penalty. Finally, within the analysis of the general provisions, we must mention the punishability of the crimes punishable by death as well and the limitation of the enforceability of the imposed death penalties, which, based on Act no. 4 of 1978, similarly to the regulation of the Criminal Code of 1961, would occur in twenty years;[7] the only exception being, as a new rule, war crimes and crimes against humanity (as of Chap.11 of the Criminal Code).[8]

When analyzing the special factual situations, we see that there were several changes compared to the Criminal Code of 1961 (namely, its form in force since January 1, 1972).[9] Although both allowed the death penalty for twenty-six crimes, the basic acts and the classified cases were not the same for all crimes. The least of the changes were probably made in the cases of crimes against the state (Criminal Code Chap. 10) as both Criminal Codes imposed the death penalty for the same nine offences, though not necessarily under the same circumstances. Out of these nine crimes, only the delict of supporting the enemy (Article 146)[10] was similar to the previous regulation and in the case of the other crimes, some of the elements of the basic factual situation, or the range of classified cases punishable by death were the ones to be modified. Thus, the mere participant of conspiracy (Article 139) could no longer be punished by death, while the initiator and leader could only be sanctioned with this penalty if the act was committed armed or during the war (Article 139 para. [3]).[11] The organizer and leader of the rebellion (Article 140) could now be sentenced to death only for committing such acts armed or during the war (Article 140 para. [4]), while earlier, the armed and serious disturbance of public order by rebellion could result the same penalty. The classified cases of damage (Article 141) punishable by death did no longer include the causing of a particularly serious damage and only the case of committing it during war was punishable by death (Article 141 para. [3]). The subjects of destruction (Article 142) did no longer include the stocks of crops, thus, its destruction, rendering it unusable or damaging it were not punishable as a crime against the state even with the presence of a motivation against the state (only if these could not be considered "assets of similar importance"); while the method of committing this crime by causing public endangerment was no longer included among the classified cases punishable by death and it could only be sanctioned by death if it caused particularly great damage, or it was committed during war (Article 142 [2]). The concept of assassination (Article 143) has slightly changed compared to the previous one; thereafter, the offender of assassination was someone who, as a member of a representative body, caused grievous bodily injury to a person in a leading position at a state body or social organization for their activity carried out in the interest of socialism (Article 143 para. [1]). The assassinator could have only been sentenced to death if he/she killed the person with the above characteristics for their activities carried out in the interest of socialism (Article 143 para. [2]), thus, causing "only" lethal bodily injury was no longer a reason for imposing the death penalty. The conditions of high treason (Article 144) that could lead to the death penalty basically remained the same as previously (Article 144 para. [2])[12] and only the definition of the method of committing the basic factual situation changed.[13] The classified cases of espionage (Article 147) punishable by death did no longer include regular committing, but those carried out in relation to a state secret, as a member of an spy organization, or during the war remained (Article 147 para. [2]). Finally, Act no. 4 of 1978, as its predecessor, ordered the same penalties for the offences against the state that were committed not to the detriment of Hungary, but other socialist states ("crimes against other socialist states"—Article 151).

The range of crimes against humanity (Criminal Code Chap. 11), as opposed to those against the state, were modified compared to the state of the Criminal Code after 1972; now the death penalty could be imposed for four crimes instead of two. Genocide {Article 155 para. [1]) is the only delict that remained the same as it was previously and continued to be punishable by death. The crime of war atrocity ceased to exist, but, among the acts punishable by death, "violence against the civilian population"[14] (Article 158), previously regulated among military crimes, as well as "criminal warfare" (Article 160) that had not existed before 1978, were included. In accordance with Article 158 para. (1) of the Criminal Code, the former is committed by the person who, on a military or occupied territory, uses violence, inhumane treatment against a civilian or prisoner of war,[15] or abuses their power in a serious way. The action was punishable by death if the offender caused death (Article 158 para. [2]). Article 160 provided on criminal warfare as follows: "The military commander, who, by violating the international legal rules of warfare, (a) carries out a military operation that causes serious damage to the life, health and properties of the civilian population, the cultural assets protected internationally and the facilities of dangerous powers, (b) attacks an unprotected place or demilitarized zone, commits a crime punishable by imprisonment of ten to fifteen years or life imprisonment or the death penalty." Finally, the fourth crime against humanity punishable by death that was previously regulated among military offences (listed as a crime violating international military law) and was punishable by death even then, was "violence against a military attaché" (Article 163), while its factual situation and case remained unchanged. According to Article 163 para. (2), the most serious legal consequence for committing this delict could be imposed on those who murdered the military attaché or their accompanying person (Article 163 para. [2]).

Instead of the former twelve types of military crimes, the Criminal Code of 1978 threatens the perpetrators of ten criminal cases with the most severe legal consequence; the most important modifications compared to the regulations of Act no. 5 of 1961 are described in the following. First, the violence against a military attaché was transferred to crimes against humanity, so it did not cease and also continued to be punishable by death, but no longer as a military crime. Secondly, the delict of absconding abroad was ceased; more precisely, it merged in the factual situation of absconding; thirdly, the crimes of "violation of the instructions of the guard" and of "violation of the rules of standby duty" were abolished; finally, fourthly, the offences of "denial of service" and "misconduct in service" were introduced as new factual situations. The offenders of these two new crimes: the person who refused military service during war (Article 347) could be punished by death and the person who violated "the regulations related to the execution of guard, standby or emergency services" (Article 348 para. [1]) was punishable by this sanction as well, if the above misconduct was committed during war and it resulted in a particularly great disadvantage (Article 348 para. [3]).

Based on the above, a total number of eight military crimes were punishable by death based on both the Criminal code of 1961 and the Criminal Code of 1978. Among these, the crime of absconding (Article 343), as we mentioned, now included the previous delict of "absconding abroad"; after 1978, absconding (which could be committed by the person who, in order to abdicate from performing military service, deliberately leaves or stays away from their station, according to Article 343 para. (1) may have resulted in capital sanction, on the one hand, if the absconding abroad was committed armed, in a group, while serving an important task, by using the service, or by using violence against a person, on the other hand, if the absconding (either domestic or abroad) was carried out during war (Article 343 [4]). The name of the crime of "absconding from performing military service" from the Criminal Code of 1961 was simplified to "absconding from service" (Article 346); the basic factual situation was reformulated. Accordingly, this crime is committed by the person who, in order to abdicate from performing military service, mutilates their body, damages their own health, or presents fraudulent conduct (Article 346 para. [1]). However, this crime did not contain essential modifications compared to the previous one and it continued to be punishable by death only if the act was committed during war (Article 346 para. [1]). The name of "misconduct on behalf of the commander in battle" was also simplified (the new name was "misconduct of the commander"—Article 364), but the crime itself remained the same as previously. Finally, the same can be said about other military offences punishable by death, such as mutiny (Article 352), insubordination to order (Article 354), the crime of "violence against a superior"[16] or the "environment of service" (Article 355), the delict of "abdication from performing battle obligations" (Article 365) and the endangering of battle stations (Article 363).

Finally, several modifications were made to the common criminal offenses punishable by the death penalty. First of all, prison mutiny was excluded from these offences: the new Criminal Code set out the punishment of this crime (now called "mutiny of prisoners," as of Article 246) as imprisonment of five to fifteen years for the most serious cases. Secondly, the terrorist act was regulated as a new factual situation. In accordance with Article 261 para. (1), this was committed by the person who deprives another person from their personal freedom, or acquires significant financial properties, and makes the release of the person, as well as the preservation and return of the properties dependent on the fulfillment of a demand addressed to a state body or social organization. The most severe sanction could be imposed for this crime if the offender caused death or other particularly severe disadvantage with these actions, or if these were committed during wartime (Article 261 [2]). Finally, the death penalty continued to be imposable for the "seizure of aircraft" (Article 262) and murder (Article 166), basically in the cases mentioned before. The legislator of the Criminal Code of 1978 omitted the criterion of "unlawful" from the name of the delict of "unlawful seizure of aircraft" included in Article 192 of the Criminal Code of 1961 by Law-Decree no. 28 of 1971, given that the concept of crime *ab ovo* includes unlawfulness and in its absence, we cannot even talk about crime. The attitude of committing the seizure of an aircraft was defined by the new Criminal Code by different words compared to the previous one: while according to the former, the crime was committed by acquiring and practicing unlawful control of the aircraft, the latter claimed that it was performed by taking possession of the control of the aircraft. In addition, among the classified cases of murder (that may result in the death penalty) those committed as a recidivist were modified to murder by a special recidivist (Article 166 para. [2) h]), where, in accordance with Article 166 para. (5), assassination (Article 143 para. [2]) and voluntary manslaughter (Article 167) were considered similar crimes from the aspect of special recidivism.

The execution of capital punishment applicable in the cases set out by the Criminal Code was regulated by Law-Decree no. 11 of 1979 and Decree no. 8 of 1979 of the Ministry of Justice (June 30) on the Policy of the Enforcement of Criminal Sanctions. The first one provided that "the death penalty, on the day following the rejection of the penalty for mercy, should be executed in a closed space, with a rope or by firearm" (Article 17 para. [1]), however, in practice, the firing squad was never applied, the only method was hanging. Furthermore, it provided who should be present at the execution and also regarding the burying of the body. According to this, in addition to the convict and the executor, the prosecutor (in the first instance), the appointed judge (also from the council of the first instance), the registrar, the doctor, the commanding officer of the prison, and the guards securing the execution must have also been present at the execution, however, the Minister of Justice may have authorized others {for example, the defense counsel and relatives of the convict, or the relatives of the victim of the crime) to be present at the execution as well.[17] The corpse of the executed person had to be buried in a public cemetery by the prison,[18] in a marked grave,[19] just like any other citizen. Decree no. 8 of 1979 of the Ministry of Justice provided details on the method of implementing the death penalty. For example, it provided that after the rejection of the petition for mercy was published, the convicted person had to be placed in a separate room (the so-called "death cell") with increased security, where a close relative (who had to be informed unless the convict did not want to be visited) could visit the sentenced person, and where the convict could write letters or make a written provisional will during the last afternoon and night[20] and, of course, prepare for the execution of the next morning.

In the Hungarian legal system, these (Criminal Code, Law-Decree on the Enforcement of Criminal Sanctions, Decree no. 8 of 1979 of the Ministry of Justice on the Policy of the Enforcement of Criminal Sanctions) were the last norms on the application of the death penalty; thereafter the process of abolition has the main role. Partly, Law-Decree no. 28 of 1971 and Act no. 4 of 1978 could be adapted in the process of abolition as these laws reduced the possibility of imposing the death penalty and, consequently, the extent of the practical application of this sanction. (While in the 1960s, the number of death penalties imposed was 129, out of which seventy-nine were given by civilian courts and fifty by military courts, this number was reduced to forty-seven (thirty-four and thirteen, respectively) in the 1970s, and to thirty-two (twenty-nine and three respectively) in the 1980s. The last execution took place on July 14, 1988 when Ernő Vadász who committed intentional killing, qualified multiple times and was executed by hanging, while the last death sentence, obviously, unexecuted, was imposed in 1989.) However, the abovementioned norms had not yet formulated the need that the death penalty should be, once and for all, in regard of all crimes, completely erased from the Hungarian legal system. Although Tibor Horváth had already prepared an expert opinion for the Criminal Code from 1978, which proposed the full or partial elimination of the most serious legal consequence from criminal sanctions, this remained unnoticed to the extent that during the codification work, it had not even been discussed. The first major step was taken in 1983, when the Criminal Law Committee of the Hungarian Lawyers Association, on December 12, held a debate entitled “The death penalty and its future in Hungarian criminal law,” where, being led by Tibor Horváth, theoretical and (mainly) practical criminal lawyers shared their opinions and views on the above topic.[21] Although the majority of the speeches (especially since the theoretical experts and defense lawyers favoring abolition[22] represented a minority at the conference compared to the prosecutors and judges) continued to support the death penalty; however, from that point on, the idea of abolition was rooted in the Hungarian criminal and general intellectual thinking of the time, which provided a good basis for both criminal lawyers and the wider public opinion to familiarize with and perhaps accept all the reasons that encouraged abolitionists to disapprove of this punishment.

Notes

1. Emphasis added.
2. Emphasis added.
3. Detailed reasoning for Article 39.
4. Ibid.
5. Criminal Code Article 39 para. (1).
6. Detailed reasoning for Article 39.
7. Article 33 para. (1) a) and Article 67 para. (1) a).
8. Article 33 para. (2).
9. In the following, I will compare the current Criminal Code (Act no. 4 of 1978) and the Criminal Code of 1961 based on the version in force at the publishing of the former and version after 1972 of the latter.
10. In the following, the cited paragraphs always mark Act no. 4 of 1978.
11. Thus, it is not applicable if the offender committed another crime in connection with conspiracy, which was punished by law with imprisonment of more than eight years; nor if the conspiracy seriously endangered the state, social, and economic order.
12. The death sentence could be imposed in case of causing serious disadvantage (according to the wording of the Criminal Code of 1961: “if the crime led to serious consequences”); by using state service or official assignment; and if the crime was committed during wartime.

13. While according to Act no. 5 of 1961, high treason could have been realized (in the case of the existence of a motivation against the state) by engaging, forming an alliance or cooperating with foreign governments, foreign organizations or their agents, Act no. 4 of 1978 simplified the method of committing this crime to engaging in a relation with a foreign government or a foreign organization.
14. This is regulated by the Criminal Code of 1961 among the crimes violating international military law, in Article 335.
15. According to the interpretative provision in Article 158 para. (3), "inhumane treatment, in particular, involves the settlement of the civilian population of the occupying power to the occupied territories or the resettlement of the population of the occupied territory, the deprivation of the civilian population and prisoners of war from their right to be judged in a regular and impartial trial," as well as "the unjustified postponement of the repatriation of prisoners of war and civilian people."
16. In Act no. 5 of 1961, the word "and" figured instead of the word "or."
17. Article 17 para. (2).
18. Article 18 paras. (1)–(2).
19. Decree no. 8 of 1979 of the Ministry of Justice (June 30) Article 153 paras. (2)–(3).
20. Article 152 paras. (1)–(3).
21. The full text of the official minutes of the debate is accessible to anyone. See: A halálbüntetés és jövője a magyar bünetőjogban (Death penalty and its future in Hungarian criminal law). (A Magyar Jogász Szövetség Büntetőjogi Bizotságának vitaülése.) In: Jogász Szövetségi Értekezések (Studies of Lawyers' Association), no. 1984/1.
22. Attorneys, in general, are against death penalty due to their procedural status. This is also the case today: out of the thirteen defense counsels of today's famous and acknowledged criminal cases, interviewed by Judit P. Gál in her book, nine are clearly against it, while only four of them support it to a lesser or greater extent. (Cf: Judit P. Gál: *Ördögök ügyvédei* (Devil's Lawyers). Alexandra, Pécs, 2003, pp. 21, 40–41, 64, 84–85, 94–95, 118–119, 135–136, 168, 187, 213, 251–253, 271, and 287–288.)

14

The End Time of the Death Penalty in Hungary: Two Steps of the Abolition in 1989/90

On the question of the existence or non-existence of the death penalty, the turning point came during the regime change. At the beginning of 1989, with the aim of abolishing the death penalty, being led by Tibor Horváth as president, the Anti-Death Penalty League was established, which was joined by hundreds of intellectuals in the coming months. The League wished to introduce the arguments against the most severe sanction to the public opinion and to convince politics to represent the issue of abolition. The former was only partially successful (the majority of people were in favor of the death penalty at the time), while the latter goal was completely unsuccessful. One of the reasons for this was that politicians were engaged in creating and debating the laws that prepared the regime change and created the new socio-economic-political system, and another reason was that the parties and their politicians simply did not dare to make a decision which would have obviously made a huge uproar among people, and thus which would have resulted in a radical decline in the popularity so important to politicians.

This, of course, did not apply to crimes of a political nature; in the unique atmosphere of the change of regime, it was a general demand that nobody should ever use criminal law as an instrument for achieving their

Z. J. Toth, *Changing Attitudes Towards the Death Penalty*,
https://doi.org/10.1007/978-3-030-47557-4_14

subtle political goals. As a result, the Minister of Justice at the time, Kálmán Kulcsár, presented a bill that aimed to abolish the death penalty from the penalties of all crimes committed against the state; this was accepted by the last, but already transitioning socialist Parliament and it was codified as Act no. 16 of 1989. The law itself consisted of only two paragraphs: Article 1 provided that:

> the imposable punishment for the crime of initiating or leading a conspiracy that seriously endangers the state, social or economic order, committed armed or during the war (Article 139 para. (3) fourth phrase of the Criminal Code), the crime of organizing or leading a rebellion committed armed or during the war (Article 140 para. (4) third phrase of the Criminal Code), the crime of damage committed during the war (Article 141 para. (3) of the Criminal Code), the crime of destruction resulting in a particularly serious disadvantage or committed during the war (Article 142 para. (2) of the Criminal Code), the crime of assassination committed by murder (Article 143 para. (2) of the Criminal Code), the crime of high treason with serious consequences, by making use of state service or official mandate, committed during the war (Article 144 para. (2) of the Criminal Code), the crime of supporting the enemy (Article 146 para. (1) of the Criminal Code), and the crime of espionage committed in regard of the state secret or as the member of a spying organization, during the war (Article 147 para. (2) of the Criminal Code), is modified to imprisonment between ten and fifteen years or life imprisonment

while Article 2 provided that "this law enters into force on the day of its publication."[1] Due to this, the punishment by death of political crimes (against the state) was definitively abolished in Hungary.

For the reasons mentioned above, this could not be expected of the Parliament in relation to common crimes (and other, non-political offences), which is why the Anti-Death Penalty League started an independent action. Because the Constitutional Court, previously unknown in the Hungarian legal system, set up by Act no. 32 of 1989 (Act on the Constitutional Court), was given the right to annul the legislation or legal provisions that are contrary to the Constitution through the subsequent abstract norm control, however, in order for the League to succeed in the case of the death penalty, something else was needed, namely the radical transformation of the Constitution (Act no. 20 of 1949), which was achieved by Act no. 31 of 1989. On the one hand, because Article 34 introduced the right to life and human dignity[2] in the text of the Constitution (precisely, in Article 54), on the other hand, Article 2 of the law incorporated in Article 8 para. (4) of the Constitution the provision which prohibits, inter alia, that the right to life and human dignity can be limited in any way.[3]

Accordingly, these fundamental rights were not allowed to be limited or suspended in a state of emergency,or situation of risk, however, the final text of Article 8 para. (4) was not determined by Act no. 31 of 1989, but Act no. 40 of 1990 Article 3 para. (2). Accordingly, the text in force since June 25, 1990 is as follows: "Exercising the fundamental rights in a state of emergency, emergency or situation of risk—except for the fundamental rights set out in Article 54–56, Article 57 paras. (2)–(4), Article 60, Article 66–69 and Article 70/E—can be suspended or limited." Act no. 15 of 1990 Article 3 para. (1) (also, with effect from June 25) modified Article 8 para. (2) of the Constitution as well (which will also be important in relation to the Decree of the Constitutional Court on the abolition of the death penalty), the effective text of which reads as follows: "In the Republic of Hungary the rules of fundamental rights and obligations are set out by the law, but the essential content of fundamental rights may not be limited." (Article 8 para. [3] was annulled by Article 51 para. [1] of this law.)

As a result, the legal conditions were ready for the Constitutional Court to determine the unconstitutionality of capital punishment. The petition in this regard was submitted by Tibor Horváth in the name of the Anti-Death Penalty League, in January 1990. The petition itself was not even one full page. The text of the statement signed on January 17, 1990, by Tibor Horváth as president of the Anti-Death Penalty League, was the following:

> Honourable Constitutional Court, In the name of the Anti-Death Penalty League, I make a constitutional complaint against the criminal law imposing the death penalty and I ask for the subsequent declaration of the unconstitutionality of these laws. Article 54 para. (1) of the Constitution amended by Act no. 31 of 1989 provides that 'In the Hungarian Republic,

> every person has the inherent right to life and human dignity'...and that 'No one can be subjected to torture, cruel, inhuman and humiliating treatment or punishment...'[4] The League considers that the provisions on the death penalty of the criminal legislations in effect do not comply with the above quoted provisions of the Constitution as they violate human rights. The death penalty as the remainder of the principle of jus talionis cannot be justified ethically, is incompatible with human right, irredeemable and irreversible, it is an unsuitable and impractical means of punishment for preventing serious crimes or deterring others from committing crimes punishable by death. Instead of the death penalty, the protection of the society can be adequately served by imposing life imprisonment or imprisonment for a determined long period—twenty or twenty-five years—for any crime committed. The detailed reasoning of the position of the League can be found in the attached expertise.

However, the study attached to it, which presented the history of abolition, and described the legal, moral, and practical arguments against the death penalty, was approximately seventy pages long. In order to determine the validity of the petition, the Constitutional Court requested three experts and asked for the opinions of the president of the Constitutional Court, the general prosecutor, and Minister of Justice.

One of the three experts, József Földvári, professor of criminal law at the Janus Pannonius University (today: University of Pécs), did not take a position on the issue of the death penalty regarding its constitutionality or unconstitutionality, but he only approached the problem from a criminal law aspect. He explained that although the death penalty is not acceptable either from the aspect of individual prevention (since an individual can be prevented from committing new crimes by imposing other, lighter punishments, such as life imprisonment as well), or from the aspect of general prevention (the impact of a punishment on others cannot be measured), the continuation of this form of punishment must be considered by the legislator. Therefore, its recognition or continuation is not a matter of a legal, but of a moral-political decision.

Criminologist and criminal statistician László Korinek analyzed the deterrent-preventive effect of the death penalty, in relation to which he pointed out the starting point of his expertise: that there is not a period long enough through which all the relevant data (except for the existence of the death penalty) would remain unchanged. The abolition of the death penalty typically implies other social transformations, regarding which it cannot be safely decided whether the potential reduction or increase of criminality was caused by the abolition or restitution of the death penalty, or the political and economic change that has also led to this decision; "thus ... in the debate surrounding the death penalty, statistics cannot provide absolute conclusive evidence."[5] Nevertheless, "it is highly probable ... that the growth or decline of homicidal crimes in a certain state is more likely the result of stable socio-cultural effects such as education and urbanization rather than whether the given legal system recognizes or rejects the death penalty. Which in turn also implies that the growth or decline of the crimes around the abolition of the death penalty may only coincide with this legislative act."[6] After this, László Korinek examined the different types of criminals (acting against life) and notes that the death penalty only has a deterrent effect on a small group of murderers (and only some of them), who cold-bloodily considered the consequences of their acts; the behavior of other types of criminals is not affected by this sanction (and of course, other punishments). Finally, he concluded that "after the abolition of the death penalty... there has not been an avalanche-like increase in criminality, because the existence of absence of the death penalty does not affect the totality of crimes, but the attitude towards crime among the population (fear and revenge)";[7] thus, according to Korinek, the death penalty does not have a preventive-deterrent function, but only one that comforts society and satisfies people's sense of justice.

Finally, András Sajó expressed his opinion as being opposed to the death penalty from every aspect. He argued firstly that it is arbitrary, because "similar crimes in the same country and in the same period may be subject to different judgments."[8] Secondly, imposing a death penalty depends on the decision of the prosecutor. The body or person evaluating the petition for mercy also makes a decision based on their own considerations. The "exceptional" phrase of the Criminal Code is objectively uninterpretable and the other conditions of application (the outstanding danger to society of the offender and the crime, the particularly high degree of guilt) are also indefinite and irrelevant. Moreover, when imposing the sentence, it is never possibly to state with 100 percent certainty that the protection of society can only be ensured through the death penalty. In addition, "in the case of the death penalty, the legal system institutionalizes the irredeemable judicial error, which, as a mistake, is undoubtedly arbitrary in its content."[9] This sanction may be used for political reasons, too, to eliminate opponents by keeping up the appearance of legality. The hanging used in Hungary is cruel and waiting for the execution also means suffering for the relatives of the convict.

In the second place, Sajó considered this punishment unconstitutional because its application violates human dignity since, during execution, the person is treated as a mere object. He explains that "dignity is not the inherent right of a person, but an endowment that cannot be eliminated"[10] and exactly because of that, the person cannot be deprived of it (the death penalty, among other things, is unconstitutional because it terminates the objective condition of the development and expression of human dignity). Finally, in the third place, the death penalty is opposed to the purpose of punishment of the rule of law and the purpose of punishment to the requirements of the rule of law, which set out that the purposes of punishment should be carried out with the least possible impairment (and there are lighter sanctions than the death penalty that have the same effect) and, in accordance, the punishment will not be considered constitutional due to its "practical necessity."[11] According to Sajó, the constitution does not authorize the legislator to introduce the death penalty into the law. As a democratic constitution of the rule of law, it cannot do so. The adopted system of penalties must define the minimum sanction required to ensure the right and obligations from the Constitution, which is then determined by the court in accordance with the proportionality principle during the imposition of penalties. Sajó sums up the reasons that make the death penalty unconstitutional: "The death penalty is unconstitutional, as it is inevitably arbitrary in its imposition in the absence of a legal definition, but in addition, by the very nature of the sentencing procedure and due to its execution, it is a cruel punishment; since it is incompatible with human dignity and the inalienable nature of human dignity, it contradicts the idea of rule of law set out in the Constitution, and extends the power to punish of the state beyond inevitable necessity, without explicit constitutional mandate."[12]

The expert opinions were completed by February 1990, and the Minister of Justice sent a written statement to the Constitutional Court in March. Herein, he stated that he considered that the death penalty was unconstitutional since it was anti-humane, morally unjustifiable, and did not serve the purpose of punishment or did not serve to a greater extent than other penalties. The Constitutional Court set the date of the trial on the issue of the death penalty on October 16, 1990. (At that time) this was a public hearing where those interested could be present and even Tibor Horváth could have spoken as an applicant. (Later, the rules of procedure of the Constitutional Court prohibited this and from that time on the constitutional judges decide only on the basis of written documents.) At this plenary meeting, the previously mentioned expert opinions were presented and the representative of the Minister of Justice (at that time István Balsai) spoke, as well as President of the Supreme Court Pál Solt and chief public prosecutor Kálmán Györgyi. Solt considered that the death penalty in general and in the present historical situation in Hungary was unjustifiable and thus unconstitutional in both legal and moral terms. Györgyi, on the one hand, stated that he was personally a supporter of abolition and, on the other hand, also drew attention to the fact that, contrary to the request of the petition, Article 54 para. (1) alone does not allow to pronounce the unconstitutionality of the death penalty, because it does not exclude the possibility of non-arbitrary taking of life, but for this purpose (to determine unconstitutionality), this must be interpreted in relation to Article 8 para. (2), because this is only way to exclude that the term "arbitrary" mentioned in Article 54 para. (1) does not imply the permissibility of the death penalty.

Subsequently, members of the Constitutional Court had one week to make their decision, to justify it, and to write their parallel or separate opinions. The life-altering decision was made on October 24, 1990, when the Constitutional Court decided in an 8:1 ratio that the death penalty is unconstitutional. The Decision entered into force on its day of publication in the *Hungarian Official Gazette*, on October 31 (Decision no. 23 of 1990 of the Constitutional Court [October 31]) and as from this date, all legislation that previously set out the conditions of the application of the death penalty were overruled. Thus, the Constitutional Court declared unconstitutional and annulled as from the date of publishing (October 31) the provisions of the Criminal Code and other statutes regarding capital punishment.[13]

The preamble of the decision of the Constitutional Court provided that:

> in Hungary, the right to life and to human dignity … is the inherent, inviolable and inalienable right of every person. The primary obligation of the Hungarian state is to respect and protect the right to life and human dignity. … According to the effective provisions of Article 8 para. (2) of the Constitution 'in the Republic of Hungary the rules of fundamental rights and obligations are set out by the law, but the essential content of fundamental rights may not be limited.' The Constitutional Court considered that the provisions of the Criminal Code on the death penalty and relevant legislation contradict the restriction of the essential content of right to life and human dignity. The provisions on the deprivation of life and human dignity by the death penalty do not only limit the essential content of the fundamental right to life and human dignity, but also allow the complete and irrevocable termination of life and human dignity, as well as of the right ensuring these therefore, it stated their unconstitutionality and annulled them.

Thereby, the possibility of executing anyone in Hungary in an official procedure, within a state-controlled framework legitimated by the state, was definitively ceased. And although isolated attempts have been made to restore the death penalty through a referendum[14] and there still are disputes over its adequacy or inadequacy, necessity or redundancy, expediency or impracticability, in the political context it seems that in 1990, the epoch of the death penalty in Hungary, after a whole millennium, ended for good and all.

Notes

1. The date of publication and entry in force of Act no. 16 of 1989 on the modification of Act no. 4 of 1978 on the Criminal Code was June 15, 1989.

2. "In the Hungarian Republic, every person has the inherent right to life and human dignity, which cannot be arbitrary deprived." (Constitution Article 54 para. [1])
3. Accordingly, these fundamental rights were not allowed to be limited or suspended in a state of emergency, emergency or situation of risk either, however, the final text of Article 8 para. (4) was not determined by Act no. 31 of 1989, but Act no. 40 of 1990 Article 3 para. (2). Accordingly, the text in force since June 25, 1990 is as follows: "Exercising the fundamental rights in a state of emergency, emergency or situation of risk—except for the fundamental rights set out in Articles 54–56, Article 57 paras. (2)–(4), Article 60, Articles 66–69 and Article 70/E—can be suspended or limited." Act no. 15 of 1990 Article 3 para. (1) (also with effect from June 25) modified Article 8 para. (2) of the Constitution as well (which will also be important in relation to the Decree of the Constitutional Court on the abolition of death penalty), the effective text of which reads as follows: "In the Republic of Hungary the rules of fundamental rights and obligations are set out by the law, but the essential content of fundamental rights may not be limited." (Article 8 para. [3] was annulled by Article 51 para. [1] of this law.)
4. This latter one, in fact, was actually provided by Article 54 para. (2). (*Note from the author.*)
5. In: Tibor Horváth (ed.): *A halálbüntetés megszüntetése Magyarországon.* (The abolition of capital punishment in Hungary). Halálbüntetést Ellenzők Ligája (Anti-Death Penalty Leage), Miskolc, 1991, p. 77.
6. Ibid.,p. 84.
7. Ibid.,p. 89.
8. Ibid.,p. 91.
9. Ibid.,p. 92.
10. Ibid.,p. 95.
11. Ibid.,p. 98.
12. Ibid.,p. 96.
13. Accordingly, the Constitutional Court annulled Act no. 4 of 1978 of the Criminal Code Article 38 para. (1), Articles 39 and 84; Act no. 1 of 1973 of the Code of Criminal Procedure Article 399; Law-Decree no. 11 of 1979 (Law-Decree on the Enforcement of Criminal Sanctions) Articles 17 and 18; Decree no. 8 of 1979 of the Ministry of Justice (June 30) Articles 151, 152 and 153). Furthermore, it abolished the provisions set out in Article 155 para. (1), Article 158 para. (2), Article 160, Article

163, Article 166 para. (2), Article 261 para. (2), Article 262 para. (2), Article 343 para. (4), Article 346 para. (1), Article 347, Article 348 para. (3), Article 352 paras. (3) and (4), Article 354 para. (3), Article 35 para 5(5), Article 363 para. (2), Articles 364 and 365 of the Criminal Code, which, in defining the penalties imposable, indicated the sanction of the "death penalty""as applicable criminal sanction.

14. See in detail in the following chapter.

Part III

The Politicization of Capital Punishment in Hungary: Renewed Controversy

In 1990, the death penalty was abolished without the intention of political parties and without the understanding of the people of Hungary. Since capital punishment was abolished by the decision of the newly established Constitutional Court of Hungary, a body without any traditions in the Hungarian public law, and not by an act of the National Assembly elected by the people and possessing democratic legitimacy, the majority of Hungarians did not embrace that decision and even the politicians did not stand by it. Directly after the abolition of the death penalty, three out of four Hungarians opposed the decision of the Constitutional Court of Hungary, and surveys carried out during the decades since then also found the society being pro-death penalty (even if the support thereof steadily decreases). The politicians tried to take advantage of all this and occasionally, mainly after brutal murders that shocked society, they raised the issue of whether the reintroduction of the death penalty or a debate thereon was necessary. Apart from a few exceptions, the reintroduction of the death penalty has been required by far-right parties and politicians; but the recent change of the last decade is that the centre-right parties governing with two-thirds majority from 2010 i.e., Fidesz and KDNP, have also taken up the issue of the death penalty—even in cases of engaging in confrontation with the bodies of the European Union or the Council of Europe.

15

Public Opinion in Hungary in the Light of the Current Legal Situation and the Facts about Trends in Murder Rates

In Hungary, the idea of the abolition of capital punishment emerged in the 1980s, when a debate regarding the adequateness of the death penalty commenced. Eventually, the abolition of capital punishment, as mentioned in the previous chapter, took place in 1990, right after the end of the political transformation, that is, the transition from a state of socialism to democracy. This abolition was performed in a special and unique way; for the first time in legal history it was implemented not by an act or through the text of the state's constitution, but following a decision by the Constitutional Court declaring this legal institution to be contrary to the regulations of the Constitution. Later, however, some states followed this example, namely, in the Republic of South Africa,[1] in Lithuania,[2] in Ukraine,[3] and partly in Moldova[4] the death penalty was also abolished by their Constitutional Courts instead of legislative acts.

Due to a widespread misunderstanding, some people believe that in the USA the Furman decision in 1972 also declared capital punishment unconstitutional, though, in fact, this was not the case. In *Furman vs. Georgia*[5] the Supreme Court of the United States declared the death penalty, as then administered, and not per se, unconstitutional across the USA, because on the one hand, it was in breach of the Eighth Amendment's

Z. J. Toth, *Changing Attitudes Towards the Death Penalty*,
https://doi.org/10.1007/978-3-030-47557-4_15

ban on cruel and unusual punishment, since imposing of the death penalty was "arbitrary and capricious," and, on the other hand, it violated the Fourteenth Amendment's equal protection clause as well. Nevertheless, this Supreme Court decision did not prevent state courts from imposing capital punishments on those found guilty of capital offenses, and what is more, state legislatures began creating new laws that complied with the requirements of the Furman decision. Especially the three pro-death penalty pioneers, Florida, Texas, and Georgia, were particularly keen on enacting new death penalty statutes, which would fulfil the demands prescribed by the Supreme Court of the United States in *Furman*.[6] In 1976 a new era began when in *Gregg vs Georgia*[7] the Supreme Court ruled that those death penalty statutes which gave the jury a discretional power to decide whether a guilty defendant had to be sentenced to death or not (the so-called "guided discretion death penalty statutes") could be constitutional. This latter decision restored the applicability of the death penalty; however, from this it follows that the Furman decision had never declared the death penalty, as such, unconstitutional in the United States.[8]

As indicated above, the Hungarian Constitutional Court declared capital punishment unconstitutional immediately after the transition to democracy, by the Constitutional Court Decision No. 23 of 1990 (October 31) on an eight to one vote. The primary and formal cause of it was, according to the majority of the court, that it violated the right to life and human dignity of every person. Due to Article 54 para. (1) of the then Constitution, in the Republic of Hungary every human being had the inherent right to life and human dignity, of which no one should be arbitrarily deprived. The court deemed that the legal regulations concerning capital punishment were in conflict with this constitutional provision and, therefore, had to be ruled unconstitutional. The curiosity of the reasoning of the decision was that the court stated that the right to life and the right to human dignity constitute an independent substantive right which differs from both the right to life and the right to dignity. According to this reasoning, "[h]uman life and human dignity form an inseparable unity and have a greater value than anything else. The rights to human life and human dignity form an indivisible and unrestrainable fundamental right which is the source of and the condition for several additional fundamental rights. … The rights to human life and dignity as an absolute value create a limitation upon the criminal jurisdiction of the State."[9] However, the stipulation of Article 54 allowed, in theory, taking someone's life on a non-arbitrary basis, but the court interpreted it in the light of the Article 8 para. (2), which regulated that the basic meaning and content of the inviolable and inalienable fundamental human rights may not be restricted by law. For Article 54 contained such a special right; the limitation of the right to life and human dignity was prohibited by the Constitution. And since permitting and regulating capital punishment in the statutes not only imposed a limitation upon the essential meaning of the fundamental right to life and human dignity, but also allowed for the entire and irreparable elimination of life and human dignity or of the right ensuring these, therefore the Constitutional Court established the unconstitutionality of these provisions and declared them null and void.[10]

The one and only dissenting opinion was that of Justice Peter Schmidt. Nevertheless, even he agreed with the uselessness and inhumanity of the death penalty, but deemed that the Constitutional Court had no power to dissolve a collision between contradictory constitutional rules, since it was the Parliament's exclusive right and obligation. As he wrote:

> [w]hile the interpretation of the Constitution falls within the competence of the Constitutional Court, it is the right and obligation of the Parliament, the body empowered to frame or to change the Constitution, to resolve the conflict between the provisions of the Constitution. Such powers may not be assumed by the Constitutional Court. Therefore, in my opinion, the Constitutional Court should state that it lacks such a power, and should call the Parliament's attention to the necessity of eliminating the conflict. This would not exclude the possibility for the Constitutional Court to list all the current arguments against capital punishment.[11]

Evaluating the Constitutional Court ruling as a whole, with this decision and its reasoning the Constitutional Court, in considering the constitutionality of the death penalty, avoided having to adopt an opinion in the legal-political debates, yet its decision is questionable from other aspects. The inseparability thesis stems from the monistic concept of man, that is, the unity of body and soul (as, according to the Constitutional Court, there is no life without dignity and there is no dignity without life), which (the monistic concept of man) is contrary to the principle of ideological neutrality of the State. The dualistic concept of man (life is expendable in order to preserve dignity), as opposed to the monistic approach, would be in accordance with the ideological neutrality of the State, because the dualistic constitutional approach does not preclude any individual from living his or her life according to the monistic concept of man as a guiding principle, but the monistic constitutional approach excludes the individual decision to live life according to the dualistic approach.[12] The inherent shortcomings of the monistic concept of man, however, arises not primarily in the assessment of the death penalty, but instead in a situation when a possibility of choosing euthanasia emerges. The ideologically neutral dualistic concept of man let anybody choose both life over death and death over life, but the ideologically biased (typically religious) monistic concept (that is, that body and soul, or life and dignity are inseparable from each other) does not let people make this choice and thus forces the former one for them, whether or not they want it. For example, in the practice of the German Constitutional Court (*Bundesverfassungsgericht*) the dualistic approach prevails and the right to life is not considered as an absolute and unrestrictable value; the only absolute value is human dignity, conceptionally separated from the value of and right to human life.[13]

The problem with the reasoning of the CC Decision No. 23 of 1990 is that it is consciously based on questionable moral ethics (and these problems were also revealed in the reasoning of the CC Decision No. 22 of 2003 on euthanasia), albeit it would have been an obvious solution for the Constitutional Court to declare the death penalty unconstitutional on the basis of that it was in breach of Article 54 para. (2) of the Constitution, which stated that "[n]o one shall be subjected to torture, to cruel, inhuman or degrading treatment or punishment." Considering that the death penalty is undoubtedly a cruel and degrading punishment, a reasoning based on this consideration would have been sounder and less debatable.[14]

The Hungarian people, however, were far from that opinion and did not agree at all with the abolition of the death penalty in Hungary as a result of the Constitutional Court's decision. After the abolition of capital punishment several nation-wide representative surveys were conducted in Hungary about the opinion of the population regarding this legal sanction. The first one was made by Szonda Ipsos right after the publication of the Constitutional Court's judgment in 1991. It concluded that 77.2 percent of the adult Hungarian population opposed the abolition of capital punishment, which means that more than three-quarters of people supported capital punishment. Only 20.4 percent supported abolition (which means that only one-fifth of Hungarians opposed capital punishment), and 2.4 percent did not answer.[15]

In 2001 the TÁRKI Institute made another survey about this issue; according to the results in the first year of the third millennium 68 percent of the Hungarian population would agree with the application of capital punishment. (This data was collected within the *Central European Opinion Research Group*—CEORG and the same question was asked at the same time in the Czech Republic, Poland, and Lithuania, which allowed the comparison of the results. Based on this it may be concluded that the Hungarian attitude about capital punishment is general in the region, because even though only 58 percent of Czechs agreed with the possible restoration of capital punishment, 76 percent of Lithuanians and 72 percent of Polish supported it.)[16] This survey also concluded that there is a reverse proportionality between the support of capital punishment and satisfaction with public safety and work of the police, which means that the safer one feels, the less they support the maintenance or restoration of capital punishment.

The third survey was made in March 2005 when Medián Public Opinion and Market Research Institute measured the opinion of the population about capital punishment on a representative sample of 1200 people. According to this two-thirds of Hungarians definitely supported capital punishment; 63 percent would consider it acceptable even in peacetime, while 7 percent would not allow it in peacetime, only in wartime. Only 28 percent said that they would not accept it at all, and 2 percent could not or did not want to answer. The next representative survey was also made by Medián upon the request of *HVG*, a popular weekly, between December 3–7, 2010 on a sample of 1200 people. To the question "Would you rather support or rather oppose the application of capital punishment in serious crimes?" 69 percent said "yes," 27 percent said "no," while 4 percent could not answer.[17]

In December 2015, Szonda-Ipsos again conducted a large-scale survey in Hungary on a representative sample of 1000 people. István H. Szilágyi and György Gajduschek re-analyzed the data of this survey in 2017 in order to determine the attitude towards crime in Hungary.[18] H. Szilágyi and Gajduschek asked a four-item question regarding capital punishment in this questionnaire. Two of them were in support of the death penalty, and two of them were in opposition thereto, asking also the basic reasons for people's opinions. This allowed respondents to choose why they support the death penalty, or why they opposed it and, in both cases, for what reason. There are two reasons for this: utilitarian or moral. Based on this, respondents had to choose one assertion from the following statements that they considered most appropriate and closest to their views. (1) The death penalty is meaningless because it has no deterrent effect. (2) The death penalty is unacceptable because the state has no right to kill anyone. (3) The death penalty should be reinstated as this would be the fairest punishment for the most serious crimes. (4) The death penalty should be reinstated, as it would protect society from incurable criminals.[19] 13.2 percent of respondents opted for the first statement, while 26.7 percent opted for the second, which is approximately 40 percent (39.9 percent to be exact) in favor of the abolitionist position. Compared to this, 31.5 percent of the respondents voted in favor of the third assertion and 23.8 percent voted in favor of the fourth, meaning that about 55 percent in total (55.3 percent to be exact) proved to be proponents of capital punishment. (forty-eight persons, i.e., 4.8 percent of respondents were unable or unwilling to answer.)[20]

Interestingly, looking at the reasons for the answers it can be seen that 37 percent formed their opinions on a pragmatic-utilitarian ground, and 58 percent in a deontological-ethical ground (either pro or con). That is, in terms of the attitude towards the death penalty in Hungary, there is a slight majority of respondents who express their views on a theoretical, moral basis, and a minority of those who form their views on a utilitarian ground. H. Szilágyi and Gajduschek also found that neither gender nor age plays a role in what one thinks of the death penalty (which is somewhat surprising according to a large number of US surveys to the contrary), but that income (and, we might add, presumably the school education which might correlate with the level of income) already has an explanatory role; the higher one's income (and most likely his or her educational background) is, the less likely he or she is to support the death penalty.[21]

The last survey was conducted specifically for scientific research, led by László Kelemen; this was done in November and December 2018, also on a representative sample of 1000 people.[22] The results of this survey are very similar to those of H. Szilágyi and Gajduschek. Kelemen, and used the same items as H. Szilágyi and Gajduschek. 18 percent chose the death penalty as meaningless because it has no deterrent effect; 22 percent thought the death penalty was unacceptable because the state has no right to kill someone; 30 percent believed that the death penalty should be reinstated because this would be the fairest punishment for the most serious crimes; and 24 percent thought that the death penalty should be reinstated because it would protect society from incurable criminals. Overall, 40 percent of those surveyed were abolitionists and 54 percent were in favor of the death penalty (6 percent of respondents did not answer.)[23]

There was a significant difference between the respondents in terms of gender and highest level of education. While 58 percent of the men who substantively responded to the answer said the death penalty should be reinstated, only 50 percent of women thought so. The difference is even more spectacular in terms of educational attainment; of those who have not completed elementary school, of those who have completed it but have not completed their profession or their baccalaureate, and of those who have completed high school (but not college or university), 57, 55, and 56 percent, respectively, supported capital punishment. This proportion, however, was only 42 percent among college graduates and only 38 percent among university graduates.[24]

It may be seen from all these figures that the Hungarian public has always been in favor of the most severe criminal sanction, even though the rate of support has been slowly but steadily declining since the early 1990s, and today just over half of the Hungarian people advocate the reinstatement of capital punishment.

As for the facts based on statistical figures, both the abolitionists and the retentionists wish to prove the rightness of their standpoints on the grounds of pure statistical analyses. The fault of these attempts (from both sides) is that whether in Hungary or abroad, they do not take into account that plenty of other social trends and flows, numerous economic impacts etc., influence the criminality in a given state. This will be shown by the example of Hungary. In Hungary, as mentioned before, the Constitutional Court declared capital punishment unconstitutional right after the end of the transition to democracy, in October of 1990 by the Constitutional Court Decision No. 23/1990 (October 31). Hence, the last year that we can consider a "year with capital punishment" is 1990 and the first year we can regard as "a year without capital punishment" is 1991. The mere statistical data show as follows. Between 1975 and 1990, from a minimum of 185 to a maximum of 237[25] murders, both premeditated[26] and not premeditated,[27] and murders of passion (or, as it is named officially in the Hungarian penal law: voluntary manslaughters committed with provocation or in the heat of passion) occurred every single year[28] (in these occurrences manslaughters as negligent crimes are not involved). This means that the number of murders in Hungary was almost the same in each year (between 1975 and 1990): approximately 210 on average, with a margin of plus/minus 10 percent. In 1991, the first death penalty-free year, this number rose up to 307; in 1992, this number was totally the same (307) and then, between 1993 and 1998 it fluctuated between 271 and 313.[29] So, it can be seen that the frequency of violent intentional killings was higher by one and a half fold in the years after the abolition of capital punishment than in the years before that.

There would be a conclusion drawn (by the retentionists) that the abolition of the death penalty made the potential murderers more unflinching, more desperate, and more fearless, but, in fact, this inference may be false, or at least, to be more exact, it lacks soundness. Why? First, the abolition of capital punishment happened just at the time when Hungary transitioned from state socialism to democracy. This transition was accompanied with the *anomic state of society* in a Durkheimian sense. This means that sharp, drastic, and rapid changes cause value crisis among the members of a society (called anomie) that appear in, among other things, more frequent deviancy (for example, an increased number of suicides, alcohol diseases, and crimes). Furthermore, in Hungary, this transition went with the liquidation of state companies and, thereby, dismissing lots of employees, making them unemployed; there was growing poverty and international organized crime turned up, all of these being criminogenic factors.

This explanation (of anomie) is also shown by the fact that not only murder rates increased during these years but the total number of crimes as well. The evidence thereof is that between 1975 and 1988 from about 120,000 crimes up to 188,000 offences were committed per year.[30] (On average, approximately, with a margin of plus/minus 20 percent, 150,000). The political transformation began, in fact, in 1989, thus the causes of the growing number of crimes started to operate in that year. This actually did manifest in the years of the political transformation, even in 1989 as well. Namely, in 1989, the total number of crimes was 225,000, in 1990 it was 341,000, in 1991 it was 440,000, and then between 1992 and 1999 it ranged from 389,000 to 600,000.[31] This means that the total number of crimes rose in a few years' time by about three- or four-fold, while the number of murders increased by only one- and a half-fold, that is, the anomic state explanation seems to be a plausible one.

And there is one more argument that corroborates this scenario. Namely, after 1999, when the shocking effects of the political transformation began to fade away, the number of murders started to decrease tendentiously. Only 253 murders were committed in 1999 and only 205 in 2000; in 2001, the figure again rose to over 250 (254 exactly), but then began to fall again: 203 in 2002, 228 in 2003, 209 in 2004, 164 in 2005, 174 in 2006, and 154 in 2007 such cases were registered. Finally, as of 2008, the number of homicides has not even reached 150: 147 in 2008, 139 in 2009, 133 in 2010, and 142 in 2011. In 2012, this figure broke the record in Hungary, with only 112 homicides recorded; and even though the number of homicides has increased slightly over the next two years from this "negative peak" (though it still did not reach two-thirds of the period of state socialism, it was only 135 in 2013 and 2014). But there was another, even more significant, decline, since in recent years the number of homicides has been around 100 (in particular, 99 in 2015, 101 in 2016, and only 92 in 2017).

In other words, one decade after the abolition of the death penalty, the number of completed murders has slowly returned to pre-1990 levels; after another decade, it has been significantly and steadily underperforming; and today, although the death penalty has not existed for a long time, it is also clearly below its lowest level during the period of state socialism, to the extent that *the average number of homicides in the last three years is only half of the average annual death penalty of the communist era.*

The anomic state scenario may be indicated not only by the increased incidence of homicides, but also by the increasing trend of total crime in the 1990s, far greater than the increase in crimes that were previously threatened with the death penalty. While between 1975 and 1988 there were between 120,000 and 188,000 crimes known per year, in 1989 (when the change of regime was apparently underway, with all its, positive and negative, effects) this number increased to 225,000;,in 1990 it was 341,000, and in 1991 it moved up to 440,000. In the following years (between 1992 and 1999), the figure was also high, between 389,000 and 600,000, an average of three to four times higher than a decade earlier; whereas, as we have seen, the increase in homicides was "only" one and a half times greater. However, this proportion has not changed significantly until now; in each of the twelve years between 2000 and 2011, the total number of crimes was between 400–450,000 (between 394–465,000 precisely),[32] whereas in recent years (partly due to purely statistical methodological-survey reasons) it dropped. (The total number of crimes between 2012 and 2017 was officially 472,000, 377,000, 329,000, 280,000, 290,000, and 226,000.) One of the reasons for the strong statistical decline is undoubtedly the fact of the new Criminal Code (Act C of 2012), and some time ago, since April 15, 2012, the old Criminal Code. (Act IV of 1978) increased the previous offense value of 20,000 forints to 50,000, that is, crimes against property (theft, fraud, embezzlement, misappropriation, etc.) for which the damage and the property damage amounted to HUF 20,001 and 50,000 is no longer a crime, just an offense, so it does not appear in crime statistics, although it is as unpleasant for victims as it was when they were officially offended. However, it is also true that other effects (such as increases in crime detection efficiency) can and do contribute—without it (due to changes in statistical methodology alone), for example, the unusually low rate of

2017 cannot be explained. (This is also likely to play a role in reducing, for example, the number of intentional assaults by one third between 1998 and 2017 and the number of robberies by less than one third.)

There also could be a conclusion drawn, in this latter case by the abolitionists, that the abrogation of the former death penalty does not have any influence at all either on total criminality or on the former death-eligible offences, however, this latter inference is unsound, too. *Since we are simply not able to learn what would have happened if capital punishment had not been abolished* (it is, theoretically, possible that if capital punishment had not been ceased then the number of murders would have dropped even more than it actually did) *we cannot infer from pure statistical figures either that this kind of penalty deterred or that it did not deter some part of the potential murderers.* In any case, it is clear from the homicide statistics that the death penalty is not strictly necessary to reduce the number of murders.

Notes

1. In South Africa, the Supreme Court (which is an ordinary court with the right to review the constitutionality of laws) declared the death penalty unconstitutional on June 6, 1995. (Cf.: The State vs T. Makwanyane and M. Mchunu, S. v. Makwanyane and Another (CCT3/94), 1995. ZACC 3; 1995 (6) BCLR 665; 1995 (3) SA 391, 1996, 2 CHRLD 164; 1995 (2) SACR 1 (June 6, 1995).) Although it formally did not erase the regulations on capital punishment from the South African laws, it made practically impossible for state authorities to impose and execute capital punishment. Ultimately, in 1997, the Criminal Law Amendment Act formally abolished the unconstitutional stipulations regarding the death penalty.
2. In Lithuania, the Constitutional Court also ruled it unconstitutional on December 9, 1998 followed by a legislative corroboration in the same month, which formally modified the Lithuanian criminal code and another bill was passed which turned death sentences into life imprisonments.
3. In Ukraine, the Constitutional Court declared the death penalty unconstitutional on December 29, 1999. However, in order for this decision to

be effective even formally, it had to be strengthened by the Ukrainian Parliament as well. It was done on February 22, 2000. Cf.: Renate Wohlwend: The Role of the Council of Europe's Parliamentary Assembly, p. 74. In: *Death Penalty: Beyond Abolition*. Council of Europe Publishing, 2004, Strasbourg, pp. 65–85.

4. In Moldova the legislative body removed this sanction from the statutes in 1995 (this act entered into force in 1996), abolishing the death penalty. In 2005, the Constitutional Court of Moldova approved an amendment to the Moldovan Constitution, which declared capital punishment unconstitutional. Consequently, from that time it cannot be revived in a statutory level (which was not true between 1996 and 2005).
5. *Furman vs Georgia* (408 US 238). This case consists of virtually three different cases (*Furman vs Georgia*, *Jackson vs Georgia*, and *Branch vs Texas*) known jointly as *Furman vs Georgia.*
6. See in detail: Most Death Penalties Are Unconstitutional: *Furman vs Georgia* (1972). H. A. Bedau (ed.): *The Death Penalty in America*. Oxford University Press, 1982, pp. 253–270.
7. *Gregg s. Georgia*, 428 US 153 (1976).
8. See in detail: The Death Penalty Is Not Per Se Unconstitutional: *Gregg vs Georgia* (1976). In: H. A. Bedau (ed.). *The Death Penalty in America.* Oxford University Press, 1982, pp. 271–288.
9. CC decision 23/1990. (X. 31.) AB [ABH 1990, 89, 93.]
10. CC decision 23/1990. (X. 31.) AB [ABH 1990, 89, 92.]
11. CC decision 23/1990. (X. 31.) AB [ABH 1990, 89, 94–95.]
12. For gains and problems of the so-called "inseparability thesis of the right to life and human dignity" see, e.g.: Renáta Uitz,: Lessons from the Abolition of Capital Punishment in Hungary: A Fortuitous Constellation Amidst and Beyond Democratic Transition. Acta Juridica Hungarica, 45 Nos 1–2, pp. 67–99 (2004).
13. See, e.g.: BVerfGE 39, 41 (1975).
14. For a criticism of the Constitutional Court's monistic concept of man, see: J. Z. Toth. The Past and Future of the Inseparability Thesis in the Light of the old Constitution and the new Fundamental Law (Az oszthatatlansági doktrína múltja a régi Alkotmány, és jövője az új Alaptörvény fényében). Tímea Drinóczi and András Jakab. (eds.): *Alkotmányozás Magyarországon* (Constitutionalization in Hungary). Vol. 1. Pázmány Press, Budapest–Pécs, 2013, pp. 275–304.

15. Cf.: András Firon, *Káinbélyeg. Nyugdíjazzuk-e végleg a hóhért?* Panoráma Kiadó, Budapest, 1991, pp. 128–129.
16. Cf.: Társadalomkutatási Intézet Rt.: Közép-európai közvélemény: Lakossági vélemények a közbiztonságról és a halálbüntetésről a közép-kelet-európai országokban. (Central European public opinion: Public opinion on public safety and the death penalty in Central and Eastern European countries) In: http://www.tarki.hu/adatbank-h/kutjel/pdf/a556.pdf.
17. Cf.: Endre Hann and Zsuzsa Lakatos: Nem kényszer, hanem...Felmérés az alkotmányozásról (Not a compulsion, but...A constitutional survey). In: *HVG*, 2010, 51–52, (December 25, 2010), pp. 14–16.
18. Cf: István H. Szilágyi and György Gajduschek: Nevelés és büntetés. A büntetési igény alakulása a magyar lakosság jogtudatában az újabb hazai empirikus kutatások fényében, különös tekintettel a nevelési elvek hatására. (Education and punishment. Evolution of the need for punishment in the legal consciousness of the Hungarian population in the light of recent Hungarian empirical research, with special regard to the effect of educational principles.) MTA Law Working Papers, MTA/Hungarian Academy of Sciences, 2017/7, jog.tk.mta.hu/uploads/files/2017_07_HSzilagyi_Gajduschek.pdf
19. Cf.: H. Szilágyi and Gajduschek: op. cit., p. 3.
20. Cf.: H. Szilágyi and Gajduschek: op. cit., p. 3.
21. Cf.: H. Szilágyi and Gajduschek: op. cit., p. 6.
22. Cf: István H. Szilágyi and László Kelemen: Miként vélekedünk a jogról? (How do we feel about the law?) *HVG-ORAC*, Budapest, 2019.
23. Cf.: H. Szilágyi and Kelemen: op. cit., p. 146.
24. Cf.: H. Szilágyi and Kelemen: op. cit., p. 155.
25. For the Hungarian statistical data, cf.: Hungarian Statistical Yearbooks, 1975–2017.
26. "Intentional killing with malicious aforethought."
27. "Homicide."
28. In detail: in 1975 206, in 1976 237, in 1977 219, in 1978 185, in 1979 230, in 1980 200, in 1981 214, in 1982 190, in 1983 215, in 1984 205, in 1985 191, in 1986 233, in 1987 203, in 1988 206, in 1989 191 and in 1990 201 murders and involuntary manslaughters took place per year. Nevertheless, the number of the latter is not worth taking into account since those criminal acts that are qualified as "involuntary manslaughters" befall very rarely, usually once or twice (or not once at all) per year.

29. In 1993 298, in 1994 313, in 1995 296, in 1996 271, in 1997 289 and in 1998, again, 289 intentional homicides eventuated.
30. Annually: in 1975 120,889; in 1976 129,424; in 1977 123,623; in 1978 126,907; in 1979 125,267; in 1980 130,470; in 1981 134,914; in 1982 139,795; in 1983 151,505; in 1984 157,036; in 1985 165,816; in 1986 182,867; in 1987 188,397; in 1988 185,344 crimes occurred.
31. In detail, the total number of crimes: in 1989: 225,393; in 1990: 341,061; in 1991: 440,370; in 1992: 447,222; in 1993: 400,935; in 1994: 389,451; in 1995: 502,036; in 1996: 466,050; in 1997: 514,403; in 1998: 600,621; in 1999: 505,716. Nonetheless, it has to be mentioned that the salient value of the crime rate in 2008 is due to a sole offender who defrauded nearly 80,000 people (committing, as a consequence of it, almost 80,000 crimes) pretending to be a parking attendant and, hence, to be entitled to get money from drivers in order for them to be able to park in places where the parking in fact was free of charge.
32. An important methodological note is that the above data do not actually show the number of *crimes committed* in a given year, but the *crimes in which the investigation was terminated* in that year. However, the figures are still suitable for illustrating trends.

16

Revived Debate on the Death Penalty in the Political Scene

There was quite a long period when the death penalty was not a key issue of politics in Hungary. As mentioned, it was not the politicians who incurred the odium of the abolition of the death penalty after the regime change; had the Constitutional Court of Hungary not declared the death penalty unconstitutional, probably none of the political parties would have taken any action for many years (at least until Hungary's accession to the European Convention on Human Rights), due to the fear of losing votes. In the 1990s, Tamás Tóth, the mayor of a settlement in Hungary (Sárszentmihály) was the only person who directed public opinion to the death penalty: he collected signatures for a referendum on whether the death penalty should be reintroduced in Hungary or not.

After his son was murdered in 1992, Tamás Tóth became the most determined devotee of the reintroduction of the death penalty in Hungary. In 1997, he commenced the collection of signatures so that the National Assembly would order a referendum on the question of the reintroduction of capital punishment. For the first time on November 26, 1997, and later on several occasions, Tóth submitted the collected signatures, but the National Election Commission—the body certifying the questions for referenda (and thereby giving permission to holding

Z. J. Toth, *Changing Attitudes Towards the Death Penalty*,
https://doi.org/10.1007/978-3-030-47557-4_16

them)—did not examine the signatures. On October 6, 1998, Tamás Tóth submitted a new set of signatures to the NEC, and asked for the examination thereof. The request was rejected by the NEC in its resolution 88/1998. (XI. 20.) based on two formal grounds.

The first ground was that the initiator had not submitted the sample signature sheet and the question thereon preliminarily (i.e., prior to commencing the collection of signatures) in order to get it verified (thus, a formulated question that could be asked in a referendum did not even exist in practice), which verification would have been a compulsory formal requirement pursuant to Act III of 1998 on national referenda and popular initiatives. The other ground was the expiry of the four-month period prescribed in the Constitution (Article 28/E in Act XX of 1949) for the initiation of a referendum. The said provision was enacted by Article 4 in Act XCVIII of 1997 with effect from 31 October 1997, and was applicable also in pending cases from that time, pursuant to Article 6 (3) in the same Act. Thus, the time available for the initiator expired on February 28, 1998, so the certification of the (actually not existing) "question" was not possible either due to the exceeding of the deadline.

On December 22, 1998, exploiting the experiences gained from the resolution's reasoning and not giving up his goals, Tamás Tóth requested the NEC to certify the following question initiating the temporary reintroduction of the death penalty: "I request the National Assembly to establish the legal conditions under which the death penalty can be reintroduced temporarily." The NEC adjudged the motion at its session held on January 14, 1999 and, this time on substantial aspects, rejected it with its resolution 1/1999. (I. 14.). The first and most important substantive ground was that the Constitution prohibited the posing of that question, since "no national referendum may be held on any obligation arising from international treaties and on the content of the Acts on that obligations" pursuant to Article 28/C (5) b) therein. Since both treaties concerned—i.e., the European Convention for the Protection of Human Rights and Fundamental Freedoms, signed in Rome on November 4, 1950 (European Convention on Human Rights, shortly Rome Convention) with the Protocol No. 6 concerning the abolition of the death penalty thereto, and the Second Optional Protocol to the International Covenant on Civil and Political Rights, also prohibiting death penalty as a punishment in case of offences other than war crimes—were enacted by the National Assembly (Act XXXI of 1993 and Act II of 1995), a referendum on the question of the reintroduction of the death penalty would be unconstitutional.

As regards the second, less important substantive ground, the NEC pointed out that the clarity requirements were not met. According to NEC, the actual intention of the majority of the people cannot be determined only on the basis of "yes" or "no" responses to the question, as the sentence indicated on the signature sheet contains no information on what the National Assembly's obligation would be after the referendum. Pursuant to the resolution:

> When a referendum on the question of the reintroduction of the death penalty could be held and the answer to the question on the signature sheets was 'yes', the National Assembly could decide either to denounce effective international treaties, or to reintroduce the death penalty only in the limited scope provided by such treaties. In both cases, however, there is a possibility of a decision that is contradictory to the true will of the citizens, which will is actually not expressible in the referendum.

Finally, the third, also substantive, ground of the rejection was that, on the basis of its content, the sentence indicated on the signature sheet qualified as a request and not as a question; thus, it might serve as basis for a so-called popular initiative, but not for a referendum. (Popular initiatives do not oblige the National Assembly to make a positive decision on the concerned question but only to examine and discuss it.)

The applicant tried to modify his motion on the basis of the NEC's resolution 1/1999. (I. 14.) considering the facts specified therein and submitted it to the National Election Committee for certification once again. This time, he attached six various sample signature sheets, indicating six questions with the same content but with different wording. The questions were aimed at the National Assembly to establish the legal conditions under which the death penalty could be temporarily reintroduced in case of serious crimes against life. This motion was adjudged and, again, rejected by the NEC with the resolution 8/1999. (III. 29.). As ground for rejection, the NEC concluded again that the questions were contrary to the prohibition stipulated in Article 28/C (5) b) in the Constitution. The aforesaid international treaties, which had become part of Hungary's legal system, prohibited the application of the death penalty for offences against life other than war crimes, i.e., the very offences the initiator proposed the temporarily reintroduction of the death penalty for. These treaties tolerate the application of the death penalty only in case of the most serious crimes committed during wartime, but the request did not seek to establish the possibility of application of the death penalty for this type of crimes. The other, less important failure (as it could be easily eliminated) that served as basis of rejection was that Tamás Tóth requested not only one question to be certified but submitted more potential questions to the NEC, so that it would sort out which one to certify. The NEC concluded that it was not entitled to such a procedure; it was the duty of the initiator to word the specific question being proposed for referendum and the NEC was only entitled to judge whether it was lawful and could be asked in a referendum.

Finally, the decision 11/1999. (V. 7.) AB of the Constitutional Court of Hungary clearly stated that, due to the undertaken international law obligations, the reintroduction of the death penalty was not possible in Hungary, which decision affirmed the NEC's prior reasoning according to which the reintroduction of the death penalty was contrary to effective international treaties, thus, no referendum could be held on that issue. Therefore, it has been unquestionably established that the death penalty cannot be applied in Hungary in any form or extent under the current circumstances.

It remains so to this day, despite the fact that neither the previous Constitution (effective until December 31, 2011) nor the new Fundamental Law (effective from January 1, 2012) included a so-called death penalty clause. Although the Fundamental Law has no specific provision on the death penalty, other constitutional provisions currently exclude the reintroduction thereof. Pursuant to Article II therein, "every human being shall have the right to life and human dignity." Article III (1) provides that "no one shall be subject to torture, inhuman or degrading treatment or punishment." Pursuant to Article Q) (2), "in order to comply with its obligations under international law, Hungary shall ensure that Hungarian law is in conformity with international law," which can be achieved only through adapting the Hungarian law to international law and not in reverse. A further implicit prohibition regarding the death penalty can be found in Article XIV (3) in the Fundamental Law: "no one shall be expelled or extradited to a State where there is a risk that he or she would be sentenced to death, tortured or subjected to other inhuman treatment or punishment." Thus, following the logic of the principle of *argumentum a minori ad maius*, if the less, namely the extradition, is prohibited (due to the *risk*, the mere *possibility*), a larger or a more serious act obviously has to be also prohibited i.e., neither imposing nor execution of the death penalty is allowed in Hungary. Holding a referendum on the death penalty is forbidden by Article 8 (3) d) in the Fundamental Law saying that "no national referendum may be held on any obligation arising from international treaties."

Despite all the aforesaid, in the 2000s, there were several politicians making statements that the reintroduction of death penalty would be necessary in order to tackle crimes against life. Most of these expressions followed serious offences, murders causing public outcry, and the obvious aim thereof was to get political gain, formulating opinions which are "likable" for voters. These expressions are the results of political populism, since these politicians know that due to the aforesaid constitutional provisions and international law obligations, the reintroduction of the death penalty is currently not possible in Hungary. Far-right politicians and parties may be the only exceptions, since they do not wish to achieve only the reintroduction of the death penalty, but they also aim at other radical goals (such as possible termination of Hungary's European Union membership and withdrawal from other international organizations).

Such far-right politicians raise the matter of reintroduction of the death penalty relatively regularly but mostly with only a slight response. For the sake of curiosity, here are a few examples.

After the elections of 2002, the national radical party Jobbik (Movement for a Better Hungary) established a working group on public safety, the leader of which, Gábor Vona—who later became also the leader of the party—formulated the opinion that it would be important to discuss the question of the death penalty. At the same time, Ervin Nagy, the then leader of Jobbik, told the magazine *Kapu* (Gate) that an important goal of the party was to initiate a public debate on the death penalty. Nagy said: "We know well that the European Union's regulation and the Constitutional Court of Hungary do not allow the reintroduction of the death penalty. But we are saying that, looking at the senseless brutality of the crimes recently committed in Hungary, if the Hungarian people's need arises to discuss the righteousness of the death penalty, then we should discuss it. We live in democracy—let the question be decided on the basis of the majority rule."[1] In February 2006, Tamás Molnár, deputy leader of the party Jobbik, said in Debrecen at a campaign event (held together with MIÉP [Hungarian Justice and Life Party], the other far-right party and with FKgP [Independent Smallholders and Civic Party]) that the death penalty had to be reintroduced.[2] A few weeks later, the deputy leader of the FKgP (the party allied with Jobbik) said the same.[3]

In the course of preparing for the municipal elections held in autumn of 2006, repeating the point he made earlier, Tamás Molnár linked the death penalty to the phenomenon he had already referred to before as "gypsy crime." He intended to strengthen public safety with a criminal policy that is rigorous in all aspects, since, in his opinion, the death penalty was the only means against violent crimes. "According to Jobbik, only the harshest possible penalisation could lead to results against criminals, including gypsy offenders…"[4] In the rhetoric of Jobbik, the issue of the death penalty arose again in October 2006, following a brutal lynching (Lajos Szögi, a 44-year-old teacher was murdered in a small village, Olaszliszka, after a local little girl ran across his car. The girl was not hurt, but the villagers, her relatives gathered around and beat Lajos Szögi to death after he got out of the car to help).[5] Inter alia, similar statements were made by Biber, József, the then deputy leader of Jobbik (which later became a parliamentary party) in December 2007,[6] Gábor Vona (as party leader by that time) in December 2008[7] and Levente Murányi, deputy leader of Jobbik, in October 2009 (the latter talked about changing prisons into labour camps, too).[8]

As a parliamentary party by that time, Jobbik (which won 17 percent of the votes cast in the parliamentary elections of 2010) proposed the reintroduction of the death penalty in the Parliament in 2011, but the pro-government majority voted against the discussion of the issue (neither the other proposals made therewith, such as the removal of the immunity and the recall of the MPs, were discussed). Afterwards, Gábor

Staudt MP urged the reintroduction of the death penalty at different times,[9] and, on behalf of Jobbik, Ádám Mirkóczki MP made a new proposal for resolution, stating that there is a need for a public debate on the question of the death penalty. (It is interesting that in his answer given to this parliamentary speech, Viktor Orbán, who previously (as discussed below) also brought up the reconsideration of the issue of the death penalty, said to Mirkóczki that "I can hardly imagine any rigorous legislation that could guarantee that no serious crimes will be committed." He also added that whilst he agreed with the MP of Jobbik as regards several philosophical approaches, with accession to the European Union after the referendum thereon, Hungary accepted that the Member States are not allowed to introduce the death penalty.[10]

During the campaign of 2014, the candidates of the party Jobbik went on with campaigning with the reintroduction of the death penalty and with advocating rigorous criminal policy in general (including for example the castration of offenders committing sexual offences).[11] In spring of 2015, after the murder of a young woman working in a tobacco-shop in Kaposvár, Jobbik initiated a parliamentary debate once again, but the centre-right majority voted against it (albeit several members of the governing party would have agreed with the suggestion personally).[12]

Concurrently with moving away from the far-right and approaching the centre-right (the result of which was an election cooperation with the left-wing parties in the parliamentary elections of 2018 and municipal elections of 2019 in order to replace the governing conservative parties i.e., the Fidesz-KDNP [Fidesz-Hungarian Civic Alliance and Christian Democratic People's Party]), Jobbik gradually left the radical tone and withdrew the question of the death penalty from the public issues. These issues were made part of the public discourse once again by the Mi Hazánk Mozgalom (Our Homeland Movement), a body founded by the radical members excluded from or having quitted the Jobbik, which, from its foundation in 2018, wished to reach the radical right-wing voters who were left without political representation because of the Jobbik's efforts to become a people's party. Even before its official registration as a party, the Mi Hazánk Mozgalom made a stand that the death penalty had to be reintroduced. In addition, László Toroczkai—the leader of the movement and the later leader of the party—beside suggesting a referendum on the death penalty,[13] raised the possibility of the detention of prisoners in foreign prisons[14] (later he specified it as "detention of prisoners in Siberian prisons" under a treaty to be concluded with Russia,[15] and he said that if the Jobbik came to power in 2022, this institute would be used in the case of "anti-fascists and right defenders"[16] as well). In January 2020, Toroczkai said that "the Mi Hazánk Mozgalom [Our Country Movement] initiates again the application of the death penalty, the preventive effect of which has been proved by research, in case of crimes committed with particular cruelty against the life of defenceless individuals, such as children and elderly people."[17]

Beside Jobbik, MIÉP was the other far-right party represented in the Parliament after the regime change. At the finish of the campaign before the elections of 2006, István Csurka, the then president of MIÉP (which was a parliamentary party at that time), made a statement on the death penalty in response to a question concerning the issue in the popular morning television magazine *Nap-kelte*. In Csurka's opinion, the death penalty was abolished when it became clear that the regime would change and "the dirty villains who ordered and executed the shootings [in the course of the reprisal following the revolution of 1956] themselves escaped to this situation" (i.e., according to Csurka, the abolition of the death penalty was the creation of the communist nomenclature, in order to avoid execution). To the question whether these people should have been hanged or not, he answered: "Damn sure, yes!"[18]

Yet the death penalty was supported not only by far-right parties (still-active ones with demonstrable backing from the society and old ones which no longer operated in effect), but (more or less) also by politicians of moderate parties.

Péter Boross, former right-wing prime minister (the second Hungarian prime minister after the regime change acting between 1993 and 1994 i.e., resigned just before the concerned statements) was one of the most illustrious persons who, in March 1995, in several fora, consistently represented the standpoint that the possibility of the reintroduction of the death penalty should be considered. He explained to the daily paper *Magyar Nemzet* that all of this was necessary having regard to the steadily deteriorating public safety (which indeed was reduced at that time), the increase in the number of crimes and the "general mood" resulting from these situations.[19] His statement was not quoted word-for-word as an interview but the summary of its content was published, thus, *Magyar Nemzet* interpreted his words as follows. According to the article, Boross explained that:

> he is aware that his statement will incense certain people. He also knows that the death penalty is contrary to the development of law in Europe, certain provisions of the UN and the decision of the Constitutional Court of Hungary, but he does not believe that this question cannot be discussed on the merits, having regard to the present situations of the European law and the public safety. He stressed that he neither believes that the shock caused in the entire society by each horrible crime could be ignored. Boross also mentioned that according to surveys of the Ministry of Interior, 80 percent of the surveyed individuals would agree with the reintroduction of the death penalty which, according to him, could be applied in case of perpetrators of crimes against life. In his opinion, in the present situation, we cannot merely recite the dogma of what norms the death penalty is contrary to. Even if it is true, it cannot restrain decision makers from reconsidering the present legal practice, especially in cases of crimes like contract killings, child murders or killing a policeman during performing his duties, which crimes are serious and cause large panic.[20]

In those days, he also explained in a television interview that "it is not about death harvesting from the judge's bench. But it is about that…crimes like contract killings or child murders or…killing a policeman during performing his duties should be adjudged more rigorously." (Pál Vastagh, the then [left-wing] minister of justice responded that reintroduction of the death penalty would entail the denunciation of international conventions which, regarding the rule of law, are more important than the death penalty, and, moreover, the death penalty is not the proper mean to prevent serious crimes.[21] In addition, he made a promise to review, later that year, the applicable imprisonment terms and to introduce a considerably longer (e.g. fifty years) imprisonment term or whole life sentence in case of crimes against life. The latter was not realized during the ruling of the socialist-liberal government, since the whole life sentence was introduced in 1999 by the Orbán government.

On June 9, 1996, Gyula Horn, the then left-wing (socialist) prime minister said at a party event on a weekend that a referendum was necessary on the question of the reintroduction of the death penalty and that he himself would vote for the reintroduction.[22] (However, it is also true that later Pál Vastagh, his minister of justice, added that in Hungary no referendum on the question of the death penalty could be held, unless Hungary exited the international conventions on human rights.)[23] Nevertheless, according to a report of *Népszava*—a newspaper close to socialist party—Pál Filló, the leader of Article of the party representing the workers' interest in MSZP (Hungarian Socialist Party) and Ildikó Pécsi MP (and also a famous actress) expressed their agreement with the opinion of Gyula Horn.[24] In the next few days, MSZP and the prime minister himself communicated that the statement was only the personal opinion of Gyula Horn, and that neither any governmental intention existed to hold such a referendum, nor was it even possible. The situation had some further added features, since Mihály Bihari, MP of the party (later a judge and, between 2005 and 2008, the president of the Constitutional Court of Hungary) argued a few days earlier that the referendum on the death penalty might be considered because "it is better to previously address controversial issues, in order to relieve the final referendum on the Constitution."[25] (The mentioned new Constitution was not created). The same (i.e., holding a referendum on the death penalty) was suggested in her parliamentary speech by Katalin Szili, MP of the socialist party, later speaker of the National Assembly.[26]

In April 1998, József Torgyán—leader of the party and the parliamentary group of then opposition FKgP (the coalition party of the winning Fidesz after the election)—proposed that the speaker of the National Assembly should convoke an extraordinary session, even before the elections, to discuss the Constitution's amendment aiming at the reintroduction of the death penalty, to which motion twenty-one supporting signatures (from FKgP) were attached. After seeking the opinion of the parliamentary groups, Zoltán Gál, the socialist speaker, rejected the motion as legally unfounded, since the ordinary session of the National Assembly was still ongoing and enough signatures (one fifth of the 386 MPs) were not attached. Otherwise, according to the speaker, the motion was an unserious campaign item, since during the few days remaining until the elections, it was impossible to discuss the question with the thoroughness appropriate to its importance.[27] On behalf of FKgP, Zsolt Lányi (who called himself a devotee of the death penalty) reacted to the accusation of using campaign items and he rejected Gál's assertion, saying that his party had been continually calling for the reintroduction of the death penalty for more than one year.[28]

However, the most well-known statements made by politicians, which had wide (domestic and foreign) resonance, were related to the events of the recent years and to the leaders of the right-wing Fidesz, mainly to Viktor Orbán who is now (in 2020) already in his fourth term of office as prime minister. While both Fidesz as a party and its leaders used to speak moderately about the death penalty and mostly expressed their rejection regarding the issue, in May 2002, following a brutal bank robbery in which eight persons were murdered in a bank branch, their attitude has changed.

The bank robbery itself was committed on May 9, 2002, when unknown offenders (according to the witnesses, there were two or three offenders—the actual number is still unknown) burst into the local branch of a bank in the Hungarian town of Mór and killed all the employees and clients present. It is curious that the investigation that was led to identify the offenders got astray twice; it soon became apparent that the two suspects of the first days, Róbert Farkas and Szilárd Horváth, who both had criminal records, had nothing to do with the brutal murders. Two months later, in July 2002, another two suspects, Ede Kaiser and László Hajdú, were taken into custody; both of them had committed armed robbery before, even an attempt of homicide in one case. They were both convicted based on the—not entirely clear—evidence collected against them: Kaiser was sentenced to life imprisonment to be served in a maximum security prison, and Hajdú was sentenced (as an aider) to fifteen years' imprisonment (even though the court found that the trigger was pulled i.e., the murders were actually committed by a third, unknown person). As it turned out later, that was the most serious mistake made in the history of Hungarian criminalistics. In 2007, the murder weapons were found in the apartment of one László Nagy (regarding whom the investigation was originally carried out due to another homicide, the murder of a postman from Veszprém, which was most probably also committed by him). Finally, the investigation revealed that László Nagy was indeed one of the perpetrators in the Mór murder case (he admitted the participation at the bank robbery but claimed to have only been the driver), and that the other perpetrator was Róbert Weiszdorn, Nagy's coactor. László Nagy committed suicide in prison before the hearing, and Róbert Weiszdorn was convicted; he was sentenced to life imprisonment at first instance, where the earliest date of release on parole was after thirty years' imprisonment; the court of second instance rendered a more severe judgment against Weiszdorn, modifying the date of the earliest possible parole to after forty years' imprisonment. The court found (in accordance with Weiszdorn's testimony) that there was no third coactor; the security guard of the bank was shot by Weiszdorn, while the other seven people were murdered by Nagy. (Since Ede Kaiser committed other crimes, he was not released from prison; thus, he was eventually sentenced to eighteen years' imprisonment to be served in a maximum security prison at the retrial, but was finally acquitted of all charges in connection with the Mór case. It is very likely (considering the criminal proceedings of cases that were punishable by the death penalty in 1980s Hungary) that if the death penalty had been applicable in Hungary at the time of the Mór case, Kaiser (and possibly also Hajdú) would not have only been sentenced to death, but also executed by the time the actual perpetrators were found.

On May 22, 2002, shortly after the Mór bank robbery and the parliamentary elections of 2002, Viktor Orbán (who was only the caretaker prime minister by then) said the following in a radio interview: "Hungary needs to seriously consider the introduction of the death penalty." He also said that he used to think that the death penalty was an undue legal institution, but his opinion changed when he met the relatives of the victims of the Mór bank robbery in person. He also made it clear that he was aware of the fact that the reintroduction of the death penalty is not possible due to international conventions, but, according to him, this might change in the future, for example, due to the fight against terrorism. He stated being aware that Hungary was not going to be able to accede to the European Union if it reintroduced the death penalty, but, according to him, the EU was changing. He expressed his view as follows: "I believe that—after what happened here, in Hungary—the place of us,

Hungarians is among the countries who argue that the issue of the death penalty should be replaced into the legislative powers of the states in Europe." The prime minister's party, Fidesz, has not commented on the issue, the right-wing politicians have not yet repeatedly supported Orbán with their comments. On the contrary e.g.Mihály Varga, deputy leader of Fidesz, tried to mitigate Orbán's words by stating that those words were not said by Orbán as a prime minister, but as a private individual.

In May 2012, István Boldog, MP of Fidesz, said the following in his parliamentary speech: "I am well aware that I am not the only one in the Parliament, or even in the parliamentary group of Fidesz, who supports the introduction of the death penalty against the most brutal criminals. Many of us think that criminals who committed the most serious crimes should not be fed and well-kept by the state, spending the money of working, tax-paying citizens, but they should be treated with the utmost rigour." Shortly thereafter, on June 4, 2012, Antal Rogán, the leader of the parliamentary group of Fidesz acknowledged that there were some members of Fidesz who—during the debate on the Fundamental Law or the new Criminal Code—mentioned the possibility of laying down the death penalty in the Fundamental Law or in the Criminal Code, but he also made it clear that the parliamentary group of Fidesz itself does not support any such suggestions.

On June 18, 2012, the aforesaid was confirmed by Róbert Répássy, state secretary of the Ministry of Justice, who—in his answer given to the interpellation of István Apáti, MP of Jobbik—clearly and consistently rejected the death penalty (for the first time in years) as the statement of a responsible government officer, indicating several arguments that suggested the appropriateness of the present regulatory situation. In his said interpellation, the far-right politician Apáti demanded the reintroduction of the death penalty, the applicability of whole life sentence from the age of eighteen instead of twenty, and the introduction of a provision based on which the killing of one's offender—regardless of the place and time of committing the offence, as well as of the number of offenders i.e., in a general manner—in case of any unlawful offense against a person would qualify as justifiable defence. Répássy started his detailed answer by listing the provisions of the Fundamental Law based on which reintroduction of the death penalty is not possible. In such regard, Répássy said the following: “Pursuant to Article II of the Fundamental Law, human dignity shall be inviolable; every human being shall have the right to life and human dignity. Pursuant to Article I (3) therein, a fundamental right may only be restricted to allow the effective use of another fundamental right or to protect a constitutional value, to the extent absolutely necessary, proportionate to the objective pursued and with full respect for the essential content of such fundamental right.” As a summary, he added: “*The Fundamental Law is on the side of life, protecting life against the death penalty.*” Thereafter, he addressed the international situation, not only in the light of law: “Furthermore, it is indeed a fact that Hungary is obliged by several international treaties. [...] There is no death penalty in all 47 Member States of the Council of Europe. In Europe, the death penalty exists only in Belarus, which is the only European country not being a member of the Council of Europe. It would be unfortunate if Hungary stood out of such unity of understanding of the European Council.” Finally, he addressed pragmatic aspects as well: “My next argument is related to judicial mistakes. I hereby remind you that in the so-called Mór case, the court—unfortunately—could have rendered such an irreversible and unalterable decision, where the mistake made by the court would have been revealed later in vain, since the life of a person, the life of an offender executed innocently cannot be restored.”

The next public debate, having been also the biggest since the regime change in Hungary, flared up due to two murders, committed not more than a few months apart in 2012: the violent death of a young police psychologist, and, later, of a child. In the early morning of July 8, 2012 in Pécs, a 25-year-old woman was raped and murdered. Her body was found only on July 11, three days after she went missing. The perpetrator, 26-year-old László Péntek was captured on July 15. Before the murder, despite his young age, Péntek had been convicted several times; he spent most of the ten-year period before his arrest in prison. The main reasons why the murder of Kata Bándy—apart from the relatively rare, therefore unusual and shocking sexual motive—differed from the other homicide cases were that the victim was a young woman, who was well known in her home town, active in social media and (as all media stressed out) definitely pretty, with a job of high reputation.

Even though there were several rape and murder cases prior to 2012, none of those triggered such flame war as the murder of Kata Bándy. After her body was found, a Facebook group of tens of thousands of members was formed in order to demand the reintroduction of the death penalty, many politicians, public figures, and celebrities commented on the case, hundreds of articles were written on debating pros and cons as regards the manner of punishment. All in all, the issue of the death penalty, since its abolishment in 1990, has never received such public and media attention. An inner group of the governing party Fidesz—which used to form the independent party of united smallholders—made it clear that they wish to reintroduce the death penalty as a punishment of murder; Béla Turi-Kovács, leader of the smallholders' group (Kisgazda Polgári Szövetségpárt [Smallholders' Civic Union Party]), MP of Fidesz said the following: "The events of the past years, more so of the past days, demonstrate that the protection of society requires the reintroduction of the death penalty." He asked a question as well: if the Criminal Code ensures the individual's right to self-defense, then why does not the state have the entitlement necessary to "apply the death penalty against criminals who left their humanity behind?"[29]

Naturally, the Jobbik party also made a comment after the murder of Kata Bándy, as always before in similar cases: Ádám Mirkóczki, spokesperson of Jobbik, said that as regards extremely serious crimes committed against life, the death penalty may be the only actually preventive instrument. Tamás Gaudi-Nagy, MP of Jobbik even said that public executions would bear the ultimate preventive force. However, regarding such suggestions, Tibor Navracsics, minister of justice in the Orbán government explicitly stated that—due to international obligations of the country and ethical aspects—the reintroduction of the death penalty is not possible; according to Péter Paczolay, president of the Constitutional Court of Hungary, the reintroduction thereof is also impossible due to the new constitution i.e., the Fundamental Law of Hungary which was drafted by Fidesz and enacted by the Parliament with the majority of the MPs of Fidesz.[30]

However, the overheated public mood was not pacified even by the fact that Kata Bándy's family did not want the reintroduction of the death penalty; the victim's mother posted the following statement on

Facebook: "I express also the request of our family when I ask the civil society and political organisations not to use either the name or the personal tragedy of our daughter as an excuse for incitement, rancour or the reintroduction of the the death penalty. Thank you."

The other homicide case with significant effect was the premeditated, brutal murder of an 11-year-old boy, Bence Szita, from the vicinity of the town of Kaposvár. The little boy's stepmother, Erika Polcz reported on October 29, 2012 that Bence went missing, and that he was last seen on a playground; as it was later proven, that was the time when he was taken away and murdered not too far away. His body was found on November 3 and the perpetrators were captured soon thereafter. Bence Szita was raised by his mother's ex-husband as a foster father; when Erika Polcz and the foster father moved in together, she soon got jealous and blamed Bence for the deteriorated relationship of the couple. Thus, she hired two homeless men, József Bogdán and József Kertész to beat the child to death, paying a total sum of HUF 192,200 (approx. EUR 600) for the brutal act. The woman and the men took Bence Szita from the playground in a car to a wooded area, and the men, called upon by the woman, beat the boy nearly to death with a shovel, also stabbing him with a knife repeatedly. Despite all that, the child was still alive when they pushed him into a previously dug hole and threw soil on his body, basically burying him alive. According to the forensic expert, the little boy's death was not caused by the assault but by soil penetrating into his lungs; basically he suffocated under the ground. The abettor stepmother, who ordered the murder, as well as the two men who executed it were convicted by a whole life sentence, both by the court of first instance and the court rendering the final judgment. It is curious (and many people in Hungary tended to comprehend it as justice done by fate) that all perpetrators—even though none of them were old, in fact, they were in their forties or fifties—died within a few years due to natural causes, illness: Erika Polcz died in 2017, while József Bogdán and József Kertész both died in 2019, only a few months apart.

As a response to a suggestion of the parliamentary group of the—persistently—far-right party Jobbik, namely to a question put forward by Ádám Mirkóczki, Prime Minister Viktor Orbán explained that even though he agreed "on a philosophical basis" with Jobbik as regards many issues of their view on the death penalty, but—revealing a pragmatist approach—he added that such suggestion is ill-timed[31] due to the environment of international law and to the prohibitions of EU law.[32] Furthermore, the prime minister expressed the following: "I can hardly imagine any rigorous legislation that could guarantee that no serious crimes will be committed."[33] Nevertheless, the extent of the public debate was almost as large as after the murder of Kata Bándy, with numerous Internet op-ed pieces, impromptu amateur polls, and with the—almost inevitable—Facebook groups, among which one of the most popular—with approximately 30,000 followers—offered a choice to the followers from among sixty-seven cruel ways for Szita Bence's murderers to die.

The next occasion when public attention was directed to support for the death penalty took place in 2014 when János Lázár—the then leader of the prime minister's cabinet, who soon thereafter, in June 2014, became the minister of the Prime Minister's Office—who was practically Viktor Orbán's deputy and the second most influential member of Fidesz, made a pro-death-penalty statement in an interview. The particular occasion was a debate on the whole life sentence, due to the fact that the Szeged Regional Court of Appeal suspended the criminal procedure pending against a person charged with multiple murders (who, according to the charges, premeditatedly murdered three people on two different occasions, for financial gain, with particular cruelty), due to that, in the court's view, the whole life sentence applicable against the accused constituted a violation of the European Convention on Human Rights, specifically, of the prohibition of inhuman punishment, and referred the case to the Constitutional Court of Hungary, requesting the establishment of whether the provision in the Criminal Code prescribing the whole life sentence violates any international treaty. Following that, on April 3, 2014, János Lázár strongly criticized the courts at a community meeting; he said that judges had no idea about reality, and that they merely implement the law, instead of serving justice. He expressed his view on that not only the whole life sentence is justified, but even application of the death penalty could be. He said that the majority of the Hungarian population supported the death penalty, and wished to reintroduce it as regards the most serious crimes. He made it clear that, personally, he also shared such view and "he feels sorry for that it is not possible," because "he considers it would be the righteous penalty" in the cases where children or old people are murdered.[34] Soon after Lázár's statement, in May 2014, Viktor Orbán himself made a comment on the case in his regular weekly radio interview, stating that in his opinion—despite all contrary statement—the death penalty does bear preventive force. In his view, it is a huge dilemma that a life is taken when the death penalty is applied, but—due to the preventive force thereof—it can also save a few lives. He also said that he was aware that the death penalty was prohibited by the European Union, but, as he put it, "this is well worth a mass, too."[35]

Finally, the most recent event that sparked a debate on the death penalty, both in society and in politics, has been the murder of a young shop assistant. In the late afternoon on April 21, 2015, a young female tobacco-shop assistant was murdered in the town of Kaposvár; the robber and murderer took all of the day's revenue, following which, even though she gave him the money voluntarily, he stabbed her on the neck, managed to take her keys, lock the door behind himself and walk away, while remaining undetected. On April 28, Prime Minister Viktor Orbán said, in Pécs, that the issue of the death penalty should be kept on the agenda because the application of the "three strikes" and a whole life sentence—even though it seemed to be a sufficient tool in the fight against crime before—is not enough in itself. "Thus, in my opinion, the issue of the death penalty should be kept on the agenda in Hungary, it needs to be addressed, and it needs to be made clear for criminals that Hungary will stop at nothing when it comes to saving our own citizens."[36] The prime minister's speech was reaffirmed on the same day in a statement made by Antal Rogán, leader of the parliamentary group of Fidesz, where he said that he found the debate on the death penalty legitimate, since "the Hungarian society did not have a chance to make a decision thereon," since it was not abolished by the Parliament or by a referendum, but by the Constitutional Court of Hungary.[37] Naturally, the opposition parties (with the exception of Jobbik) did reject the suggestion immediately, pointing out that it is unrealistic due to legal causes; they expressed their opinion that reheating the topic was merely an attempt to gain political benefits, nothing more than mere populism. András Schiffer, co-leader of the opposition party Lehet Más a Politika (LMP [Politics Can Be

Different]) summarized his view by saying that the prime minister had "lost his marbles."

Nonetheless, the heated debate continued in the following days. Antal Rogán stated: if a 20-year-old girl is murdered in the town where, just a few years before, her stepmother had Bence Szita murdered, one starts wondering if such perpetrators would deserve the death penalty. In his opinion, despite the prohibition of the EU law, if the citizens of a Member State want to reintroduce the death penalty, the issue should be raised at EU level.[38] However, other MPs of Fidesz did not support the suggestion and openly turned against the prime minister's communication. Lajos Kósa, who was to become the leader of the parliamentary group of Fidesz a few months later—stated the following: "I am pro-life, so to speak. In my opinion, what you cannot give, you shall not take away."[39] Bence Rétvári, a member of KDNP, the smaller governing party beside Fidesz, and of KDNP's parliamentary group, reaffirmed his view expressed in a statement made in 2012, where he said that stressing pro-death-penalty arguments "mean a clear break-up with Christian values," and that "no politician who is a devout Christian can support the death penalty without contradicting the Church teaching."[40] György Schöpflin, MEP of Fidesz, interviewed by the journal *Népszabadság*, said that he rejected the death penalty, since it violated human dignity and the principal that God created man in his own image.[41]

However, the debate exceeded Hungarian domestic politics and was elevated to an international level. Martin Schulz, President of the European Parliament, initiated a phone call with Viktor Orbán as regards his statements on the death penalty (which, by his own admission, was welcome by the Hungarian prime minister, since he would be happy to continue a consultation on the topic on a European level). The phone call followed a question put forward by Jörg Leichtfried, MEP of the Socialist Group on April 29 i.e., the day before, asking Schulz's opinion on Orbán's suggestion regarding the reintroduction of the death penalty, which, in Leichtfried's view would be an infringement of the EU law and "would be barbaric."[42] At the same session, Guy Verhofstadt, chair of the liberal group in the European Parliament, and former Belgian prime minister also spoke, expressing his opinion that "under Orbán's policies, Hungary would no longer qualify for admission to the EU if it applied to join now.

Orbán's statements go against the fundamental values that Europe represents. If the European People's Party take their own manifesto seriously, it is high time that the leadership stands up to Orbán."[43] (Nevertheless, Manfred Weber, chair of EPP, responded in an evasive way, and did not comment on the words of the Hungarian prime minister. He only said, addressing his words to the chair of the Liberal Group in the European Parliament that "fortunately, the death penalty belongs to the past in Europe, and it is no issue of debate.")[44] Orbán's words were also condemned by Christian Wigand, spokesperson of the European Commission. But the Hungarian prime minister's statements not only received a reaction in the European Union, but also in the Council of Europe, the organization created to protect human rights by the democratic states of Europe. Nils Muiznieks, Commissioner for Human Rights in the Council of Europe said the following: "The idea of reintroducing the death penalty, raised by Prime Minister Orbán, is incompatible with Hungary's obligations under the European Convention on Human Rights and runs contrary to the values that Europe stands for."

On April 30, at his regular Thursday governmental press conference called Kormányinfó (Government Info), János Lázár, minister of the Prime Minister's Office said the following as regards the phone call between Viktor Orbán and Martin Schulz: "The Prime Minister wishes to inform you that he spoke to Martin Schulz at half past 2 [...] and informed him that there is an ongoing debate regarding the death penalty in Hungary, as well as that the Prime Minister does not intend to introduce the death penalty. The fact that an ongoing debate exists does not mean that a plan exists to introduce the death penalty." On May 2, Viktor Orbán gave a lengthy interview on Echo TV, where—refining his earlier words—he said the following: "I consider answering the question on whether or not we should introduce the death penalty premature. However, I find the discussion thereon important." Then, on May 8, at his regular Friday radio interview that took place after the debate held by the European Parliament Committee on Civil Liberties, Justice, and Home Affairs (LIBE) on Viktor Orbán's comments on the death penalty (where the MEPs who spoke during the debate reaffirmed their commitment to the death penalty-free Europe), the Hungarian prime minister made the following statement: "I am on the side of life, therefore, my approach is to consider what is necessary to protect innocent, law-abiding people. If we can protect them without introducing the death penalty, then we should protect them in such a way; however, if there is no other way, then we should introduce it." He also said the following: "We want to develop a European public opinion which tends to reinstate the issue of introduction or non-introduction of the death penalty into the jurisdiction of Member States. This was taken away from the Member States and became a centrally controlled one. Prohibiting the death penalty even was put in the most important legal documents, but I think every Member State should decide this on their own; there's no reason for all countries to think the same way about this issue." (In the radio interview, the prime minister did not address his ideas about non-European obligations i.e., about international treaties which Hungary joined voluntarily; with such treaties, Hungary obliged itself not to reintroduce the death penalty.) It is apparent from the statements made by the prime minister that he is not against the death penalty on theoretical grounds, and he is basically not concerned about international treaties on human rights or even the Charter of Fundamental Rights of the European Union, since, in his view, the latter could be modified if a debate conducted with the participation of the people showed that the citizens of the Member States find the death penalty necessary, or more precisely, in such cases where it should be modified in accordance with the people's opinion.

Notes

1. Gábor Szabó: "Öltöztessük nemzeti színekbe a világot!" Interjú Nagy Ervinnel, a JOBBIK elnökével. ("Let us dress the world in national colours." Interview with Ervin Nagy, the leader of the party Jobbik]) *Kapu*, 15 (2002: 6–7): 21.
2. *Magyar Nemzet*, February 13, 2006, p. 3.
3. *Vas Népe,* March 18, 2006, p. 3.
4. *Vasárnapi Hírek*, July 9, 2006, p. 4.
5. At the commemoration of the tragedy, Csanád Szegedi, one of the prominent members of the party argued that the death penalty has to be reintroduced (*Vasárnapi Napló*, October 29, 2006, p. 2).

6. *Háromszék*, December 10, 2007, p. 2.
7. *Népszabadság*, December 9, 2008, p. 4.
8. *Népszabadság*, October 17, 2009, p. 2.
9. *Vas Népe*, August 13, 2011, p. 2; *Napló*, March 24, 2012, p. 2.
10. *Magyar Hírlap*, November 6, 2012, p. 2.
11. E.g. Lóránt Budai (cf.: *Népszabadság*, January 8, 2014, p. 2); János Árgyelán, leader of the party's Fejér county Article (*Fejér Megyei Hírlap*, January 21, 2014, p. 2); Lajos Kepli (*Napló*,April 5, 2014, p. 5).
12. *Magyar Nemzet*, May 2, 2015, p. 1.
13. *Népszava*, August 14, 2018, p. 3.
14. Cf. e.g.: *Napló*, July 27, 2018, p. 2.
15. *Magyar Hírlap*, January 8, 2020.
16. *Magyar Hang*, May 21, 2019.
17. *Magyar Hírlap*, January 8, 2020.
18. *Népszabadság*, March 24, 2006, p. 2.
19. *Magyar Nemzet*, March 6, 1995, p. 4.
20. Ibid.
21. *Magyar Nemzet*, March 8, 1995, p. 6.
22. *Új Magyarország*, June 11,1996.
23. *Népszabadság*, June 10, 1996, p. 1.
24. *Népszava*, June 10, 1996, p. 2.
25. *Magyar Nemzet*, June 7, 1996, p. 5.
26. *Népszava*, June 6, 1996, p. 2.
27. *Napló*, April 16, 1998, p. 2.
28. *Népszava*, April 16, 1998, p. 2.
29. *Népszava*, 20 July, 2012, p. 3.
30. Ibid.
31. "We can debate on whether we need the death penalty or not, or on whether it is right or not. But I would rather say that such debate is ill-timed at the moment." (*Népszava*, November 6, 2012, p. 3.)
32. *Napló*, November 6, 2012, p. 2.
33. *Magyar Hírlap*, November 6, 2012, p. 2.
34. Cf. e.g.: *Magyar Nemzet*, April 4, 2014, pp. 1 and 5.
35. *Népszava*, April 29, 2015, p. 3.
36. *Magyar Nemzet*, April 29, 2015, p. 3.
37. Ibid.
38. *Magyar Nemzet*, April 30, 2015, p. 3.
39. Ibid.

40. Ibid.
41. *Népszabadság*, April 30, 2015, p. 1.
42. *Népszava*, 3April 30, 2015, p. 13.
43. Ibid.
44. Ibid.

Index[1]

A

Abolition, 5, 10, 14, 22, 26, 39, 53, 57, 68–70, 75, 84, 89, 120, 155, 156, 159–166, 169, 171, 174, 175, 178, 180, 185, 186, 192
Anomic state of society, 178
Anti-Death Penalty League, 159–161
Arrow Cross, 90, 95–97, 100, 101

B

Bándy, Kata, 198, 199, 201
Baze v. Rees, 20
Beccaria, Cesare, 11, 16, 22, 25, 26, 32n2, 52, 57, 69
Belarus, 3, 198
Boross, Péter, 192, 193
Brooks, Charles, 19

C

CC Decision No. 23 of 1990, 174
Code of Csemegi, 76, 86, 120, 131
Constitutional Court (CC), 10, 13–15, 75, 160–162, 165, 166, 167n3, 167n13, 169, 171–175, 178, 181n2, 181n3, 182n4, 182n14, 185, 188, 190, 193, 194, 201, 202
Costs, 19, 29, 55–59, 59n2, 60n4, 60n7
Court-martials, 98, 109
Crimes against humanity, 133, 145, 150–152
Crimes against the state, 87, 131, 133, 138, 145, 150
Crimes of passion, 10

[1] Note: Page numbers followed by 'n' refer to notes.

Z. J. Toth, *Changing Attitudes Towards the Death Penalty*,
https://doi.org/10.1007/978-3-030-47557-4

Cruel and inhuman punishment, 17, 162, 174
Csurka, István, 192

D

Death brigades, 65, 66
Death row, 20, 21, 23n9, 36, 58, 72n16
Deterrent effect, 4, 5, 9–12, 25, 31, 50, 163, 176, 177
Discrimination, 5, 41, 66, 68

E

Electric chair, 18, 19
Electrocution, 17
Elimination of perpetrators, 51, 52
European Convention on Human Rights, 185, 186, 201, 204
Evans, John Louis, 19
Execution, 3, 5, 15–22, 23n6, 38–40, 43, 44, 50, 56–59, 62–65, 72n16, 76, 78n2, 84, 90, 91n22, 97, 102, 104, 110, 121, 124–127, 129n16, 131, 138, 152, 154, 155, 164, 189, 192, 199
Expert opinion, 10, 36, 155, 165

F

Fair trial, 67
Fidesz, 169, 194, 195, 197, 199, 201–203
Firing squad, 17, 110, 121, 138, 154
FKgP, 190, 194, 195
Forced labor, 22, 26, 32n2, 52, 57, 102, 142n1
Francis, Willie, 19
Furman v. Georgia, 171, 172, 182n5

G

Gas chamber, 17–19
Goal of punishment, 32n1, 49–53, 140
Györgyi, Kálmán, 14, 165

H

Hanging, 17, 84, 85, 91n22, 102, 110, 154, 155, 164
Hippocratic Oath, 64
Horn, Gyula, 194
Horthy era, 77, 81–90, 106, 107
Human dignity, 13, 14, 161, 162, 164, 166, 167n2, 172–174, 182n12, 188, 198, 203
Hungarian National Independence Front, 98

I

Imprisonment, 22, 27, 29, 31, 32, 35, 39–41, 45, 57–59, 61–63, 68, 69, 85, 99, 120, 121, 125, 127, 131–141, 149, 152, 153, 156n11, 160, 162, 193, 195, 196
Incapacitation effect, 32n1
Incompetence of the defense lawyer, 37
Indirect suiciders, 11
Individualization, 69

J

Jobbik, 189–192, 197, 199, 200, 202
Jon, Gee, 18
Jury, 36–38, 45, 64, 66–68, 172

K

Kaczyński, Jarosław, 3
Kaczyński, Lech, 3
Kaiser, Ede, 40, 195, 196
Karr, Alphonse, 63
KDNP, 169, 203
Kemmler, William, 19

L

Law & economics, 56, 57
Lázár, János, 201, 202, 204
Le Pen, Jean-Marie, 3
Le Pen, Marine, 3
Lehet Más a Politika (LMP), 202
Lethal injection, 17, 19–22, 73n21
Life imprisonment, 9, 22, 27, 29–31, 33n8, 39, 41, 51, 55–59, 60n4, 84, 102, 121, 125, 126, 140, 141, 142n1, 152, 160, 162, 181n2, 195, 196
Life sentence, 22, 27, 193, 197, 200–202
Lipšic, Daniel, 3

M

Mares, Eliseo J., 17
Martial law, 75, 77, 82–84, 86, 88–90, 90n3, 91n9, 92n38, 107, 108, 111n1, 116n69, 116n72, 123
Matuska, Szilveszter, 84, 91n15
Mental disintegration, 21
Mercy, 101–103, 124–126, 132, 138, 139, 141, 149, 154, 155, 163
MIÉP, 190, 192
Military crimes, 73n21, 84, 91n16, 92n26, 109, 131, 133, 135, 138, 145, 148, 151, 152
Military criminal law, 109
Miscarriage of justice, 20, 35–45
Murderers for hire, 11

N

National Council of People's Tribunal (NOT), 96, 99, 103

O

Orbán, Viktor, 191, 193, 195–197, 199–204

P

Paczolay, Péter, 199
People's tribunals, 96–102, 107, 109, 121, 124–126, 128–129n15
Poena ordinaria, 76
Political killings, 64
Political perpetrators, 11
Political transformation, 171, 179
Presidential Council, 122–124, 139, 141, 149
Prevention, 49–53, 62, 70, 132, 138, 140, 144n12, 148, 162
Procedural irregularities, 36

Protection of society, 29, 49–52, 132, 140, 148, 149, 162, 164, 199
Provisional National Assembly, 95, 102, 103, 111n2
Psychological pain, 21
Public outrage, 45, 68
Pusoma, Dénes, 42, 43, 45

R

Referendum, 166, 185–189, 191, 192, 194, 202
Répássy, Róbert, 197
Resocialization, 50, 51, 53n1
Retribution, 49, 50, 52, 127n6
Right to life, 13, 15, 27, 61, 62, 161, 162, 166, 167n2, 172–174, 182n12, 188, 198
Right to self-defense, 15, 199
Riley, Leandress, 18
Russia, 3, 192

S

Schmidt, Péter, 14, 173
Schulz, Martin, 203, 204
Situation of emergency, 16
Slippery slope, 70
Slota, Ján, 3
Sólyom, László, 14, 15
Soviet Republic of Hungary, 77, 81–83
Stevens, John Arthur, 3–4
Suicidal murderers, 11
Summary jurisdiction, 107–109, 115n64, 115n67, 116n71, 116n72, 121, 123, 124, 126
Surveys, 21, 68, 69, 169, 175–177, 193
Szántai, Attila, 40, 41, 43
Szemere, Bertalan, 16
Szita, Bence, 200, 201, 203
Szögi, Lajos, 190

T

Tafero, Jesse Joseph, 19
Torgyán, József, 194
Toroczkai, László, 191, 192
Tóth, Tamás, 185, 186, 188
Tuti, Mario, 30

U

Usury courts, 98, 105–107, 109, 113n36, 115n62

V

Vastagh, Pál, 193, 194
Verhofstadt, Guy, 203
Vona, Gábor, 189, 190

W

War criminals, 95, 96, 100, 101, 103
Wartime legislation, 87, 88
Weiszdorn, Róbert, 196

The manufacturer's authorised representative in the EU is Springer Nature Customer Service Centre GmbH, Europaplatz 3, 69115 Heidelberg, Germany. If you have any concerns regarding our products, please contact ProductSafety@springernature.com

Printed and bound by CPI Group (UK) Ltd, Croydon, CR0 4YY

22/09/2026

02221058-0001